NATURAL LANGUAGE PROCESSING TECHNOLOGIES IN ARTIFICIAL INTELLIGENCE
The Science and Industry Perspective

ELLIS HORWOOD SERIES IN ARTIFICIAL INTELLIGENCE

Joint Series Editors: Professor JOHN CAMPBELL, Department of Computer Science, University College London, and
Dr JEAN HAYES MICHIE, Knowledgelink Limited, Edinburgh

* In preparation

NATURAL LANGUAGE PROCESSING TECHNOLOGIES IN ARTIFICIAL INTELLIGENCE
The Science and Industry Perspective

KLAUS K. OBERMEIER, Ph.D.
Intelligent User Interfaces
Battelle Laboratories (Columbus Division)
Columbus, Ohio

ELLIS HORWOOD LIMITED
Publishers · Chichester

Halsted Press: a division of
JOHN WILEY & SONS
New York · Chichester · Brisbane · Toronto

006.3
0 12

First published in 1989
ELLIS HORWOOD LIMITED
Market Cross House, Cooper Street,
Chichester, West Sussex, PO19 1EB, England
The publisher's colophon is reproduced from James Gillison's drawing of the ancient Market Cross, Chichester.

Distributors:

Australia and New Zealand:
JACARANDA WILEY LIMITED
GPO Box 859, Brisbane, Queensland 4001, Australia

Canada:
JOHN WILEY & SONS CANADA LIMITED
22 Worcester Road, Rexdale, Ontario, Canada

Europe and Africa:
JOHN WILEY & SONS LIMITED
Baffins Lane, Chichester, West Sussex, England

North and South America and the rest of the world:
Halsted Press: a division of
JOHN WILEY & SONS
605 Third Avenue, New York, NY 10158, USA

South-East Asia
JOHN WILEY & SONS (SEA) PTE LIMITED
37 Jalan Pemimpin # 05–04
Block B, Union Industrial Building, Singapore 2057

Indian Subcontinent
WILEY EASTERN LIMITED
4835/24 Ansari Road
Daryaganj, New Delhi 110002, India

© **1989 K. K. Obermeier/Ellis Horwood Limited**

British Library Cataloguing in Publication Data
Obermeier, Klaus K.
Natural language processing technolgies in artificial intelligence: the science and industry perspective.
1. Natural language computer systems
I. Title
006.3'5

Library of Congress data available.

ISBN 0–7458–0562–0 (Ellis Horwood Limited)
ISBN 0–470–21528–3 (Halsted Press)

Printed in Great Britain by Hartnolls, Bodmin

TABLE OF CONTENTS

6

8

PREFACE

The question is not whether natural language will play a role in years to come, but whether natural language products warrant a closer look today. [*Computerworld*, December 1986]

So far, natural language processing [NLP] is still in an embryonic state. But it will help to usher in an exciting new age in computer technology – the understanding computer. This new breed of software includes programs that model language behavior – something conventional computer languages can't do. For this development to take place radical changes in the theory, design and implementation of NLP systems have to take place. When it comes to NLP systems for tomorrow, current technology won't do.

With the advent of computers people became fascinated with the idea of just talking to the computer in English, German or any other "natural" language. Apart from sheer expediency, a NLP system being able to carry on a conversation could prove to be something more than just an advance in a new field of technology: it may generate answers for some of the enigmas connected with what language is and how it developed; maybe even pass the Turing test. Why, then, so little progress in an exciting field with immense commercial potential? What are the academic, scientific and commercial issues? On the surface, there are two reasons for the current, less than glamorous state of the art of NLP: (1) the lack of a clear definition of what NLP as a science is, and (2) the initial failures to make NLP technology a commercial success and to garner widespread market acceptance.

There are almost as many definitions of NLP as there are researchers studying it. In fact, there are almost as many variations of language itself as there are people using it. Anyone who ever asks linguists what they do for a living realizes the multiple aspects of studying language, ranging from the structure of sounds to that of conversations. The variations within any one language, and more so across languages, have not only puzzled linguists but also long intrigued philosophers, psychologists and anthropologists. Enter computers. Studying syntax and parsing methods in compiler theory has been the bread and butter of computer scientists from the beginning of the computer age. On the surface, there are a number of similarities between computer languages and natural languages: they all have grammars and syntax to determine the allowable statements in a particular language. But no one has dared successfully to leave it up to the computer to end a DO-WHILE loop in C; and human languages allow for such a multiplicity of meanings [i.e., ambiguities] that the mere thought of having computers interpret them causes scepticism in computer aficionados and high tech grammarians alike.

NLP has been a controversial issue for the two academic disciplines that primarily deal with NL: artificial intelligence [AI] and linguistics. AI scientists are concerned with building models of the language user and adequate knowledge representation schemes, whereas linguists construct models of grammar and formalisms. The eclectic nature of NLP research thus has to give way to a more autonomous discipline dealing exclusively with the issue of NLP by computers, with neural networks as a prime contender as an integrating force for such a development. Current NLP research has been caught between the ideologies of the various academic disciplines. NLP systems of the future have to be based on more innovative linguistic and conceptual models if they are to become useful and accepted on a large scale.

Enter venture capital and government. Being able to use plain English with the computer conjures up a lucrative market for investors, and a strategic edge for defense and federal agencies. Unfortunately, innovations are often excluded from funding while entrenched research directions perpetuate dead-end reports. In NLP, more than in any other advanced technology area, the pay-off lies in exploiting the do-able, and not in pursuing the impossible. It is not necessary to solve all NLP problems to make money with this technology; in fact, knowing how to get around these problems is often more profitable than solving them. Unfortunately, university professors, with very few exceptions, have never been known to be savvy businessmen.

The lack of commercial success and market acceptance, however, can be attributed to two factors: (1) an emphasis of the remaining – mostly academic – open research problems that limit large scale applications, and (2) a fundamental misconception of what current-day NLP systems in general and natural language interfaces [NLIs] in particular should and should not be. An NLI, for instance, should make it easier for the user to manipulate data without having to learn another computer language, and ideally should integrate existing software programs into the retrieval process. Ultimately, an NLI should be the "lingua franca" for all computer application programs. An NLI program should not be considered the panacea for all the information processing problems, the magic wand against computer illiteracy, nor the pinnacle of AI research, and yet, NLP systems are considered by many to be just that. NL (e.g., English) should be the fifth generation language possibly being used in conjunction with other interface options.

Because of the diversity of controversial issues, NLP is one of the most often debated subjects in AI and computer science. The host of books on NLP attest to this diversity. Adding another one to the market needs some justification. Currently, available books on NLP are mostly written for the NLP professional and graduate student, or try to promote exclusively one particular aspect of commercial and scientific thrust. The foremost goal of this book is to provide a viable introduction especially for the data processing professional and businessman new to the field of NLP, in brief, to give a science and business perspective of its infrastructure and help provide answers to the following questions [see Epilog]: *Will NLP increase productivity, and if so, how? What criteria are relevant for evaluating NLP systems? What products are available now and will be in the future?* The second goal is to differentiate succinctly what is currently do-able from what could be possible in the future. The third goal is to present to the reader an up-to-date compendium with relevant pointers to further resources.

Because the book is written for the novice, I have tried to stay away from using many footnotes and attributions in the text to make it easy for the reader to follow the arguments. Consequently, practicing NLP researchers may become frustrated by the lack of scholarly debate. Specific references are listed in the "Suggested Reading" section at the end of each chapter. A list of generally useful publications (e.g., journals, conference proceedings) is given at the beginning of the bibliography. I have also included addresses of companies and organizations specializing in applications at the very end of each chapter in Part II in the section "Useful Contacts".

PLAN OF THE BOOK

NLP is no longer just an academic endeavor; its commercial potential and its integration in future computer technologies has been widely recognized. Thus, understanding the impact of NLP includes an understanding of both technology and marketplace as well as their interconnections. This book is a survey across academic and commercial sectors related to NLP technology. Its purpose is to assess and help transfer current NLP technology. Focusing on ideas rather than names, the book is highly analytical. Starting with a description of the nature of NLP systems, the book then addresses the major areas of applications of NLP, concluding with a look at "the bottom line" of NLP academically and commercially.

Consequently, the book is divided into three parts. Part I, "NLP in Perspective", introduces in its first chapter the components of NLP systems with reference to the broad theoretical issues. Chapter 2 describes the approaches to NLP. Chapter 3 looks at formalisms for implementing NLP systems. If you are less technically inclined, you may want to skip or skim chapter 3. Part I is meant to be a gentle introduction without going into great technical detail. For the NLP neophyte to follow the arguments in Parts II and III, it is necessary to have a basic understanding of the nature and approaches of NLP systems – even more so, since it will "de-mystify" the procedures that enable computers to process NL in the first place. Part I will substantiate the claim that there are shortcomings with the entrenched approaches in mainstream NLP based on their sentence-level methodology. Contrary to textbooks on the subject of NLP, current approaches will not be presented as "God-given" [Allen 87a, Grishman 86, Harris 85, Cullingford 85, Winograd 83]; rather, their obvious strengths and weaknesses are shown. This book will not enable you to build NLP systems. Books for this purpose are given in the section on "Suggested Reading" at the end of chapter 3. And none of them will substitute for the hands-on experience that you get from actually working with the technology.

Part II, on the other hand, gives an analysis of the various applications of NLP, ranging from the popular NLIs to the commercially popular spell- and grammar-checkers. The information presented here is intended especially for demonstrating the potential and the currently feasible applications. Based on information presented in Part I, the reader will be able to understand conceptually what problems are addressed in various applications and how shortcomings of the technology are rooted in its methodology. In particular, the orientation of sentence analysis supported the notion that the focus of NLP should be syntax.

Part III draws together the presented information in an open issue chapter where general problems with existing NLP technologies are discussed, an assessment of commercial ("The NLP Business") and scientific ("NLP – A Science by Itself") viability of NLP as an autonomous business sector and field of study, respectively. Part III addresses the issue of differentiating the current state of the art from future possibilities of NLP technologies. Part III in particular relates the overall picture of NLP infrastructure and its place in the infrastructure of general computing.

Whereas ten years ago it was possible to describe all existing NL interfaces in one journal article [Hendrix 78], recent surveys [Johnson 85] show that the number of operational NLP programs at the prototype stage is now in the thousands, and off-the-shelf products are in the hundreds. The NLP systems mentioned throughout the book are of some notoriety and significance, references to further resources are limited to the most recent publications that are easily accessible, exceptions are only made where a particular publication was a landmark. The annotated bibliography at the end of each chapter and at the beginning of the "Bibliography" will assist you in finding resources for your special interest.

IN MY OWN WRITE

This book is based on my personal, 10-year experience with the NL technology, first in academia, then in the R&D arena, and finally in the NLI product business. The objective of this book has been to provide within 250 pages a glimpse of the technology and complete this project within a year, starting May 1988. My message regarding NLP technologies is: it's desirable for certain applications, somewhat do-able, definitely needed, but has to get a whole lot better before being generally acceptable. Moreover, to focus more on exploiting the currently do-able rather than dwelling on the some-day-possible, requires a change in the mind-set from a university professor to a data processing professional. Because I have tried to point out some inadequacies of current approaches, the book may have a debunking flavor to it. Nevertheless, I do believe that the field of NLP technology is ripe for exciting innovations and lucrative ventures.

It has become fashionable to discuss science in terms of Kuhnian paradigms whereby entrenched theories survive for a long period of time just because most researchers take them as sacrosanct. Kuhn's contentions that innovations are hard, revolutionary and very time-consuming apply fully to NLP per se. Currently, there is no NLP system out there that provides a reasonable amount of coverage based on a comprehensive linguistic/cognitive theory. New fads and outdated algorithms are often favored to serve as the underlying theories and formalisms for NLP.

It has become common practice for people to render unto semantics what they rendered unto syntax many years ago. Meager success stories are misleading given the substantial research effort in the field. Today's only viable commercial applications of NLP besides spell and grammar checkers are NLIs for database management systems [DBMS], and selected machine translation applications (e.g., bank transfer telexes that are translated from French into English). The tremendous market potential for applying NLP technology to text database management remains untapped because orthodox academic approaches will not work. The current state of NLP provides a sobering experience otherwise:

- real alternatives between existing linguistic theories for NLP are only beginning to emerge,

- most approaches are rule based and favor linear, sentence level processing,

- many applications that people want are unrealistic and un-doable.

In my opinion, for NL technology to have any major impact on the computing infrastructure and on life itself, fundamental breakthroughs must occur. Three factors will bring about this needed change:

- new theories and formalisms: neural networks will force speech to become a commodity, and will greatly change the notion of parsing at the end of the 20th century; fractals and chaos theory will influence substantially our thinking about language in the 21st century.

- new applications: information needs will demand natural language capability to cope with the complexities of the computing tasks, and with the proportionally growing computer illiterate public. English will become the next major programming language; as gigabyte databases become common, CASE technology establishes itself, and parallel processing advances, the NLP practitioner will have to overcome the current sandbox and soapbox mentality.

- new science: changes in the politics of science will establish natural language as an autonomous field, outside of entrenched dogmas, while funding agencies will realize many of the dead ends currently being pursued in government and industry. The commercialization of the NLP technology will help select applications that are bound to be successful because they solve real problems and fulfill real needs.

Some time ago, Fortran was viewed as a means to eliminate the need for programming. English may well be the next candidate. Many truly phenomenal applications of NLP have not yet been fully appreciated, text processing/understanding being a case in point. Again, NLP is an exciting field where it takes an uncreative mind to spot the wrong answer but a creative mind to spot the wrong question.

ACKNOWLEDGEMENTS

I would like to thank James MacDonald (The Ohio State University), Bill Stockwell, Bobbi Riemenschneider (Control Data Corporation), Jessie Pinkham (DePaul University, Chicago), Janet Barron (Byte Magazine), and John Campbell (University College London) for commenting on drafts of the book. I appreciated Sue Horwood's encouragement expressed in many telefax messages. I thank Nancy Tenuta (Battelle) for many insightful discussions on real life issues in NLP and for letting me use her research on spell checkers. Many people helped to make this book come to life: thanks to Rejane Chaves de Souza (Brazil) for continued support, Sally Cleary and Stephanie McClellan (Battelle) for lay out and initial diagrams, Joy Hoyte (The Ohio State University) for all the final graphics, Amy Jordan (Battelle) for final editing on a sunny day, and especially Ruth Krech (Control Data Corporation) for dedicated customer services on weekends; last, but not least all my colleagues in the Intelligent Systems Group at Battelle Columbus for keeping the spirit alive.

I would like to thank the following publishers for giving me permission to use their materials: D. Reidel Publishing Company for excerpts from [Obermeier 83], BYTE Magazine for excerpts from [Obermeier 87, Obermeier 88]. Kluwer Academic Publishers, Boston for Figure 8-1 from [Church 87, page 47], and Dataquest,Inc. for Figure 11-3. In addition, the publications that contained the sources for some of the other Figures are cited at the appropriate places in the book.

PART I - NLP IN PERSPECTIVE

There are almost as many definitions of natural language processing [NLP] as there are researchers studying it. But, for simplicity, I will define NLP, on the one hand, as the ability of a computer to process the same language – spoken or written – that humans use in normal discourse, and, on the other hand, as that field of study within cognitive science which deals with linguistic behavior.[1] Research of linguistic behavior has proceeded within the theoretical and methodological confines of the disciplines which concern themselves with language: linguistics, artificial intelligence [AI], psychology and philosophy. NLP spans the activities of formulating and investigating computationally intelligent [AI], cognitively viable [psychology], and epistemologically cogent [philosophy] mechanisms for communication through natural language [linguistics].

Linguistics has been concerned with the structural properties of language, rather than with its use. In the 1950s and 1960s, the noted MIT linguist Noam Chomsky instigated a revolution in which Modern Linguistics was defined as an autonomous discipline that would provide a formal account of language. Linguistics as Chomsky and his followers saw it was a science that dealt with universals of language, the idealized speaker-listener, and mathematical models of language. In the 1980s, a new era of linguistics began that included an orientation on psychological realism of grammars and the building of tools for computational analysis of language. For AI research, NLP is seen in the context of finding out what intelligence is and how it can be put into a computer. AI researchers construct computational models for NLP to create cognitively interesting and often practically viable systems [Schank 81]. Cognitive psychologists model the use of language in a psychologically plausible way [Johnson-Laird 81] in the form of experiments that measure response time with respect to linguistic phenomena. Philosophers look at computational NLP from an epistemological viewpoint. A major issue for philosophers is the question of what it means for a computer to understand and use language [Pylyshyn 84].

For the computer to be able to process the same language that humans use in normal discourse, three issues have to be resolved: (1) what are the levels of structure for a NLP system? (2) how do they interact? and (3)

---

[1] In chapter 12, I will argue for NLP as an autonomous discipline.

what formalisms are used to model that interaction and its outcome? To resolve issue (1) – levels of structure, NLP is broken down into nice components with a clearly defined functionality, an idealization of sorts. To resolve issue (2) – approaches, each component is assigned an information processing task depending on what aspect a particular theory emphasizes, a prioritization of sorts. To resolve issue (3) – formalisms, computational concerns determine how the particular system based on a given approach is best implemented, an optimization of sorts.

The levels of structure within NLP systems reflect the five components commonly postulated in linguistics: (1) the sound level, which includes phonetics, the study of how linguistic sounds are produced and perceived, and phonology, the study of how sounds are combined from smallest meaning–differentiating elements (i.e., phonemes), (2) morphology, the study of how words are formed from smallest meaning–carrying units (i.e.,morphemes), (3) syntax, the study of sentence structure, (4) semantics, the study of meaning, and (5) pragmatics, the study of how context impacts on the use of language. These levels of structure have been explored to some degree from the perspective of linguistic segmentation and classification within a given theory. Current NLP systems rarely include a speech component because their scientific and commercial viability is only emerging. Moreover, the still prevalent distinction between speech and language processing stems from the traditional view that speech belongs into the realm of signal processing and electrical engineering rather than linguistics proper. Current NLP systems usually need a substantial amount of world knowledge to process information; in fact, for the more powerful systems the knowledge representation is the component that drives NLP in the first place.

Approaches to NLP focus on the three different schools of thought that promote approaches to NLP systems: (1) the traditional linguistic approach that aims at determining the details of sentence structure based on a grammar, (2) the AI approach that aims at modeling language according to appropriate knowledge representations, and (3), the connectionism approach that aims at modeling language according to neural network algorithms. These approaches differ as to what role the various NLP components have, what the analysis level of NLP should be (e.g., sentence, text), how language is viewed in general, and what significance is attributed to the computer program manipulating NL.

Formalisms for implementing NLP systems include the choice of a parsing algorithm and, if needed, a knowledge representation schema. While an approach to NLP is determined on a theoretical basis, the choice of formalism(s) is often based on practical considerations. While the formalism only supports the computational modeling of a theory, the question of what the formalism contributes to the theory arises at times. If this is the case, the role of the computer program in assessing a theory can become controversial. Is the program a theory? Is the theory the program itself? In general, if NLP is viewed as a symbolic process, similar to the processing of formal languages, the computer program assists in testing the power of the formalism in a stringent fashion; if NLP is investigated as a cognitive process, the behavior of the program may speak to the psychological realism of the theory itself. In the first case, the program acts as a tool for testing a theory; in the second case, the program may well be intended to be part of the theory. Nevertheless, the question of the psychological realism of the approach, i.e., whether there is empirical evidence in human language behavior to support a postulated theory, should not affect the evaluation of computational theories.

CHAPTER 1

THE LEVELS OF STRUCTURE

To understand a sentence means to understand the language. To understand the language means to be master of a certain technique.
[Ludwig Wittgenstein, *Philosophical Investigations*]

What really comes before our mind when we understand a word, a sentence, language? Before presenting a neat and at the same time misleading picture of how natural language can be analyzed and used by computer programs, a brief thought experiment may illustrate best the complexities and dimensions involved in understanding language.

Imagine hearing a word – "cube". The word all by itself has four different entries in an English dictionary. A person, upon hearing the word might associate it with a linguistic definition (e.g., "a regular solid of six equal square sides"), or a pictorial representation, or even an anecdotal reference (e.g., "the sculpture in Greenwich Village in the middle of Astor Place"). Understanding a word in isolation is fortuitous since the representation and retrieval of "meaning" by the listener is not determined by either linguistic or nonlinguistic context.

The meaning of "cube" in a linguistic context differs considerably, thus giving rise to a meaning conflict between the uses of cube–1, cube–2,... cube–n in sentences such as (1)–(5).

(1) The cube fell in my lap.
(2) The cube destroyed Oscar's confidence.
(3) The cube turns if two people push it.
(4) The cube is enough for one cup of soup.
(5) The robot saw the cube on the hill with the telescope.

There is a common denominator for the meaning of "cube" in these examples which makes up our concept of a cube. This concept is instantiated upon hearing the word, then modified according to the context in which it is used. The overriding principle in question is plausibility; if it is possible to use the picture of a cube that came to mind differently, it has to have a meaning inherent in language that is congruent with its specific use in the given context. If we were to design a model of NLP that describes the physical world, at least four processing steps are involved [Waltz 81]: judging the plausibility; representing meaning; retrieving information from memory; taking appropriate linguistic or nonlinguistic action. Whenever the listener encounters a word, its meaning gets modified by the various uses it is subjected to. Thus meaning equals use. Consequently, NLP involves modeling the use of language and not merely describing the structure of a sentence.

When a person hears sentence (1), he presumably constructs a semantic representation from memory, and, assuming he is familiar with the other words in the sentence, tries to fit them into context. Since "lap" refers to something tangible and concrete, these properties might be transferred to the semantic representation of "cube"; moreover the size of a lap limits the representation of "cube" for the present context. This representation could depend on linguistic, logical, or geometrical modeling. This example suggests strongly that visual representations of propositions seem to play a role in language understanding.

The representation of "cube" must again be modified after the person hears sentence (2): confidence, an abstract and intangible concept is acted upon by a concrete object; a meaning conflict between (1) and (2) is encountered. For a native speaker the concept of a cube entails further properties (e.g., ability to challenge, puzzle, bewilder someone). For a person whose domain of discourse is so far limited to "cube" and cubes that fell into my lap, the meaning of "cube" in (2) has to appear utterly opaque. Neither visual nor logical operations can prevent this. If knowledge of the outside world could help to determine the meaning of "cube" in (2), it would have to be added to the representation of the meaning of the language used in the sentence. This addition might only hold for the situation at hand; Oscar might be exceptional when it comes to confidence-destroying cubes in that he had been confident that there were no such things as cubes, or that he was confident that he could solve the puzzle of

Rubik's cube for good. If that is the case, (2) has added only a very limited property of cubes to its semantic representation.

The varying qualities of cubes become evident in (3) and (4). When it comes to size and weight of cubes, both qualities can differ greatly, not to mention the "purpose" of cubes. In (3) the person not only imagines the size of the cube but also its position and what direction it is being pushed. By the same token, the representations of "cube" in (3) and (4) consist of a common denominator with respect to shape and particular features in terms of weight, size, purpose, etc. that are instantiated in the particular sentences.

In (5), an added dimension, the structure of the sentence, becomes crucial for understanding. This sentence in some form or another puzzles students of introductory NLP courses because of its five different (syntactic) structural descriptions.   (5) points to the need for representation schemes beyond those of sentence diagrams, logic, or any other linear methods, representation schemes of visual types that capture the essence of what is shown in Figure 1-1.

To be master of a technique, to understand language, one must have stored the meanings qua use of the words, and, more importantly, must be able to adapt and assimilate new meanings in novel ways to the current use in a given context. This is a linguistic process that can be succinctly analyzed in terms of plausibility, representability and computability of a sentence. These properties in turn enable us to come to an understanding that is guided by inferences and expectations. The storage and retrieval of information enable a native speaker to function successfully in terms of language. The emulation of this ability by a computer program is contingent on the use it makes of information that has been presented to it. If a program can handle linguistic information, relying on the function of the individual words in context and acting according to established rules, it is capable of understanding, not in a biological but in a functional sense.

The "thought experiment" brings up the following fundamental issues for NLP: (1) the philosophical issues of what "understanding language" means for humans on the one hand, and, on the other hand, to what extent and in what form it can be embedded in computers and (2) the practical issue of what can realistically be expected of NLP systems and how can it be achieved. While the philosophical issue has been popular with the cognitive intelligentsia and high tech grammarians alike, we will turn our attention in this book exclusively to the practical issue, with a fleeting appreciation of the underlying – epistemological – problems of NLP. For me, understanding is a functional and not a biological process.   Therefore, computers able to respond to questions in a natural language can understand language, even though they do not have the same physiological make-up as humans.

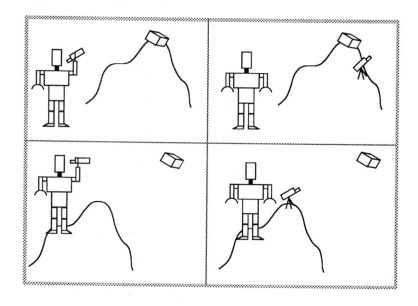

Figure 1-1: Four interpretations of the sentence
"The robot saw the cube on the hill with the telescope."

The "thought experiment" also shows the necessity for being able to analyze language, breaking it down into meaningful and theoretically viable components. While theories as part of science at large help to explain phenomena, they also require choices and hypotheses concerning their components. Components function as building blocks for theories. Theories differ as to the nature of the building blocks and how they are combined. Consequently, describing the information processing tasks for the components of NLP systems in order to illustrate the differences in approaches requires a somewhat idealistic attitude for dealing with the complexities of NLP – idealistic in the sense of presenting the data and phenomena in a cut-and-dried fashion and not in their actual fuzziness. The obligation of orthodox science to impose order on chaos comes at a cost – stipulating and demonstrating there exists order in the first place.

In this chapter we look at the   information processing tasks and the functionality of the five levels of structure commonly postulated in NLP systems. The preliminary look at their tasks and relevance in the overall architecture will help you to appreciate the complexities of any approach to NLP that one has to deal with. In Figure 1–2, the diagram shows a walk-through of a NLP system, distinguishing components, their theoretical underpinnings, and their implementation techniques. We will come back to the theoretical approaches and implementation techniques in chapters 2 and 3, respectively. Suffice it to say that there is a fundamental difference between the approach as theory, the implementation as technique, and the levels of structure as processing components.

In general, the five commonly postulated levels of structure are: (1) the sound level for the analysis of the spoken utterance; (2) the word level that contains information about word classes (e.g., nouns, verbs) and word meaning (animate, count); (3) the syntactic level that contains information about structure of the utterance; (4) the semantic level that provides account of meaning; and (5) pragmatics, the study of how context impacts the interpretation of a given utterance. As in most academic disciplines there are disputes about the exact boundaries of these levels; even more so when it comes to the interactions between them.

While the different levels of structure attest to a stipulated modularity of NLP systems, modularity does not require a linear processing strategy, going strictly from one level to the next without ever allowing any other form of interaction between them. The major advantage of modularity lies in the possibility of formulating constraints for individual components while using an explicit control structure for regulating the "dynamic" interaction between the "static" components. In brief, the flow of information may well be determined by control structures that call for an interaction between levels of structure. The interaction may become necessary in cases when the NLP

Theory	Levels of Structure	Implementation Techniques
Template-matching Rule-based	Sound (Phonetics, Phonology)	Linear Predictive Coefficient Filter Bank Analysis Backpropagation
Morpheme-based Word-based	Word (Morphology)	Hash-Tables

Generative Transformational
   Grammar
Generalized Phrase Structure
   Grammar
Lexical Functional Grammar
	Utterance (Syntax)	CF rules
		ATN
		Chart
		Unification
		Parallel Parsing

Model Theory Case Grammar Semantic Primitives	Meaning (Semantics)	Production Rules Conceptual Dependency Scripts Frames
Memory-based Reasoning Speech acts Discourse Grammar	Context (Pragmatics)	Semantic Networks Logic

Figure 1-2:   Components and levels of structure
within an NLP system.

system encounters a snag in the analysis. Classic examples are sentences like "The prime number few", in which most NLP systems would analyze "number" as the noun initially and only after trying to analyze "few" would it be possible to re-label "number" as the verb of the sentence. Based on the metaphor of a blackboard, the most common control structure in AI technology, the sentence is analyzed by allowing the various levels of structure ("knowledge sources") to communicate with each other. The communication takes place via the blackboard in the form of posting hypotheses that are evaluated by a predetermined metric. Other types of control mechanisms are (1) the generate and test method (a.k.a., analysis by synthesis) in which the system generates all possible solutions that are evaluated by a testing procedure only to eliminate options that are not promising, and (2) the external inference engine method, in which the processing strategy is independent of the data.

The issue of recognition versus production of NL is under discussion with respect to the possibility of using the same mechanism for both processes. This form of "reverse engineering" has not been successful for the following reason. Imagine the sentence "I saw the Jones flying over Columbus". A production NLP system has to provide rules that would account for stylistic variations and ultimately, as is the case here, for rendering the sentence ambiguous. A recognition system would never be able to recover the original form of the sentence because it would have no information as to which rules applied nor in what order. Thus, most algorithms in NLP are geared towards either production or recognition. In the first part of the book, we will mostly discuss the recognition algorithms of NLP systems. Chapters 7 and 8 (section 8.2) will contain a detailed discussion of the topic in the context of text generation and speech synthesis, respectively. In chapter 7, we will also discuss the issue of bi-directional grammar models, and if there have to be generation-specific theories of NLP.

1.1 THE ROLE OF SPEECH

youhaveanicechest

Human speech is hard to process for digital computers and at times for humans, too. Take the utterance above and think of how many interpretations could be given. There are the two obvious ones distinguishing the words "a nice chest" and "an ice chest". But there are also the different intonations that could render the utterance a statement or a question – not to mention the variations based on the physiological, psychological, sociological and phonological aspects of speech. The information processing task on the speech level involves the segmentation and classification of sounds to identify words and their boundaries. The complexity of this task becomes obvious when listening to foreign languages that do not seem to have word boundaries, when in fact, the recognition of these boundaries is part of the native speaker's linguistic capability.

The physiological aspects of speech include primarily the way the articulators interact, and also parameters related to the shape of the vocal tract, the sex, and the age of the speaker. Physiological models of speech recognition in humans postulate that the listener goes through an analysis-by-synthesis process whereby he tries to detect the invariant characteristics of sounds (e.g., "phonemic intentions"). Phonemes are, by definition, the smallest meaning differentiating elements in a language. The sound structure of every language can be described by a fixed number of phonemes (about 40 for English) while the actual pronunciation of a word or sentence has many variations of individual phonemes. According to motor theories, like analysis-by-synthesis, the listener tries to break up the continuous speech sounds into discrete elements without recourse to acoustic properties. While the process takes place without the listener being aware of it, these motor theories of speech are based on the assumption that the listener analyzes the input by converting what he hears to how he thinks it is produced. The motor theories are not without problems. They do not, for instance, have a plausible explanation of how mutes can process and recognize spoken words.

The psychological aspects of speech include concentration, fatigue, which in turn can lead to slips and slurs, and other forms of mispronunciations. Psychological theories of speech recognition are typically independent of physiological evidence. Psychology starts when cognition takes place. Psychological studies of on-line NLP in humans suggest that many analysis processes interact with each other. Beginning with the word recognition, the listener can identify the word shortly after it has been half pronounced. In general, "on-line sentence processing involves the rapid and sophisticated integration of at least three different sources of information – lexical, structural, and interpretive" [Marslen-Wilson 78]. Speech processing is tied to other linguistic processes as is evidenced by research in speech and machine translation, and speech and syntactic analysis.

The phonological aspects of speech includes the way the individual sounds are pronounced and how sounds change their pronunciation based on adjacent sounds. Each natural language has a limited number of sounds, a finite repertoire of how to modify the sounds under certain circumstances, and a finite set of how sounds can be combined. Above the sound segment level – the suprasegmentals – are rules for stress and pitch to form intonation patterns, necessary for conveying important information about the sentence, e.g., questioning, emphasizing, threatening. Let's listen to the pronunciation

of the sound [p] in words like [pit], [tip], and [spit]. The sound typically
is pronounced by forming a complete closure of the mouth at the lips and
then releasing the air by moving the lips apart. The characteristics of the
sound are overlaid based on the surrounding environment.   In word–initial
position, [p] is pronounced with a puff of air following the release of the
closure; for [p] after [s], there is no such puff of air; and in word–final
position, the lips do not have to come apart – [p] remains "unreleased".
The problem of actually recognizing the words becomes more complicated
once processes like deletion and insertion occur, as in the pronunciation of
the word "family", in which the [i] is often deleted, or in the
pronunciation of "warmth", where some people insert a [p] after the [m].
While the variations within word boundaries are hard enough to detect, the
problem is compounded across word boundaries in continuous speech.

   While the phenomena of language such as dialects and intonation are
commonly understood and rule–governed, slurs and slips, idiosyncratic
pronunciations and spurious mispronunciations introduce many parameters
current speech systems cannot cope with. Although there is a good deal of
redundancy in every utterance, a robust speech processor for speaker–
independent and continuous speech has not been built. For the same reasons,
most NLP systems do not contain a speech processor.   For many research
projects, constraining the input parameters to isolated words, and focusing on
one speaker at a time has provided a means to at least get started with
building speech recognition systems. Often, the size of the vocabulary is
limited to anywhere between 50 and 20,000 words. The methodology ranges
from building a speech recognizer to constructing a speech understanding
system, the latter being capable of functioning realistically with the cognitive
aspects of speech, the former dealing primarily with the signal processing
aspects of speech. In speech understanding systems, syntactic and semantic
information about the utterance is often used to analyze the input at the
cost of not using phonetic information.   Most variations of speech are
considered to be noise. In recent years, however, there is a trend towards
using the knowledge we have about variations in the analysis process without
recourse to syntactic or semantic information.

   In Figure 1–3, four processes to analyze speech before the word is
identified are shown. The digitization of the sound wave is the conversion of
the analog to digital signal. The next step is the analysis of the invariant
sounds, the phonemes. Allophonic variation is the changes that occur when
the phonemes are actually used in normal speech. While the number of
phonemes in English is around 40, the allophonic variations are too numerous
to count. The suprasegmental level analyzes what is above the sound
concatenation, e.g., intonation, pitch, stress. After going through these levels
of structure, a process that is not necessarily linear, the speech recognizer is
able to retrieve the word from storage.   Allen Newell, a leading AI veteran

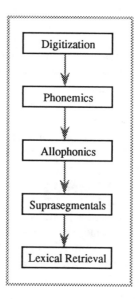

Figure 1-3:   Processing levels of
a system's speech component

from Carnegie Mellon University in Pittsburgh, once remarked that "artificial speech understanding systems provide a major step of getting a ballpark within which man can be found". Current systems have brought us to second base.

1.2 THE ROLE OF THE LEXICON

The Wesleyan housemother announced that henceforth a bell would be rung five minutes before the end of the visiting hours to give the young men time to withdraw.

Children learn words effortlessly by attaching them to things, overgeneralizing at first (e.g., referring to all men with beards as "daddy") but usually getting it right eventually. Two theories have been proposed to explain this process: one, the prototype theory postulates that children grasp the essential meaning of a term and later modify it according to the tokens or exemplars they encounter along the way; the other theory postulates that words are learned by adding features to compose the meaning. Besides referring to things, words carry information as to how objects and ideas are related to each other in time and space. Suffixes and prefixes add more structure to the word stems or roots. Word formation is a complex process, even without issues such as synonyms, antonyms, metaphors, oxymora and all that is Greek to many native speakers.

The information processing task of the lexicon is that of a repository of how words are defined and analyzed. It contains a word look-up table that labels the incoming words according to some predefined categories [e.g., noun, verb] so that other processors can analyze them further. The structure of the lexicon has spawned two separate schools of thought: on the one hand, proponents of the morpheme-based approach hold that all non-derived morphemes, the smallest meaningful units of a language, are listed in the lexicon and derived by rules (e.g., in Figure 1-4, the words "fit" and "fitting" can be analyzed as having different morphemes, which would depend on the utterance in which they are contained); on the other hand, proponents of the word based lexicon [Jackendoff 77] hold that all words are listed as independent lexical entries, which would make the necessary look-up table quite large but would save on on-line retrieval time. Depending on the particular view of the lexicon, a typical entry contains besides syntactic (e.g., noun, verb) or semantic features (e.g., animate, count) the stem of a word, or the entire word.

In the example of "fit" and "fitting" in Figure 1-4, each word can have different interpretations. "Fit" could refer to the noun or the verb "fit". The

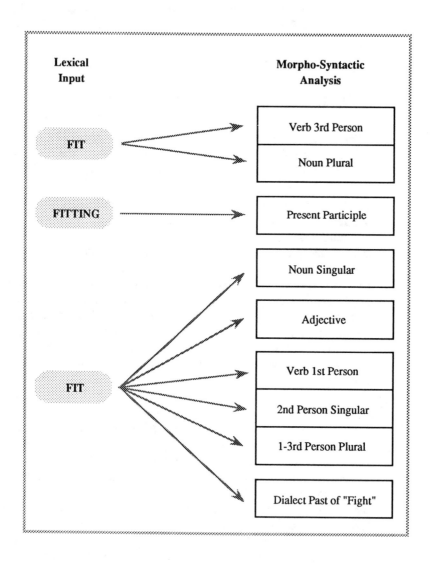

Figure 1-4:   The structure of the lexicon

lexicon look-up often introduces ambiguities that the NLP system has to contend with. In the sentence "He threw a fit", the interpretation of "fit" can be determined structurally, e.g., the word "throw" requires an object. Grammar rules, however, often cannot determine what role a certain word has in a sentence: idioms like "fit to be tied" and sentences like "fit as he seemed, no one could defeat him" cause problems for a sentence analyzer because the position of the word makes it hard to figure out what word class and what interpretation a particular lexical item has. If the word has multiple senses, e.g.,"bachelor", semantic features are necessary to analyze the sentence adequately. These problems show that a purely syntactic analyzer only generates ("describes") the many interpretations from which to select by means of semantic criteria. An exclusively syntactically oriented NLP system passes the burden of analysis onto the next – semantic – level. The lack of satisfactory lexical treatments stems from the preoccupation with syntax in linguistics. In AI, the word is analyzed more in terms of its conceptual function and content in a given sentence. In connectionism, the role and importance of the individual word increased so that individual words and their different senses determined procedurally the meaning of the entire utterance. The lexicon of an NLP system has been an under-researched area; current systems usually adopt the morpheme based approach, viewing word-formation as a dynamic process, e.g., word expert parsing, connectionism.

1.3 THE ROLE OF GRAMMAR IN NLP

President Bush swears in his new cabinet.

The grammatical formalism of an NLP system contains a set of rules to capture the structure and meanings of all the sentences a language consists of. A grammatical formalism is a metalanguage to describe an object language [e.g., English]. Just as differential equations are a means to an end, a grammatical formalism is only as good as the freedom it provides to implement grammars [see Figure 1-5]. The difference between other scientific fields and linguistics is the relation of linguistic theory to the notion of metatheory in linguistics. While theories in other scientific contexts describe observable phenomena to provide analyses for specific examples of these phenomena, in linguistics, a theory encompasses two levels of analysis, that of classes of grammars for the language, and that of particular sentences within one grammar/language. These analyses predict grammaticality of sentences with respect to a grammatical theory. Therefore, in linguistics, "the term 'theory' is primarily reserved for a characterization of general properties of or relationship among analyses – what would in other fields be considered a 'metatheory" [Shieber 87, page 5].

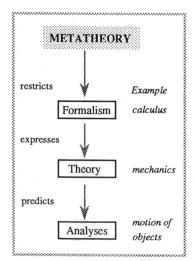
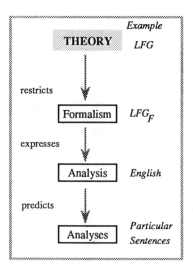

Figure 1-5:   The differences between linguistic and other scientific
theories and formalisms [Shieber 87, page 4-5]

Grammatical formalisms function as precise tools to help delimit the class of possible [natural] languages. The grammar for a particular language is a formalism that predicts what sentences are part of a language. Because it is impossible to simply list all possible sentences of a language, the question of what type of formalism is best to potentially describe all and only those sentences of a language becomes a mathematical issue. Besides being able to state structural and semantic principles of a particular language, linguists are often interested in finding universal principles of language and grammars per se. The search for language universals, according to Chomsky, was intended to shed light on the issue of language acquisition:

> Let us recall the basic character of the problem we face. The theory of UG [universal grammar; KKO] must meet two obvious conditions. On the one hand, it must be compatible with the diversity of existing (indeed, possible) grammars. At the same time, UG must be sufficiently constrained and restrictive in the options it permits to account for the fact that each of these grammars develops in the mind on the basis of quite limited evidence [Chomsky 82, page 3].

An essential part of NLP analysis is the segmentation and classification of linguistic data into structures or "phrases" to determine the "meaning" of the sentence. Similar to other academic disciplines, researchers in linguistics perform a structural analysis of the data based on the smallest meaningful elements and their relation to each other. This analysis is reminiscent of particle physics in the linguistic universe. And much as sanitized data makes for neat and clean theories, it does so at the cost of describing not the actual occurrences of phenomena but picture-perfect idealizations of reality. Nevertheless, sanitized data and theories shed some light on the complex issues of cognitive processes such as NLP. The post-Chomskyan linguists emphasize the biological/psychological aspects of grammars, e.g., lexical functional grammar [Bresnan 82]

Three major types of grammars for analyzing the structure of a sentence developed over time before evolving into specific theories of NLP [see Figure 1-6]. The arbitrariness of their employment becomes evident since their significance varies with geographical location and sub-area of NLP: in Europe, dependency grammars predominate in NLP; for language generation, functional grammars [Halliday 85] are the prime choice in the US. Immediate Constituent Grammars are based on the notion that the linguistic structure can be characterized by a number of recurring patterns that are hierarchically related to each other in the form of a sub-part relationship. Dependency grammars are based on the notion that the central element of

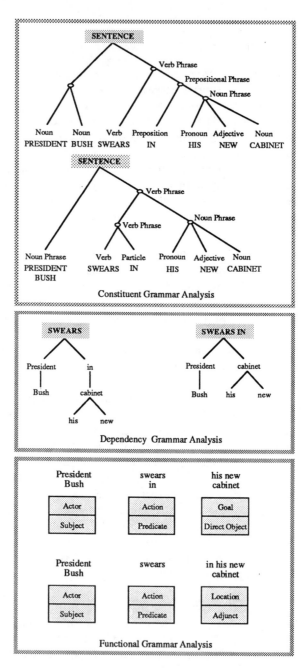

Figure 1-6:   Three different structural analyses of the
                   sentence "President Bush swears in his new cabinet".

the sentence (its "head") is modified by subordinate elements in the sentence. Functional grammars are based on the notion that there exists a level of analysis that assigns a role to a structure independent of the concatenation of individual elements. The models of grammar capture different aspects of linguistic analysis – structural versus functional. The output of such an analysis is therefore theory–specific.

During the process of analyzing an input string, the NLP program matches the incoming words based on their labeled lexical categories onto the rules contained in the grammatical formalism. We make a distinction between grammars whose rules are syntactically motivated (e.g., containing word classes such as noun, verb) and those whose rules depend on the semantics of a particular domain. In conjunction with the parsing formalism and the lexicon, the grammar based NLP programs match an incoming sentence recursively onto the rules contained in the grammar. The output of the program produces an interpretation of the syntactic or semantic information of a sentence. Historically, the dichotomy between syntactic and semantic processing arose when Chomsky [Chomsky 65] claimed that syntactic information is processed autonomously, and that semantic information is not necessary to assign structural description to sentences. The majority of linguists have acquiesced recently to the fact that semantic and even "real world" knowledge is necessary to process sentences or texts adequately [Winograd 83].

Grammar, as we know it, is really a fiction from traditional Latin based nomenclature and Greek philosophy. None of the grammatical categories [e.g., nouns, verbs] are psychologically real. Nor do any of the classifications capture the essence of any one particular language. Tradition lives on. It is unfortunate that most linguistic analyses have been based on languages with a fixed word order, thus definitely skewing the overall analysis of language.   Take English, for example. Most structural pronouncements made in modern linguistics are based on the fortuitous fact that English is a fixed order language in which the verb follows the subject and precedes the object.   Take German as an example of a free order language, and all the structural niceties exploited in modern linguistics have to be reworked.

So, defining grammar as a device that describes ("generates") the sentences of a language gives a functional definition of what a parser should provide. For purposes of convenience, and lack of many viable alternatives, NLP traditionally and currently has dealt with componential analysis of language, at times looking beyond the syntax of a sentence, but rarely beyond the sentence itself. The basic building block of language as we know it, is, however, the word; the next level the phrase, the clause, the sentence; and finally, the text. The underlying assumption is that all of this structuring and combining of elements is done on the substrate of "meaning". While there is no general consensus on how words are best analyzed, there is a greater dissent about how sentences are analyzed, and an even greater dispute of how "meaning" enters into all of this. As polemic as this statement may sound, there is no overall consensus when it comes to how language should be analyzed and the role a grammar has to play within linguistics or outside of it.

Suffice it to say that choosing the sentence as the primary focus of study is misleading because there are very few native speakers of any language that utter sentences resembling those of the grammar book. This phenomenon is one reason why current NLP systems have so many problems with "naturally" occurring language. Oddly enough, the fact that it is very hard for an NLP system to process "ungrammatical" sentences, has spawned a whole new area of linguistic investigation, that of sentence processing programs that have to contend with ill-formed input. The question arises: "Are ungrammatical sentences exceptions to rules or should the rules encompass them in the first place?" We see in this case that Kuhn's paradigm theory comes full circle in NLP. Rather than looking at the empirical evidence, more elaborate constructs are created to maintain the current theories for NLP. As we will see in chapter 12, there are many good reasons for NLP to be a discipline by itself, the need for more empirical models being an obvious one. It has become customary to pass problems with syntactic analyses on to semantics in a part-and-parcel fashion. There are a number of alternatives to this approach. It would make sense, for instance, to treat syntax as a phrase level phenomenon. Rather than producing structural descriptions of entire sentences, the role of syntax would be to form structural units ("phrases") that are combined through semantic and contextual processing.

1.4 THE ROLE OF SEMANTICS

life↑: the meaning of "life" in Montague grammar representation.

The central role of meaning in understanding language has led most researchers in AI and only recently in linguistics to rely primarily on semantic information and only secondarily on syntax in linguistic processing. These researchers do not deny the need or usefulness of structural information; in fact, they use the syntactic analysis to complement the semantic processing: "Ideally, syntactic processing might better be thought of as yielding meaning without building up explicit syntactic structures" [Johnson-Laird 81, page 106].

Significant differences in the definition of "meaning" (semantics) distinguish psychological theories of meaning from those that philosophers advance. Apart from psychological and philosophical theories, there is a third type of semantic (meta)theory referred to as procedural semantics that postulates procedures to express the relationship between truth conditions of a sentence to perception. Following the claim of the linguists Katz and Fodor that every utterance in English can be rendered ambiguous if one tries hard enough, semantics is indeed as important as the recent trend in NLP has made us believe. Just to give a flavor of some issues that are involved in semantics, we will look briefly at the three different types of semantic theories.

Four semantic theories within psychology influence NLP [Johnson-Laird 81]: (1) decompositional theories analyze words in terms of feature matrices, e.g., "bachelor" has the features "male" and "unmarried"; (2) network theories suggest that words are linked via semantic relations, e.g., "bachelor" has the link "is a" to "male" and "adult", etc.; (3) theories that require meaning postulates to define the relations between words, e.g., "FOR ANY X, IF X IS A BACHELOR THEN X IS HUMAN AND X IS ADULT AND X IS MALE AND X IS..."; (4) mental model theories that postulate internal representations for each sentence, e.g., "a picture in the head". Needless to say, each theory has its drawbacks and their scholarly debate is rampant.

In philosophy, semantic theories take one of two forms [Woods 81]: a specification of semantic interpretations either in a more or less well-defined notation or in a formal specification of truth values that characterize under what conditions a (declarative) sentence is true or false. Model-theoretic semantics of first order logic and "possible world" semantics are based on Frege's assumption that the reference of a sentence – and hence its meaning – is its truth value. A theory of meaning is therefore a theory of truth conditions. Model-theoretic semantics works under the assumption that the meaning of a sentence can be studied independently from the context and facts about the utterance. Rather, model-theoretic semantics rebuilds the universe by postulating a construct for every element in its formulas. Context and real world knowledge have become the basis of situation semantics which is based on compositional semantics like Montague grammar, but instead of having sets of possible worlds, situation semantics includes set-theoretic entities built from objects and relationships in the world. Rather than denoting truth values directly, a statement designates a set of situation types which are evaluated to a truth value. David Israel characterizes the problems with model-theoretic semanticese [sic] as a "throw in everything but the kitchen-sink" attitude and concludes that it is "impossible to translate directly and systematically from a natural language into the language of first-order logic" [Israel 83, page xxiii].

Procedural semantics is associated with the idea that meaning arises from computations: simply put, programs are meanings. Identifying the meaning of the utterance with procedures does not by itself provide adequate theories of meaning: "Procedures are devices linking truth conditions to perception. In general, the procedural semantics approach is a paradigm or framework for developing and expressing theories of meaning rather than being a theory of meaning itself" [Woods 81]. Thus, procedural semantics is a metatheory. Procedural semantics has been under attack from many critics because it can be (falsely) construed as reductionism and verificationism. The procedural semantics approach was used in some classic NLP applications (e.g., LUNAR, SHRDLU).

Psychological theories and procedural semantics had a primarily practical impact on NLP whereas model–theoretic semantics had a more theoretical influence.   Critics of the dominant psychological and philosophical theories in the 1980s argued (jokingly) that by following Chomskyan theories (based on decompositional semantics) one would never learn language, whereas by following Montagovian or other model–theoretic theories one could never actually speak or use language. While these logically inspired theories are prevalent in linguistics, procedural semantics has been a staple in the AI community. Within AI, semantics is viewed as a necessary requirement for building models for problem solving. Following Wittgenstein's dictum that the meaning of the language is its use, AI research, rather than focusing on mathematical aspects of a theory, is more interested in how closely the computer can simulate intelligent behavior. Consequently, semantic theories in AI are mostly psychologically inspired. For linguistics, semantics serves the structural analysis of language, while for AI, semantics serves the psychological analysis of language.

1.5 THE ROLE OF DISCOURSE MODELS/PRAGMATICS

> *And since I was not informed – as a matter of fact, since I did not know that there were excess funds until we, ourselves, in that checkup after the whole thing blew up, and that was, if you'll remember, that was the incident in which the attorney general came to me and told me that he had seen a memo that indicated there were no more funds.* [Excerpt from an interview with President Reagan on April 28, 1987, as reprinted in the May 4, 1987, issue of *Roll Call*]

The anacoluthon, the would–be sentence, in Figure 1–7 illustrates to what extent the processing of real world knowledge is needed. Even the surface structural analysis given in the diagram does not capture, much less explain,

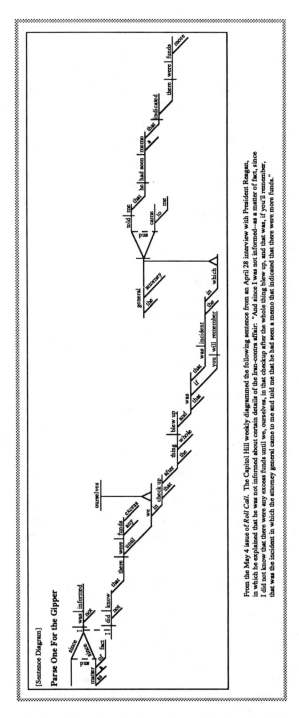

[Sentence Diagram]

Parse One For the Gipper

From the May 4 issue of *Roll Call*. The Capitol Hill weekly diagrammed the following sentence from an April 28 interview with President Reagan, in which he explained that he was not informed about certain details of the Iran-contra affair: "And since I was not informed—as a matter of fact, since I did not know that there were any excess funds until we, ourselves, in that checkup after the whole thing blew up, and that was, if you'll remember, that was the incident in which the attorney general came to me and told me that he had seen a memo that indicated that there were more funds."

Figure 1-7:   Diagram of the excerpt from an interview with President Reagan on April 28, 1987, as reprinted in the May 4, 1987, issue of *Roll Call*.

the complexity of the sentence, and its ramification. Pragmatics describes the linguistic world knowledge, the relationship between language and language user in a given context. An NLP system using pragmatic information is more concerned with modeling the speaker/listener, than processing the structural information embedded in a given discourse. Computational models of discourse have been proposed over the past ten years which focus either on the speaker and his communicative intent, or on the hearer and his reconstruction of the speaker's message [Brady 83]. As illustrated in Figure 1-8, different phenomena in the discourse process are the basis of the models. The challenge lies in integrating the many different aspects of NLP and discourse into one coherent model.

Domain knowledge and "common sense" knowledge play a significant role in NLP systems. NLP systems require the use of domain/task knowledge and not just "grammatical niceties" [Barrow 79]. The problem with constructing a knowledge base for an NLP system "in a principled way" has been that, in the past, only a few kinds of knowledge (e.g., sort hierarchies) had been encoded, or that facts in only very narrow domains were put into the knowledge base [Hobbs 84]. The trend to knowledge based NLP has been a result of active NLP research in AI [Schank 75] with special emphasis on knowledge representation and knowledge use [Brachman 85]. The use of real world knowledge for NLP involves the cognitive modeling of language use, rather than the mathematical modeling of language structure as is done by linguists. Chomskyan linguists, the dominant group in the 1960s and 1970s used formal language theory to model natural language while trying to cope with the resulting discrepancies: e.g., pervasive ambiguity in NL but not in formal language, psychological factors in the use of language. Chomskyan linguists view language as a closed system of rules that are used by an idealized speaker/listener based on his linguistic competence to encode and decode single utterances. The aspect of how and when language is actually being used in context is relegated by Chomskyan linguistics to the realm of linguistic performance.

The modern view of NLP has been under the influence of linguistics with the emphasis on syntax, and starting in the mid-seventies, on semantics. Currently, linguists, while still relying on theories that are more concerned with the structure than the use of language, are more cognizant of psychological implications of NLP and discourse level processes than in the 1970s. Linguists consider NLP primarily as a structural process, whereas AI researchers emphasize the role of knowledge to (1) resolve contextual ambiguities (e.g., I saw the Grand Canyon flying over Arizona), (2) handle ill-formed input (e.g., the car needs fixing), (3) process information contained in the text and not just single sentences, and (4) enable a dialog between the user and the NLP system itself. The knowledge base in conjunction with the appropriate control structure can be the primary component for driving the NLP analysis. In the 1980s, a convergence of AI and linguistic research on investigating discourse level processes has taken place.

1.6 CONCLUSION

In this chapter, we have seen how difficult it is to qualify or quantify the notion of understanding language. We introduced the notion of levels of structure (at Carnegie Mellon University a.k.a., knowledge sources) to distinguish the information processing tasks to be performed by various components of the NLP system. We looked at some of the tasks that humans perform and some of the theories that resulted from empirical analyses of NLP.

The five levels of structure commonly postulated in NLP systems can be characterized as follows: (1) the sound level for the analysis of the spoken utterance; (2) the word level, which contains information about word classes (e.g., nouns, verbs) and word meaning (animate, count); (3) the syntactic level, which contains information about structure of the utterance; (4) the semantic level, which provides an account of meaning; and (5) pragmatics, the study of how context impacts the interpretation of a given utterance.

The two disciplines dealing primarily with NLP issues, linguistics and AI have different goals and methodologies. While linguistics is trying to capture the structural description of language, AI is interested in exploring how different models fare using NLP in real world applications. The potential cross-fertilization between the disciplines has started in the 1980s. Both disciplines seem to converge on the following new premises for NLP:

- the importance of discourse level processing,

- the need for phrase level (as opposed to sentence level) processing,

- the necessity of using knowledge based NLP,

- the possibility of employing neural networks ("connectionism") to solve some of the problems that NLP has encountered, and

- the synergism between speech and other levels of structure

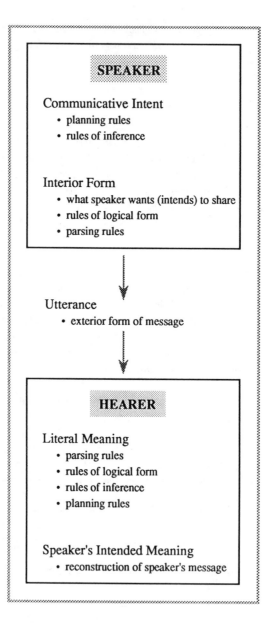

Figure 1-8:   An expanded version of the model
of language use [Brady 83, page 29]

1.7 SUGGESTED READING

Because I have excluded philosophical issues related to NLP in this book, I recommend two books on the subject for those who already read [Hofstadter 79]. Anyone interested in exploring the philosophical issues of computation and cognition should read [Pylyshyn 84]. If a more introductory book for philosophy and language is needed, I recommend "Language and Reality" [Devitt 87]. The treatment of the fundamental philosophical issues is refreshing avoiding technicalities for want of introducing the newcomer to the philosophical aspects of language, e.g., "the work [on modal logic] is complex, difficult and technical. All of it depends to some extent on modern logic. We shall, therefore, spare you an exposition of these results" [Devitt 87]. The authors' placement of ** before and after very technical subjects allows for rapidly skimming and grasping the basic concepts.

A very good anthology of articles on discourse understanding is presented in [Joshi 81]. A host of introductory textbooks on NLP has been published in the 1980s. All of them provide a lot more technical details than this book and will appeal to readers with academic aspirations [Allen 87a, Harris 85, Grishman 86].

CHAPTER 2

APPROACHES

On closer analysis we even find that science knows no 'bare facts' at all but that the 'facts' that enter our knowledge are already viewed in a certain way and are, therefore, essentially ideational. This being the case, the history of science will be as complex, chaotic, full of mistakes, and entertaining as the ideas it contains, and these ideas in turn will be as complex, chaotic, full of mistakes, and entertaining as are the minds of those who invented them. [Paul Feyerabend, *Against Method*]

Designing an NLP system means choosing from among various options what linguistic information should be processed (e.g., the structure of the sentence, the conceptual structure of the words), what level of linguistic or conceptual structure is the driving force for interpreting the input, and what formalism should be selected for the implementation. Currently, three approaches on processing ("parsing") NL exist: (1) the traditional linguistic approach concentrating on sentence level processing based on a grammar formalism; (2) the AI approach developing models for larger bodies of text/utterances based on a knowledge representation scheme; and (3) the connectionism approach creating models of NLP based on models inspired by the behavior of neurons and their connections in the brain. Each one of the three approaches tackles the problems of NLP from a different view point; thus they can be considered complementary in many aspects, rather than competitive.

2.1 THE LINGUISTIC APPROACH

The goals of linguistics are, first and foremost, completeness (characterizing all possible natural languages), and restrictiveness (characterizing only the possible natural languages), and secondarily, such goals as rigour, simplicity, elegance, and declarativeness [Shieber 87, page 8].

Traditional linguistics provides only a modicum of insight into computational NLP. Reasons include the overall goal of linguistics – the search for a description of language universals, the methodology – cute facts of language to produce cute theories without stringent formalisms the nature of the curriculum – no training in developing formalism required [Gazdar 87a]. The basic assumption of modern linguistic research – starting with Chomsky – was to investigate the syntactic structure of language. The arbitrarily chosen unit of scientific investigation was the sentence. The orientation toward the sentence seriously flawed the NLP endeavor. Not only were people misled in thinking that syntax and the sentence is the main focus of an investigation of language; many linguists brought up in the Chomskyan tradition of the 1960s thought that syntax was an autonomous phenomenon with its own rules that were independent of the rest of language. Some scientists even went so far as to postulate that the mind was modular and that grammar, perceptual mechanisms and conceptual knowledge were its major components. Each of these components can contain well-formed objects independent from the other. Sentences are objects that are well-formed in each of the three components. Represented in a Venn diagram, sentences are the objects that lie at the intersection of the three components [Lightfoot 83].

The prevalent thesis, that syntax was autonomous and the best way to find language universals, skewed the analysis. The emphasis was on finding many details about as many languages as possible, preferably exotic, to come up with cute analyses for language. At the core of the linguist–turned–polyglot craze was the quest for a description of Language [sic], determining a universal structure and universal rules for the underlying structure based on an analysis and synthesis of many languages. Unfortunately, many modern linguists seem to focus their attention on notorious examples without going through the pain of actually learning the language whose structure they have analyzed. The harvest of language universals is disappointing thus far.

Finding common denominators amongst languages, be it sentence or word structure, is hard and to some extent not enlightening because denominators often being too broad.   Nevertheless, in the late 1980s, Chomsky's "Government-binding" theory [Sells 86] is cherished amongst some insiders because it allows the derivation of grammars for individual languages from a host of universal principles that are mostly syntactically motivated.

Going back to the analysis of sentences. The methodology of linguistics with (Methodology of linguistics) respect to empirical evidence is introspection. The way to test a theory is to get a number of sentences, judge them according to your language ability and use them as evidence. Besides the obvious idiolect traps – the notion that everybody has language variations germane to himself – the underlying assumption that Chomsky introduced was that language should be analyzed on two levels: the level of competence and the level of performance. On the level of competence, language is analyzed according to cut-and-dried rules based on the idealized language user. On the level of performance, the psychological side of language, the process of language and its use should be analyzed. Slips and slurs, all "ungrammatical behavior" was to be accounted for in performance models of language. The hiatus between linguists and AI researchers became apparent when AI judged the performance models as more pertinent to its own language analysis than competence models.   It also became clear that competence models were mathematical figments that put natural language on the level of formal languages.

Within the competence models of language, Chomsky introduced another distinction that made history. A grammar not only was made up of different components for the lexicon, the sound and the semantic level, but at its core was a component that would transform the underlying structure of every sentence into the final utterance that we perceive as the final output of our grammar processor.   The dichotomy between the underlying "deep structure" and the final "surface structure" was a convenient way of explaining common phenomena in language such as synonymity and ambiguity. Synonymous sentences, assuming they exist, have the same underlying structure and their only distinction is that through a series of processes whose motivation is not quite clear these sentences have been "transformed" into their final surface structure. Ambiguous sentences follow the opposite pattern: they come from different underlying structures and by chance have been transformed into the surface structure (e.g., "Flying planes can be dangerous"). The postulation of transformations affords Chomsky et al the opportunity to discuss language in terms of syntax and in terms of transformations. The natural ordering and applicability of transformations was the subject of the better part of linguistic endeavor in the 1960s and 1970s.   Computationally, the transformational grammarians were left with a production model, not a recognition model.   Because transformations could delete, add, and move constituents within a sentence the final surface structure could have come from just about any underlying structure, the analysis of sentences was up to human imagination. Computationally there was no way to sensibly "reverse-engineer" transformational grammars to make them work as recognition systems.

Modern linguists concentrate in their study of NL on the details of the sentence structure based on a grammatical theory. In general, the grammar consists of syntactic/semantic rules, supports linear processing and is restricted to individual sentences. Linguistics, the discipline with a long history of dealing with the intricacies of language, has spawned three branches of research combining computers with the study of language: (1) the traditional, grammar-oriented linguists that view the computer simply as a tool to test their grammatical formalisms; (2) the computational linguists that create, extend, and reorganize formalisms for non-computer specialists to take advantage of computers in writing grammars; and (3) the model-oriented linguists that try to model human parsing by exploring constraints and representations, mostly addressing discourse-level processes often from a syntactic point of view.

2.1.1 Grammar based approaches

Here is the history of linguistics in one sentence: once upon a time linguists (i.e. syntacticians) used augmented phrase structure grammars, then they went over to transformational grammars, and then some of them started using augmented phrase structure grammars again, <space for moral> [Gazdar 87b].

The term "grammar" refers in the context of formal language theory to a device or a set of rules that describes ("generates") what sentences are part of a particular language. For linguists, the notion of formal grammar as a generative device became significant after the noted linguist Noam Chomsky used the properties inherent in formal languages to describe grammars for natural language and to formalize their expressiveness [Chomsky 63]. A formal language consists of (1) syntactic categories, (2) terminal symbols, (3) rewrite rules and (4) a start symbol. Noam Chomsky devised four types of grammars, based on the types of rules they used. The simplest grammar, Type 3, also known as a finite-state or regular grammar, can produce only simple "sentences". The Type 2 grammar is also known as a context-free grammar. In this grammar, the left side of each rewrite rule can consist of only a single non-terminal symbol. Note that this symbol can always be rewritten as the right side of the rule, regardless of the context in which that non-terminal appears. Most syntactic parsers use a context-free grammar. The next most complex grammar in this scheme is a Type 1, or

context-sensitive grammar. In this   type, more than one symbol can appear
on the left side of the rewrite rule. There is only one requirement for these
rules: there must be more symbols on the right side than on the left.   The
most complex grammar, Type 0, has rules that do not follow any set
patterns or requirements save that they have a left and a right side which
can be empty. This grammar is very difficult to parse. Indeed, researchers
have proved that Type 0 grammars have the full computational power of an
unrestricted Turing   machine.   Chomsky's major contention was that a
natural language such as English could not be completely described by a
context-free grammar, but required either a context-sensitive or a Type 0
grammar.

There is an on-going dispute in linguistics, however, as to whether English
does in fact conform to a context-free grammar.   One argument in support
of English being a context-sensitive language involves the fact that singular
nouns and plural nouns require singular verbs and plural verbs, respectively.
It is generally accepted in linguistics that finite state grammars were too
weak, while transformational grammars were too powerful which in turn led
to the increased interest in context-free grammars. In the late 1980s, slightly
non-context-free grammars (e.g., government-binding [Sells 86]) are in the
mainstream of linguistic investigations [Savitch 87].

Grammar based approaches consist of a set of rewrite rules to capture the
structural syntactic information of language, a lexicon containing terminal
symbols for the set of rewrite rules, and a control mechanism that helps to
assign the terminal symbols to the output of the rewrite rules.   During the
processing, the program matches an incoming sentence recursively onto the
rules contained in the grammar. The most common non-deterministic control
mechanism for assigning structural descriptions to natural language input are
top-down and bottom-up NLP systems.

2.1.2 Computational linguistics

*Once upon a time computational linguists (i.e. builders of parsers)
used augmented phrase structure grammars, then they went over to
augmented transition networks, and then many of them started
using augmented phrase structure grammars again* [Gazdar 87b].

While linguists in general try to find interesting theories of language,
computational linguists try to find interesting algorithms and formalisms to
implement some of the grammatical theories. Following our discussion in
section 1.3 and in particular the diagram in Figure 1-5, while traditional
linguists are interested in performing analyses of sentences and discovering

grammars for particular languages, computational linguists focus their efforts on the level of traditional scientific metatheory, what is called in linguistics a theory [Figure 1–5]. The point of the discussion is to distinguish the role of a formalism used on the one hand as a tool, and on the other as a theoretical device.

The brief history of computational linguistics has three major paradigms: context–free grammars [CFG], augmented transition networks [ATN], and unification grammars [for a detailed discussion, see section 3.1]. CFGs and unification grammars are in a sense augmented phrase structure grammar formalisms.   Historically, COMIT, the first computationally motivated formalism, developed by Yngve in 1958, was a CFG formalism allowing linguists to implement their grammars.   Currently, PATR II, among many other unification based formalisms, functions as a tool for implementing grammatical theories that are non–transformational and context–free. ATNs are still very popular. But because they are unconstrained, hence too powerful, their use is decreasing.   The current philosophy behind grammar formalism is best described as: "The characteristics of grammar formalisms promoted by the goals of NLP are, first of all, *weak completeness* and *computational effectiveness*. Secondarily, they are the goals of computer language design in general: *expressivity, simplicity, declarativeness, rigour*, etc." [Shieber 87, page 12].

2.1.3 Modeling discourse based on autonomous syntax

The primacy and autonomy of syntax in NLP has divided linguists and academic disciplines dealing with NLP. Chomsky's original autonomy of syntax thesis contains the idea that syntactic information is processed in a module separate from any other linguistic information, and that the syntactic processes follow rules and representations of its own. An outgrowth of the MIT school of autonomous syntactic analysis was Mitchell Marcus' deterministic parser, Parsifal [Marcus 80]. In contrast to non–deterministic parsers, Parsifal did not backtrack or allow for multiple concurrent analyses of the sentence. Parsifal used limited look–ahead, allowing the parser to analyze two constituents of the sentence coming after the one which the system was focusing on.   The limit to two–constituent look–ahead caused the parser to analyze certain types of sentences erroneously, very similar to actual human processing. Those sentence types are labeled "garden–path" sentences (e.g., "The horse raced past the barn fell") and are the test cases that require semantic information to complete the parse. "garden–path" sentences promote usually one erroneous reading which the listener detects at a later stage during processing. In the sentence "The horse raced past the barn fell", the listener has already completed one analysis before realizing that the second verb "fell" is the main verb of the sentence and "raced" is part of a reduced relative clause. Parsifal, without unlimited look-ahead will parse the sentence erroneously just like a human would.

Parsifal consists of (1) a grammar interpreter, (2) a pushdown stack for active nodes that eventually have to be dominated by non-terminal symbols, e.g., noun phrase, and (3) three to five buffers that contain constituents whose grammatical function is still unknown. The processing proceeds from left to right, pushing a node onto the active node stack to suspend formation of a constituent. If a word enters into the buffer, the grammar, consisting of a set of production rules, determines whether a new constituent has to be formed. If a new constituent is required, it is put into the active node stack which grows downward. The interpreter looks at the contents of the three buffers and at the bottom of the active node stack.

Parsifal was one of the few attempts by linguists to create a model of language use based on a linguistic theory. The model based on Chomsky's transformational grammar successfully showed some inherent limits of syntactic processing. Parsifal failed to show, however, what impact issues such as lexical ambiguity have. In language generation, the system called Mumble, developed by David McDonald [McDonald 81] at MIT, makes similar theoretical claims about syntax as Marcus made for Parsifal. While Marcus' Parsifal deals with language recognition and is concerned with avoiding backtracking and with the limits of syntax, McDonald's Mumble system is concerned with the opposite: unconstrained linguistic planning and the role of syntax in planning. Another similarity between Parsifal and Mumble was their relationship to the psychological reality, the possibility of showing that syntax based process models have some empirical evidence from actual human linguistic behavior. Parsifal showed that syntax could be used to process sentences without backtracking, except for "garden-path" sentences. Mumble [see description in section 7.4] showed that certain generation errors found in human utterances correspond to those produced by the program.

The linguistic approach to the problems in NLP that we have discussed thus far can best be summarized as the process of determining the details of the structure of a sentence based on a grammar. The grammar is primarily based on syntactic rules that favor linear processing which is usually restricted to sentences. The grammar and accompanying formalisms help determine classes of languages which ultimately may help discovery of universals of language. The study of and search for universals of language is motivated ultimately by being able to constrain linguistic theories to adequately explain language.

2.2 THE AI APPROACHES

The goals of AI are, first and foremost, completeness (characterizing all possible knowledge representations), and restrictiveness (characterizing only the possible knowledge representations), and secondarily, such goals as rigour, simplicity, elegance, and declarativeness.

If "language" from the original quote [Shieber 87, page 8] is replaced by "knowledge representation", the methodology and goals of AI and linguistics do not seem quite as far apart as commonly believed. Moreover, the quest for language universals may be on the same level of abstraction as that of knowledge representation.

In AI the focus of NLP is on the knowledge necessary to "understand" NL. NLP systems based on AI use "common sense" and domain knowledge, try to develop models for language use and go beyond sentential processing analyzing larger contexts. AI injected new aspects into NLP, in a negative form through polemic attacks about what the object of study for NLP should be, and in a positive form by orienting AI NLP research around cognitive aspects that dealt with the full spectrum of human language use. Mutual influences between cognitive psychology and AI promoted a solid research thrust for both disciplines, not to mention the formation of a new discipline – cognitive science. With the advent of AI and its role in cognition, philosophers of science dramatized the question "Can computers think?" through "thought experiments" and biological phenomenology in the vein of Searle and Dreyfus.

The methodological issue in AI when it comes to knowledge use is that of representation. In Figure 2-1, the complexity of knowledge representation schemas is illustrated. Considering a piece of discourse/text dealing with entering and ordering in a restaurant, the various levels of knowledge and their necessary interaction becomes apparent. What is represented in Figure 2-1 are two descriptions of scenes that make up a "restaurant script". Scripts are data structures that try to capture stereotypical events [see also section 3.2.5] by outlining what conditions potentially apply and how they interact during the NLP stage. Each event is made up of individual actions that are analyzed in terms of language primitives or "conceptual dependencies" [see section 3.2.4]. Utterances are analyzed in terms of these primitives, and larger chunks of discourse are analyzed in terms of scripts. While the terminology is germane to this particular theory and model, the underlying components are similar in all models of NLP proposed within the AI approach: characterize the problem solving task, determine relevant knowledge sources, define processing strategies, e.g., control structures.

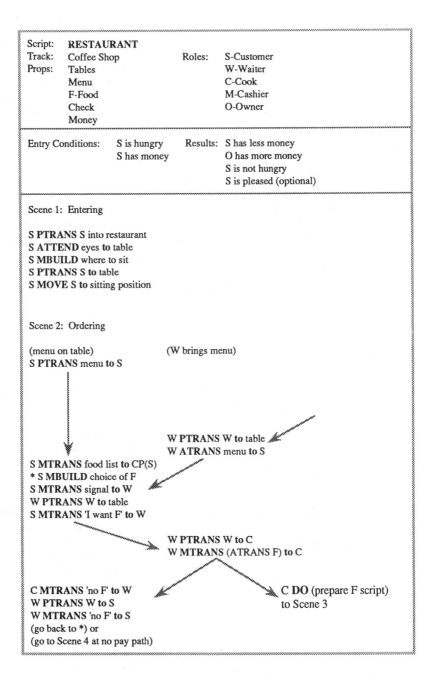

Script: **RESTAURANT**
Track: Coffee Shop   Roles: S-Customer
Props: Tables   W-Waiter
           Menu   C-Cook
           F-Food   M-Cashier
           Check   O-Owner
           Money

Entry Conditions: S is hungry   Results: S has less money
                     S has money   O has more money
                                                    S is not hungry
                                                    S is pleased (optional)

Scene 1: Entering

S **PTRANS** S into restaurant
S **ATTEND** eyes to table
S **MBUILD** where to sit
S **PTRANS** S to table
S **MOVE** S to sitting position

Scene 2: Ordering

(menu on table)   (W brings menu)
S **PTRANS** menu to S

                                          W **PTRANS** W to table
                                          W **ATRANS** menu to S

S **MTRANS** food list to CP(S)
* S **MBUILD** choice of F
S **MTRANS** signal to W
W **PTRANS** W to table
S **MTRANS** 'I want F' to W

                              W **PTRANS** W to C
                              W **MTRANS** (ATRANS F) to C

C **MTRANS** 'no F' to W   C **DO** (prepare F script)
W **PTRANS** W to S   to Scene 3
W **MTRANS** 'no F' to S
(go back to *) or
(go to Scene 4 at no pay path)

Figure 2-1:   The restaurant script [Schank 77, page 43].

Methodologically, AI research tries to encode the domain of the application
in the appropriate knowledge representation to model linguistic behavior. The
modeling of linguistic behavior can be in the form of constructing and
implementing (1) semantic theories, (2) entire domain models, and (3)
memory based models.

2.2.1 Semantics

The central role of meaning in understanding language has led some
researchers to rely on predominantly semantic rather than syntactic
approaches.   These researchers do not deny the need for some structural
processing: rather they use the syntactic analysis to complement their
semantic considerations.   Three semantically oriented approaches to NLP are
case grammar, semantic grammar, and conceptual dependency theory.

Case grammar has been used in a number of NLP implementations since
its development in 1968 [Fillmore 68]. The idea behind case grammar is
that every sentence has an underlying representation of its meaning. This
representation includes the verb and the various noun phrases related to the
verb. For example, in the sentence "John opened the door with a key", we
designate "John" as the agent, "door" as the object, and "key" as the
instrument for the verb "opened".   Note that the cases remain the same for
the sentence "The door was opened by John with a key."   The founder of
case theory, C. Fillmore, a linguist by trade who became disenchanted with
the ideological myopia of Chomsky's autonomous syntax thesis, referred to
the relationships between these nouns and the verb as cases. You may recall
that Latin and some modern languages have similar cases for nouns.
Fillmore postulated a number of cases, none of them occurring more than
once in a sentence. That very fact was the beginning of extensive criticism
of case grammar and a self critique by Fillmore who went as far as
denouncing the validity of case grammar.   Nevertheless, case grammar is one
of the few linguistic theories that was firmly adopted and accepted by the
AI community [Bruce 75].   Moreover, the more abstract notion of "case"
has been a cornerstone of Roger Schank's theory of "conceptual
dependencies", described below.

Semantic grammar consists of a lexicon and a series of rewrite rules. It is
similar to a syntactic grammar, except that word classes (e.g., noun, verb) are
replaced by specific semantic classes (e.g., ships, ship properties). The
advantage of this approach is that the size of these semantic classes is much
smaller than the size of an equivalent word class. This results in a much
more efficient parsing strategy, since the program has to check a smaller
number of possibilities. The disadvantage of semantic grammar is the
difficulty of transferring rewrite rules from one domain of applications to

another. The principle behind semantic grammar is half way between the syntactic grammars and the early AI systems that try to model domains by determining the most basic templates. One of the most prominent implementations of semantic grammar was LADDER, developed in 1978 by Gary G. Hendrix. LADDER was designed as a natural language interface to a database for the US Navy. Figure 2-2 shows an example of some of the rewrite rules used by LADDER. Hendrix later went on to form the company Symantec and developed the database manager/word processor Q&A.

Schank's notion of "conceptual dependencies" stems from the idea of reducing complex concepts to basic ones. Each word or concept, according to Schank, can be further reduced until a limited number of primitives, entities no further analyzable, remain. In language, according to Schank, verbs can be reduced to some basic meaning elements, just like the noun phrases in Fillmore's theory can be further reduced to a limited set of deep cases. This reduction principle is further developed in other areas of AI, e.g., Minsky's notion of agents that form a society of mind [Minsky 85] that can account for problem solving behavior. Schank's conceptual dependencies [Schank 75] are part of his psychologically based model of NLP.

2.2.2 Domain knowledge and world knowledge

Early NLP systems were based on the idea that parsers can look for recurring linguistic patterns in a sentence without using any explicit grammatical formalism. During sentence analysis, the system merely looks for a possible match with a fixed number of patterns. If a match is found, the system performs a certain action (e.g., rearranging the input according to another pattern). The process is similar to template-matching in other areas of AI (e.g., vision).

ELIZA, also known as Doctor, the best-known pattern-matching program, was designed to simulate a Rogerian psychologist. The program, still popular today, was written by Joseph Weizenbaum in 1966. ELIZA consists of a set of patterns [see Figure 2-3] with each pattern having a number of replies associated with it. For example, the pattern *"x always y"* had the following class of replies associated with it: *Can you think of a specific example?, When?, Really?*. Thus, the patient's input *People always stare at me*, would trigger the response *Can you think of a specific example?* by the program. Another activation of the pattern *"x always y"*, *I always think of my parents*, would trigger the response *When?* It is obvious that ELIZA performed so well because it operated in a limited domain and ignored most of the input.

Pattern-matching programs without a grammatical basis proved to be of

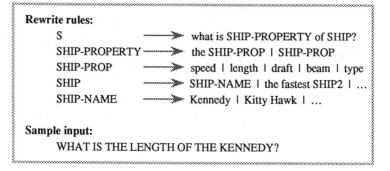

Rewrite rules:

S	⟶	what is SHIP-PROPERTY of SHIP?
SHIP-PROPERTY	⟶	the SHIP-PROP | SHIP-PROP
SHIP-PROP	⟶	speed | length | draft | beam | type
SHIP	⟶	SHIP-NAME | the fastest SHIP2 | ...
SHIP-NAME	⟶	Kennedy | Kitty Hawk | ...

Sample input:

WHAT IS THE LENGTH OF THE KENNEDY?

Figure 2-2:   A semantic grammar

limited   use. They are useful only if partial analysis is required or if other components of the system can make up for the loss of syntactic information. In the 1960s, a host of these pattern based programs were created ranging from answering questions about baseball to tutoring students in algebra. These programs demonstrated on the one hand, how easy it is to build a NLP system based on a specific domain or task, and, on the other hand, how hard it is to embed "common sense" knowledge into these systems [see [Tennant 81] for a discussion of these early NLP systems]. The basic concept of pattern matching, exploiting domain-specific information at the expense of grammatical analysis, however, has been further developed and was used in semantic grammars and research of sublanguages, which we will discuss later.

Instead of relying solely on the structural or semantic information of a sentence, some NLP systems also using the AI approach have access to a knowledge base for a specific domain of knowledge. This contrasts with most grammar based theories that look at NLP simply in terms of a set of rewrite rules for sentence level processing. Two types of knowledge based systems are being pursued: on the one hand, people try to model domain knowledge to construct interfaces, understanding systems; on the other hand, research into discourse modeling incorporates pragmatic knowledge into the NLP systems. Domain knowledge can be represented in frame-like structures in which stereotypical situations from everyday life are encoded in the system. The task of the NLP system is to determine which of these represented structures are to be accessed at any given time during processing.

2.2.3 Memory based models

Processing NL input in the context of a conversation requires linking what is said to experiences in the past. Restaurant scripts are plausible because we create the memories of the stereotypical situations we have been exposed to in order to learn and understand. Moving up higher in the level of abstraction of processes required for NL understanding, Schank and his colleagues postulate abstraction units that organize scripts by extracting the essential underlying structures into memory units. These memory units, referred to as memory organization packages [MOPs], help organize memory, recall, reminding [see Figure 2-4]. Memory based models try to find answers to many of the questions surrounding NLP, e.g., reminding. Schank contends that the process of reminding, for instance, consists of an expectation failure in the following sense. Based on their experiences, humans expect certain things to happen, e.g., entering a restaurant, ordering, leaving a tip. If something goes wrong, i.e., not according to expectation, the person has encountered a new situation, "learned" a new thing [Schank 82].

Hello	Hello
HOW DO YOU DO? PLEASE STATE YOUR PROBLEM	HOW DO YOU DO? PLEASE STATE YOUR PROBLEM.
I want a good example for my book.	I have been very depressed lately.
YOUR BOOK?	YOU SAY YOU HAVE BEEN VERY DEPRESSED LATELY?
Yes, my book about computers. Can you help me?	Yes.
YOU ARE BEING SOMEWHAT SHORT WITH ME	YOU ARE BEING SOMEWHAT SHORT WITH ME.
I didn't mean to be.	What about my mother beating me?
YOU SAY YOU DIDN'T MEAN TO BE?	TELL ME MORE ABOUT YOUR FAMILY.
That's right. What do you know about computers?	
DO COMPUTERS WORRY YOU?	
Not at all. I think they can be very useful.	
CAN YOU ELABORATE ON THAT?	
APPLICATION: ADVISORY SYSTEM	APPLICATION: ROGERIAN PSYCHOLOGY

Figure 2-3:   Sample output from ELIZA [Raphael 76, page 199]

Memory research has spawned many theories related to NLP: Anderson spreading activation models, Quillian semantic networks, to name just a few. It is apparent that the objective of these approaches is to analyze the process of language and not like linguistic theories to describe the structure of language. The issue of how to model and implement these theories has been a matter of knowledge representation and control strategies. For NLP the task of creating these representations is hard and constantly fraught with the problem of scalability. Many of the open issues within the memory based research activity, however, have pointed to a different theory of information processing – neural networks or connectionism.

2.3 CONNECTIONIST APPROACHES

Everything of interest in cognition happens above the 100–millisecond level – the time it takes you to recognize your mother. (H. Simon, quoted in [Hofstadter 85])

The increased interest in neural networks (NN), using results from brain research to form theories for human information processing that were based on the behavior of neurons and their connections, advanced speech processing technology, and spawned research in NLP under the label of "connectionism". Connectionism uses the powerful metaphor based on biological mechanisms that suggest information processing takes place by "spreading activation" of multiple processors, similar to the firing of neurons in the brain. The connections between the processors are determined by attached weights that either promote or inhibit the activation of a processor.

The basic idea behind NNs stems from the models that were developed to explain the workings of the human brain, in particular the behavior of neurons and their synapses [see Figure 2–5]. The biggest enigma is their speed. Whereas the operations of conventional computers are measured in nanoseconds, neurons operate in milliseconds, and yet they perform complex operations fast and without fail. Given that most cognitive processes take no longer than a few hundred milliseconds, Feldman in his "100–step program constraint" postulates that most of these processes take no more than 100 serial steps to perform, while individual neurons compute operations at a rate that is as slow as a single instruction of a digital computer. Therefore, the brain must perform its processing feat through massive parallelism.

Massive parallelism affords NNs, silicon or carbon based, a high degree of (1) fault tolerance, the ability to recover gracefully from processor failure, (2) associative recall, the ability to retrieve information instantaneously based on content, (3) graceful degradation, the ability to guess when there is no

MOPs	Scripts	TAUs
M-BAR	$CHANGE-CLOTHES	TAU-BROKEN-SERVICE
M-BORROW	$CALL	TAU-BROKEN-CONTRACT
M-CONTRACT	$SEX	TAU-CLOSE-CALL
M-EDUCATION	$WRITE	TAU-DIRE-STRAITS
M-LEGAL-DISPUTE		TAU-HIDDEN-BLESSING
M-MARITAL-CONTRACT	**Settings**	TAU-RED-HANDED
M-MEAL	BAR	
M-REPRESENT-CLIENT	BEDROOM	
M-RESTAURANT	COURTROOM	
M-SERVICE	HOME	
M-LETTER	RESTAURANT	
M-PHONE	ROADWAY	

Reasoning	Physical Objects	Relationships/Roles
rM-JURIS-PRUDENCE	ALCOHOL	R-MARRIAGE
	CAR	R-ROOMMATES
Interpersonal	CLOTHES	RT-JUDGE
	LETTER	RT-LAWYER
IPT-LOVERS	LIQUID	RT-TEACHER
IPT-FRIENDS	MONEY	
IP-FAVOR	PHONE	
RENEW-IPT		
SUSPEND-IPT		

ACEs	Affects
Commiseration	Gratitude
Felicitation	Relief
Reassurance	Anger
	Surprise, etc.

(Most goals, plans, events are associated with MOPs)

Figure 2-4:   Memory based models [Dyer 83, page 376–377]

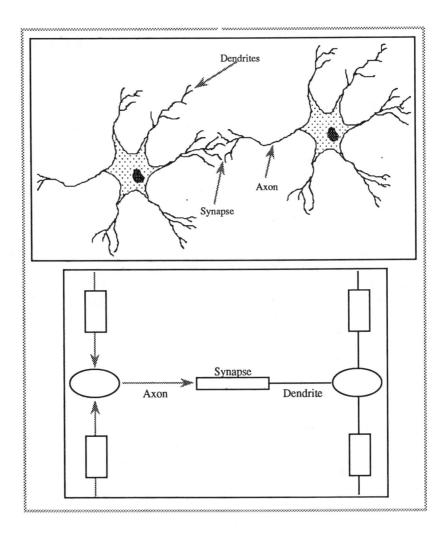

Figure 2-5: Biological and artificial neural networks

exact match for the requested information. Consequently, NNs are said to
outperform conventional computers when it comes to tasks that require the
processing of incomplete, unpredictable, and often inconsistent data (e.g.,
speech processing, pattern recognition).

Neural networks, the "reborn" science, has gone from great promises in the
1940s (e.g., McCulloch and Pitts) and 1950s (e.g., Widrow, Rosenblatt),
through misguided attacks in the 1960s (e.g., Minsky/Papert) to legitimate
and stronger than ever revival in the 1970s (e.g., Grossberg, Kohonen) and
1980s (e.g., Hopfield, Rumelhart).   NNs are being studied under two
theoretical aspects, (1) efficiency of neural based electronic architecture, and
(2) understanding of biological functions of NNs. NNs are being
used/produced either in the form of neurocomputers, hardware that models
the parallelism of neurons, or netware, software that emulates neurons and
their interconnections on conventional serial computers.   The interdisciplinary
nature of NNs makes it hard to delineate its legitimate boundaries. In
general, NN research is concerned with the subsymbolic level whereas
cognitive science, including AI, is interested in the symbolic level of
processing, subscribing to Herbert Simon's remark that "everything of interest
in cognition happens above the 100-millisecond level – the time it takes you
to recognize your mother". In particular, NN research in theory is thought
of as complementary to AI and cognitive science: NNs deal with the
biological underpinnings of processes like visual perception, speech
recognition and proprioception that have been, so far, out of reach of any
other science. NN research addresses biological as opposed to psychological
phenomena, focuses on the unconscious or subcognitive activities, and assumes
massive parallelism.

A fairly recent approach to NLP involves setting up a network of neuron-
like computing units for individual words. In Figure 2-6, the network
processing of the sentence "The astronomer married the star" simulates how
word sense disambiguation works. The various word senses are activated as
the sentence is fed through the network. After a large enough number of
repetitions [note the different activation of word meanings after multiple
cycles in Figure 2-6], the network "settles" on one interpretation over the
other.   Each processing element in the network has a number of inputs.
Each input to the processing element has a weight value, which can vary
from −1 to 1.   When a processing element is activated, it evaluates all its
inputs and weighs them according to their respective weight values. If certain
conditions are met, the processing element generates an output value that is
used as an input by other processing units.   In the example in Figure 2-6,
the network illustrates how the lexical layer and the word sense layer
interact with the syntactic input layer.   Note that only the weights between
units of the inputs may be changed during "learning": the connection pattern
itself is "prewired".   In currently competing configurations of NLP neural

network systems, various configurations, processing elements, and models are used. Neural network applications range from speech recognition systems [see section 8.1] to handwriting recognition systems. In the following discussion, the better-known models are described.

In the Small et al. approach to NLP [Small 82], word experts are considered to be the basic processing element. Linguistic knowledge is distributed among a group of procedural experts that know how the interpretation of a word changes in particular contexts. A common characteristic of many linguistically oriented NLP systems is that they are based on non-deterministic rewrite rules for sentence-level processing. This assumption is embodied even in some AI systems for syntactic analysis. In spite of their different outlook on NLP, both AI and linguistics promote the idea that NLP is best described by rules that deal with the study of discourse constituents (e.g., paragraphs). Consequently, the words of a language are reduced to tokens that are relevant for comprehension only as part of sentence and concept level rules [Rieger 79].

Evidence against the rule based approach has led to the theory of word expert parsing, which takes the word as the basic linguistic unit; linguistic knowledge is distributed among a group of procedural specialists that diagnose the word's contextual usage. As the word experts are invoked, they determine what analysis path should be taken. Arguments in favor of word experts are: (1) words have a rich linguistic and conceptual structure, (2) psychological evidence shows that lexical access is a deciding factor in language comprehension, (3) it is unlikely that language can be reduced to a number of rewrite rules. The multiple applicability of rules that are similar requires a control structure that is internal to the sentence in order to monitor the sequences of constituents – it is plausible to embody this control structure within the single word, and (4) word sense ambiguity cannot be captured plausibly by existing rewrite systems. The extension of the idea of word experts in the form of connectionism has been the basis of NLP models that deal with word sense disambiguation. The idea of word experts was made public long before the renaissance of neural networks and connectionism became popular.

In Rumelhart's et al. system [McClelland 86] the neural-network parsing model contains three levels of "neurons". The first level is the lexical level, which serves as the input level of the network. Here, the neurons are mapped to particular words. On the second level, the word sense level, the inputs from the lexical level are combined to activate the neurons that represent the meaning of the words. On the third, case logical level, the meanings are combined to form predicates and objects. Their approach is very similar to Small's, and Cottrell's [Small 82] recent research that also shows a case layer rather than a surface syntactic layer in the example shown in Figure 2–6.

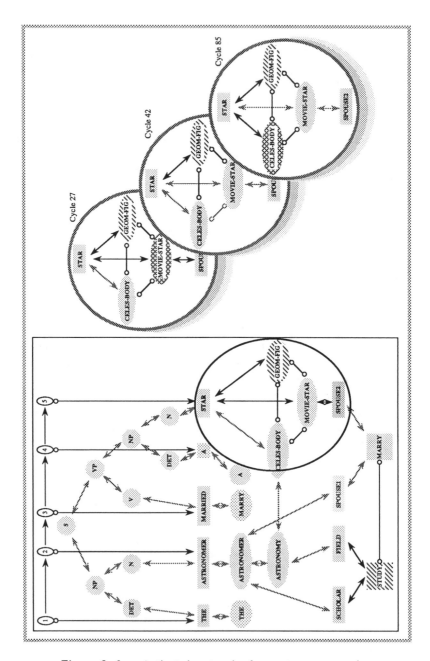

Figure 2-6: Activated networks for sentence processing
at three different stages [Pollack 86, page 191]

2.4 CONCLUSION

Alan Kay's adage "sentences are pointers into shared metaphors" is as much an implicit criticism of current approaches to NLP as it is a possible starting point for a research program. The current issues involving NLP are polarized around three schools of thought – linguistics, AI, and connectionism.

While linguists investigate language by means of mathematical formalisms, AI deals with language as a phenomenon of knowledge representation and use. The two disciplines reduce the phenomenon of NL to logical operations on a grammar that describes all possible sentences, and a knowledge base that contains all possible concepts, respectively. What is at the core of the phenomenon of NL and what makes NLP possible for humans are three abilities [McClelland 86]: (1) pattern matching, (2) modeling of the world, and (3) manipulating our environment so that it represents something. To capture and model these abilities at least three levels of analysis are required: the structural, the functional and the subsymbolic level. While the structural level has been the domain of linguists, the functional level that of AI researchers, and connectionism focuses on the subsymbolic level, together they will promote the following developments in the NLP arena:

- Parsing NL will become a knowledge based phenomenon.

- NLP will take place on a symbolic and subsymbolic level.

- The trend to more empirical studies within NLP will mean the death of some weak theories while at the same time bringing NLP closer to practical applications.

- NLP will move from investigating structural phenomena of units and elements to pursuing process-oriented theories

However, caution is necessary, as Teuvo Kohonen at the *First Annual International Conference on Neural Networks*, 1987, pointed out: "You can lead a horse to water to drink, but if it can float on its back, you got something".

2.5 SUGGESTED READING

For the linguistic approach, the transcripts of a workshop on "Linguistic Theory and Computer Applications" [Whitelock 87] provide an up-to-date and very lively discussion on the current picture of (computational) linguistics.   In addition Sell's "Lectures on Contemporary Syntactic Theories [Sells 86] and Savitch et al.'s anthology of "The Formal Complexity of Natural Language" [Savitch 87] are for those who are seriously interested in syntactic theories past or present.   Brady and Berwick's anthology on "Computational Models of Discourse" is a good, if slightly dated overview of the field.   For the AI approach to NLP, Schank's book on "Inside Computer Understanding" [Schank 81], and Kolodner's "Retrieval and Organizational Strategies in Conceptual Memory" [Kolodner 84] are good introductions. For the connectionist approach, the two PDP volumes [Rumelhart 86] give a thorough introduction into the paradigm.   Helen Gigley's work on computational neurolinguistics and her "Hope" system [Gigley 85] provides a good introduction into the field of connectionism from a linguistic perspective.

CHAPTER 3

FORMALISMS

> Just because somebody's got an implementation of something doesn't mean that they've got a theory of it. [gazd87]

Formalisms do not say anything about the validity or psychological realism of a theory; they are merely a vehicle expressing the theory in computational terms. Formalisms can be evaluated on the basis of (1) how well they fit with the theory they try to implement, (2) how well they express the theories, and (3), how efficient they are. The purpose for a formalism after all is to be a tool for the implementation of a theory.

3.1 PARSING FORMALISM

The central problem for NLP is the transformation of potentially ambiguous utterances into an unambiguous internal representation or data structure the computer can work with to produce the desired output. The transposition from a linguistic to an internal representation is generally referred to as "parsing". While the internal representations differ from domain to domain, from application to application, ranging from expressions in database query languages (e.g., SQL) to ordinary parse trees and sophisticated knowledge constructs, the most common usages of the term "parsing" can be summarized as follows:

In its original meaning (*pars orationis*, i.e., part of speech), parsing referred to the human overt activity of analyzing, for pedagogical purposes, the grammatical properties of a natural language based on heuristics learned by people. The notion of parsing changed over time to accommodate the specific research activities of various scientific disciplines dealing with natural or artificial languages. In linguistics, parsing is used to define the scientific endeavor of describing the structural properties of the sentences of language by an abstract device based on a given algorithm with the result of providing a formal representation of sentence structure. In computer science, parsing, for the designer of a computer language, is the algorithmic, computational operation on symbolic input that results in groupings of symbols and their interpretations as changes in machine states. In AI, parsing is an algorithmic or heuristic operation, performed by a computer on sentences of language, "resulting in successive (partial) groupings of symbols into larger units of particular types, and the interpretation of these groups as changes in machine states". [Dowty 85]

In general, parsing is a formally defined process that deals with abstract mechanisms for applying structure determining rules to input strings. Parsers, in the narrow sense of the word, perform the initial task of assigning structural descriptions to sentences or, on an even more elementary level, simply test for the grammaticality ("well-formedness") of the input string; in a wider sense, they also encompass the process of how the knowledge is represented and used. In general, three types of NLP programs can be distinguished: (1) recognition programs that determine if a given input string is well-formed; (2) parsing programs that assign structural descriptions to sentences on the basis of a grammar formalism; and (3) NLP systems that transform linguistic information into internal knowledge representations. Once an NL developer has decided on a particular NLP approach, he must then choose a grammar formalism for describing ' language.   Parsing formalisms fall into two groups: non-deterministic and deterministic.   The non-deterministic parsers can be further divided into top-down and bottom-up parsers. Other specialized parsing programs are based on combinations of these three major types.

Top-down parsers   try to match the grammar rules against the input, starting at the top-most rewrite rule (which usually involves the start symbol or sentence symbol S) and recursively moving toward lower, more specific rewrite rules. The parse is successful if a sentence can be constructed that matches the input sentence.   Top-down parsers are easy to write and modify. Rules that are more likely to be used can easily be placed ahead of less likely rules, enhancing performance. And the number of generated sentences can be arbitrarily limited. Top–down parsers can be slow, however. If all the rules at a particular level fail, the parser backtracks up to the previous level to try another rule there. During backtracking, the same constituents may be analyzed many times. Top–down parsers also have trouble handling ill–formed input and require a separate module to decide which of several successful parses is best.

Bottom–up parsers start by combining the lowest–level elements first and then building up larger constituents. For example, in the simple grammar in Figure 3–1, the first steps of a bottom–up parser would be to substitute the non–terminal DET for "the", ADJ for "new", NOUN for "program", and NP1 for ADJ NOUN. Bottom–up parsers can at least partially parse ill–formed input. Also, scoring mechanisms can be applied to reduce the combinatorial explosion of possible parses. Since bottom–up parsers are not goal–directed, however, they generate numerous spurious parses. And the correctness of the parse can be determined only after all the parses are performed.

Deterministic parsing is different from top–down and bottom–up parsing in that there is no backtracking. Deterministic parsing is also called wait–and–see parsing (WASP). The formalism creates new nodes in a bottom–up fashion but uses a limited look–ahead feature to determine which node to use. One advantage of a deterministic parser is increased speed because it avoids the combinatorial explosion of possible parses. The disadvantage is that most algorithms used for NLP are based solely on syntactic information. The best known of the deterministic NLP systems was Parsifal, created by Mitchell Marcus in 1980. One result of Parsifal was a clear delineation of when such a parser would have to use non–syntactic information to analyze the input.

The parsing formalism together with the knowledge representation schema represent the computational aspect of NLP; the complexity of the parsing formalism is determined by how many knowledge sources are involved in the NLP system. NLP that relied on lexical and syntactic/semantic information had top–down, or bottom–up algorithms, whereas the currently developed knowledge based NLP rely on more complex processing agendas. Common parsing formalisms are context–free, augmented transition networks, chart parsing and unification based. A formalism is nothing but a tool for implementing a theory. In academic parlance, a formalism is a metalanguage to analyze an object language such as English. Most formalisms used in NLP are very powerful, i.e., they allow for many alternatives in the linguistic analysis. A dilemma for NLP systems arises when ideally the formalism should not have many constraints while a universal theory of language, for instance, should be constrained to be scientifically more interesting.

3.1.1 Context-free parsing

> Context-free grammars are also known as *immediate constituent grammars* (by traditional linguists), *Backus normal form* (by programming language designers), and *recursive patterns* (in some computer applications). They are one particular kind of a more general class of *phrase structure grammars*, which are the basis for generative linguistics and for most computer systems that manipulate either natural language or computer languages. [Winograd 83]

The best known parsing formalism for NLP in terms of a grammar (e.g., a set of rewrite rules) is a context-free grammar [CFG]. A simple set of grammar rules to describe a sentence like "The program compiles slowly", can be written as shown in Figure 3-1. A grammar is called CF if the rules that replace non-terminal symbols do not make reference to the context in which they apply. These rules are often called rewrite rules or productions. Two simple rewrite rules are as follows:

S-->NP VP
S-->VP

These rules stipulate that a sentence (S) must have a noun phrase (NP) and a verb phrase (VP), or just a verb phrase by itself. With these rules you can build a tree structure showing unambiguously how the words in a sentence interact (see Figure 3-1). It is common practice to call the words at the ends of tree limbs terminals. The other symbols in the tree, which are usually capitalized, are called non-terminals. Rewrite rules usually establish how a non-terminal symbol can be rewritten as a string of terminals or other non-terminals.

For example, the grammar in Figure 3-1 is a simple context-free grammar. You can expand this grammar by adding two rewrite rules, both of which are allowable:

NOUN-->programs
VERB-->compile

Now, however, the grammar will allow a sentence that is not allowable in English:

*The programs compiles slowly.[2]

2
An asterisk indicates an ungrammatical sentence.

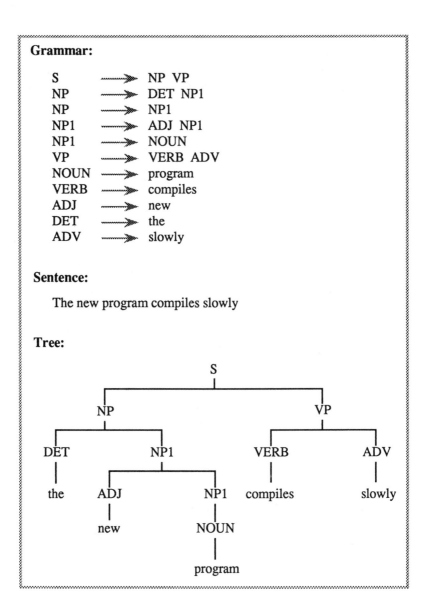

Grammar:

S   ⟶ NP VP
NP   ⟶ DET NP1
NP   ⟶ NP1
NP1   ⟶ ADJ NP1
NP1   ⟶ NOUN
VP   ⟶ VERB ADV
NOUN   ⟶ program
VERB   ⟶ compiles
ADJ   ⟶ new
DET   ⟶ the
ADV   ⟶ slowly

Sentence:

The new program compiles slowly

Tree:

Figure 3-1:   Example of parsing a
sentence in a CFG

You can add rules to the grammar that would disallow such sentences, but these rules would destroy its present simplicity. Other problems are caused by the word "respectively" in sentences such as "Singular nouns and plural nouns require singular verbs and plural verbs, respectively" [see section 2.1.1 for a discussion of context-freeness of NL].

3.1.2 Unification based parsing

A phrase type is defined by a set of constraints. A grammar rule is the set of constraints between the type X of a phrase and the types X1...Xn of its constituents. The rule may be applied to the analysis of a string so as the concatenation of constituents s1...sn if and only if the types of si are compatible with the types Xi and the constraints in the rule. *Unification* is the operation that determines whether two types are compatible by building the most general type compatible with both. [Pereira 85]

Unification based formalisms for parsing originated somewhat independently in separate areas of NLP research. As part of linguistic theory proper, the idea of unification, an information-combining operation that determines if two elements are compatible by building the most general element compatible with both, is found in Generalized Phrase Structure Grammar, and Lexical Functional Grammar [Bresnan 82]. As part of a computational formalism for implementing grammars, unification is used in Definite Clause Grammars [DCG], Functional Unification Grammars [FUG] [Kay 85], and PATR-II [Shieber 85].

Unification is an operation on "feature structures" that consist of features and their values, e.g., the feature "number" can take the value "third person". Every sentence has a set of feature structures for each word. Unification takes the union of two consistent feature structures. While formalisms such as CFGs that use grammatical labels require tests for equality between symbols, unification includes a test as to whether two (non-atomic) feature structures "unify". Unification percolates values between nodes. Take the following example:

S--> NP VP
number(S) = number(VP)
person(NP) = person(VP)

In this example, the equations indicate that the value of the feature "number" (e.g., "singular") percolates from NP to S; while at the same time enforcing agreement between the "person" value (e.g., "third person").

Because these are declarative and order independent statements, unification provides a simple formalism for expressing feature agreement and percolation between nodes in a phrase structure grammar. Compared to the ways of how previous formalisms had to go about expressing the same constraints on agreement, unification is indeed a much better formalism.

Within the logic programming paradigm (e.g., Prolog) Pereira and Warren used definite clause grammars [DCGs] as the basis of their versions of unification based formalisms. With the advent of Prolog [Clocksin 81], the relationship between parsing and deduction has been used successfully in working on NLP systems [Mellish 85, Dahl 81, Pereira 80]. Unification in Prolog consists of a pattern-matching formalism that operates on general data structures. The data structures in Prolog are called "clauses". Each of the clauses contains a "head" (the initial entry point) and a "body" that consists of "goals". Prolog procedures are activated by providing a goal to the program, which will be subsequently matched against the head of a clause. Trying each clause in a linear order, the process of "unification" is successful if the goal and the head of the clause "match", i.e., appropriate values for the variables in the procedure are found. If no match is found, the system backtracks in the program to the point of the last match and explores alternatives. If more than one match is found, the system provides "non-determinate" results, i.e., lists the possibilities. Since the Prolog-10 system consists of a macroexpansion facility that "translates a CF grammar into a logic program that functions as a recursive-descent parser" [Shapiro 83], the grammar for a particular language can be input directly into the Prolog clause form. The linguistic side of DCG is very similar to the computational implementation of this grammar: the (context-free) grammar is axiomatized in "definite clauses", a subset of first order logic. Thus, parsing is similar to executing a finite set of proof procedures. Although the proof procedures can be implemented efficiently, problems similar to those for top-down, backtrack parsing procedures are found [Pereira 83].

As we can see from these two examples of the use of unification the unification operation can take the form of pattern matching (e.g., Functional Unification Grammar [Kay 85]), or strict first order logic (e.g., Prolog [Mellish 85]). In addition, unification is part of many linguistically motivated theories (e.g., Lexical Functional Grammar [Bresnan 82] and Generalized Phrase Structure Grammar [Gazdar 81]) The simplicity of unification is attractive because feature agreement and percolation are expressed easily in such a formalism. In unification based formalisms the feature structures carry linguistic information (e.g., syntactic, semantic) and manipulate the information via a well defined operation, i.e., unification. The idea behind the unification formalism is akin to that of CFG: the rules of a grammar determine how phrase types are concatenated. The significant difference between the unification formalism and that of a CFG lies in the finite number of non-terminals in the latter, and the potentially unlimited phrase types the unification based formalism can account for. The use of unification, only recently hailed as answer for providing a satisfactory formalism, is spreading rapidly. At this point, it is easy to foresee that unification will definitely be part of the linguistic paradigm of the 1990s.

3.1.3 Augmented transition networks

Although first developed in 1970, the augmented transition network (ATN) is still the most widely used formalism for NLP, being applied to sentence level [Woods 70] as well as to discourse level processing [Reichman 85]. But before we describe ATNs, we discuss regular transition networks.

A transition network consists of a series of states connected by arcs (see Figure 3-2. Each arc is labeled by a word category (e.g., noun, verb) or a specific word. The program starts at a given state and then checks the next word in the input string for a match with one of the arcs. If a match is found, the program proceeds to the next arc, and thus "traverses the network". The advantage of transition networks is that they can be easily implemented on a computer. Each state can be implemented as a function that checks its input against the arcs emanating from that state. If a match is found, the function (or state) at the end of that particular arc is called. Recursive transition networks have an additional feature in that some arcs may be labeled with other, subordinate, transition networks (see Figure 3-2). These arcs let a given network call another network or even call itself recursively. Usually these arcs are labeled with non-terminal symbols (e.g., PP for prepositional phrase). These networks are considerably more powerful than transition networks.

Even more powerful are augmented transition networks. ATNs are similar to recursive transition networks but have three additional features: registers, which can store conditional information on a global basis, regardless of which particular subnetwork is being processed; conditions, which let arcs be selected if registers indicate certain conditions; and actions, which let arcs modify the structure of data. Note that the arcs in an ATN can be labeled, not only with words, word classes, and non-terminals, but also with arbitrary tests that depend on the state of the global registers. These global registers and their associated tests make it possible for the program to go beyond checking only adjacent elements. Obviously, being able to store and act on these conditions makes possible a much more efficient parsing than earlier transition networks did. For example, the presence of a form of the verb "be" before the main verb in a sentence can set a trigger to check for the preposition "by", which in turn can corroborate evidence for a passive or an active sentence.

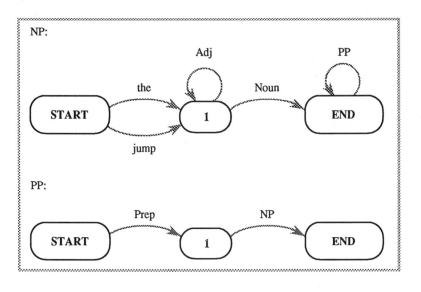

Figure 3-2: The ATN example

Although ATNs are powerful, they experience problems with ungrammatical sentences for which no relevant networks have been provided. If the program encounters a construction for which it does not have a structural description, it simply stops. Subsequently, the algorithm would instruct the network to pick up the analysis at the last junction where it had to make a decision as to what path to follow. Obviously, a major drawback of ATNs is thus the repeated processing of constituent structure until the NLP system has stopped at the sentence boundary.

Based on [Woods 70], ATNs were originally conceived as parsing formalisms and not theories of language. Nowadays, ATNs have developed into a grammar-like concept, especially for computational linguists. ATNs are also being used for processing units beyond the sentence, e.g., paragraphs and entire texts [Reichman 85]. The biggest drawback of ATNs is their potential power to accommodate almost any exceptions without being outside of the algorithm. ATNs have the power of Turing machines because they can be used for any operations within processing the sentence and they cannot be sensibly restricted without totally changing the flavor of the algorithm. Many functioning systems and products are based on ATNs: Intellect, and Clout, but also RUS, to name just a few. The drawbacks outlined above have forced most of the ATN projects to either limit the power of the algorithm or use it to their advantage by interleaving semantic procedure calls to syntactic processing.

3.1.4 Chart parsing

The chart parsing idea was implicitly stated in Earley's classic paper on context-free parsing algorithms for compilers and compiler generators [Earley 70]. A chart parser combines constituents of the input sentence according to the rules of a particular grammar as they are encountered and stores the output in a well-formed substring table (the chart). The parsing mechanism keeps track of the constituents it has built and the contexts in which they are expected, so that no work needs to be duplicated for combining words that potentially are part of several parses. A chart parser combines the goal-directed processing of a top-down parser with the data-driven processing of a bottom-up parser.

Computationally, chart parsing is based on two ideas: the use of the chart as an indexing procedure for constituents in a well-formed substring table; and the use of active edges to keep track of partial constituents. A chart is a data structure that contains an up-to-date record of the constituents or phrases found during the parsing process. Once a well-formed constituent is established and recorded in the chart, its constituents do not have to be re-parsed. A grammar for NL can be stated as a finite state transition network.

A finite state transition network consists of a number of states organized in the form of a labeled directed graph. The chart resembles a transition network, having vertices called states, and edges called arcs. Arcs represent words, phrases and constituents in general, vertices refer to the specific combination of words in the graph. The interpretation of a sentence is a traversal of the states in one direction, determining the sequence in which edges are encountered. Thus, multiple edges leaving a vertex represent multiple meanings of a particular constituent.

We will now look at how the parsing is done. In Figure 3-3, we provide a parse of the sample sentence "Plows changed life in Europe". The first step of the chart algorithm - initializing the chart - requires the labeling of every element in the string that is to be parsed. Initializing the chart means to give word class labels to every word in the utterance. Any lexical ambiguities are copied from the lexicon into the initial structure. Structural ambiguities are recorded as they are encountered. The second step after the "initialization" of the chart, is for the parser to extract all possible combinations of elements in the given sentence, and to mark them in the chart. Upon encountering an element, two basic operations are performed: (1) to see if the current element fits into an already established constituent, and add the element to the constituent; and (2) to see if the current element potentially starts a new constituent, and establish a constituent.

Chart parsing can be viewed as a complex interaction between two transition networks: a grammar containing NL rules, and a chart containing the output of the parsing process. The grammar part remains fixed, being a repository of syntactic or semantic rules for constructing and labeling parse trees. The chart is a dynamic data structure that is being built out of the structural descriptions of the incoming sentence. The chart parsing formalism incorporates a very powerful procedure for finding all the possible parses. In order to prevent the uncontrolled application of rules, flags can be used to block the application of rules at certain points during the parse.

The brief description of the chart algorithm shows how the grammar network is independent of the actual computational factors. It also shows that, using the idea of a chart, any grammatical formalism can be accommodated by modifying vertex operations on their edges. However, the most straightforward grammatical formalism used in conjunction with a chart is of the context-free variety. Context-free rules are best suited for chart parsing since they are easy to formulate, implement and update. A chart parser is flexible as to what grammatical formalism, rule invocation strategies and search strategies can be incorporated. Along with the advantage of flexibility comes the disadvantage that all plausible and implausible parses are recorded, which leads to increased storage requirements and to NLP systems that contain grammars of "Byzantine complexity that are difficult to

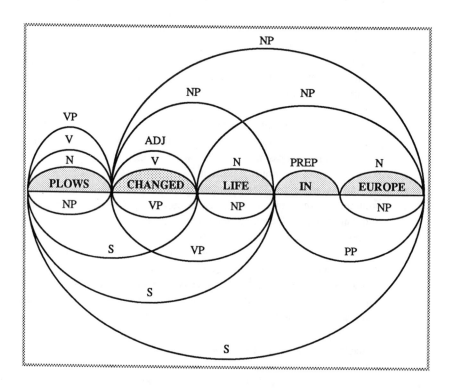

Figure 3-3:   The chart parser [Tennant 81, page 78]

understand and modify" [Winograd 83, page 390]. The very nature of the chart algorithm leaves it up to the designer as to what data structure is stored in the chart and how the parsing procedure arrives at the final outcome.

The unconstrained power of the chart parsing mechanism becomes apparent when allowing edges to have syntactic and semantic properties. The inception and development of the chart parsing idea has been for the most part due to the shortcomings of existing formalisms at the time (e.g., top-down and bottom-up), and the theoretical re-orientation of linguistics from the Chomskyan view of transformational grammar to the view that English for the most part is a context-free language, describable in terms of phrase structure rules without transformations. Another trend in using the chart parsing idea is the increasing importance for semantic processing. Semantic routines in the first chart parsers [Kay 67, Kaplan 73] had been ancillary and feature-oriented, whereas NLP systems of the 1980s treat semantics as having the predominant role in NLP [Frederking 88].

The first chart parser, "The Powerful Parser", for natural language processing was built by Martin Kay (then at Rand), in the 1960s [Kay 67]. The same year, Thompson started the REL system [Thompson 69]. It was originally written in assembler code for an IBM360. It consisted of a database and an English parser. REL's modified version of the chart rewrite algorithm contains a set of semantic transformations and features for verbs similar to the case grammar formalism. REL can process a subset of English ("REL English"), e.g., "What was the average between 1964 and now of the income of each woman who was not married?". Kay and Kaplan further developed the chart parsing idea in their MIND [Kay 73, Kaplan 73] system in the early 1970s. Henry Thompson introduced MCHART [Thompson 81] as a grammar testing tool for linguists in the early 1980s. Attempts to use the chart in conjunction with semantic processing [Frederking 88] have been shown to be useful from the very beginning of the chart parsing paradigm.

3.1.5 Parallel parsing

Parallel processing [PP] is the ability of a computer to perform operations using more than one processor simultaneously. The conventional serial computer as we know it suffers from one serious drawback: the way the CPU accesses memory. While data is being retrieved from memory it is actually written into a processor register and after incrementing the register the new value is put back into memory. During all this time, the CPU remains idle. This phenomenon, generally known as the "von Neumann bottleneck", accounts for the slowness and inefficient use of the resources in a conventional serial processor. Especially in NLP, the many different levels of structure suggest a parallel parsing approach in which different knowledge sources operate on the same input, providing each other with enough information to avoid the combinatorial explosion of too many blind alleys and too many strategies to keep the processing linear in real time.

The central problem of PP systems in general and parallel parsers in particular is the efficient use of more than one active processor at the same time. The effective use depends on identifying a problem that lends itself to parallelism, determining the algorithm and mapping it onto a suitable architecture. As you can imagine, problems arise if there is more than one processor requiring access to the same memory location, or if processors try to increment data in the same memory location. Thus, the common argument that more processors are always faster than one holds true only for systems that cope with problems such as contention and have appropriate synchronization mechanisms in place. In NLP, we distinguish two types of parallelism: data level parallelism and genuinely parallel programming for parser implementation. Both methods have been successfully used for NLP.

Data level parallelism takes the programming method of serial machines but stores the data in separate processors. While the serial program for a single processor machine would iteratively operate on the data, for a parallel processor the serial program would simultaneously operate on the data. A well-known production system for bulk processing of NL on a parallel computer called "Connection Machine" finds phrases to be indexed for a document retrieval system [Waltz 87]. The parsing operation is illustrated in Figure 3-4. Phase one combines the input of the original text, assigning the parts of speech in parallel with preliminary elimination of non-indexable terms and the marking of proper names (e.g., famous person, name of the month) at a rate of about 64,000 words in 70 msecs. During the second phase, a number of ATN parsers run over the text and determine all noun phrases simultaneously in a non-deterministic fashion (i.e., more than one analysis per noun phrase may be recorded). A special symbol "Q1" [see Figure 3-4] is attached to every processor that contains a determiner. "Q1" is used for further analyzing the noun phrase structure in detail before the syntactic analysis of the noun phrases is completed.

Algorithms for genuinely parallel parsing are discussed in [Grishman 88]: the Cocke-Younger-Kasami algorithm for CFGs, for instance, takes time proportional to n^3 (n = length of input string) on a single processor, while time n using n^2 processors. Bolt Beranek and Newman and New York University are active in comparing the performance of various formalisms (e.g, chart parser, unification grammar). In fact, as part of the DARPA NLP project [see section 11.3 and Figure 11-2], NYU (responsible for the PROTEUS [PROtotype TExt Understanding System] project) uses its

Ultracomputer, a shared–memory MIMD parallel processor for benchmarking a parallel implementation of a chart parser. While parallel algorithms for parsing existed for quite some time now, the suitable experimental facilities are slowly becoming available.

3.2 KNOWLEDGE REPRESENTATION

The usefulness of a particular type of knowledge representation is based on its "expressive adequacy", that is, what the system can understand and say, and "notational efficacy", that is, how powerful the notation is [Woods 83]. The four most commonly used knowledge representation schemas include logic, production rules, semantic networks, conceptual dependencies and frames/scripts. While these are formalisms of how to represent knowledge, they are representationally equivalent in the sense that whatever can be expressed in one schema can also be expressed in another.

3.2.1 Logic

Logic, the formal way of representing relations between facts by means of a propositional or predicate calculus, was one of the first formalisms used by AI researchers to represent knowledge structures in computers. Each sentence expresses a proposition that can be represented by a logic formula. Based on established rules of inference in logic, new facts can be evaluated and checked against facts already known to be true.

The most commonly used logical knowledge representation formalism in NLP programs is written in Prolog, a programming language based on symbolic logic [Clocksin 81]. Prolog is based on a pattern–matching mechanism referred to as "unification" that operates on general record structures. The record structures in Prolog consist of clauses, each of which contains a head as the initial entry point, and a body that consists of goals in the form of procedure calls. A Prolog program is a collection of logic statements or clauses whose execution depends on the deduction from the clauses forming the program. Clauses can be interpreted: (a) as facts, for example, *married(pete), divorced(cindy)*, which states that Pete is married and Cindy is divorced; (b) as rules, for example, *relationship_stability(PERSON) if married (PERSON) or length_of_relationship(PERSON,X) and X>2*, which states that a person shows a stable relationship if he/she is married or has been in a relationship for more than 2 years.

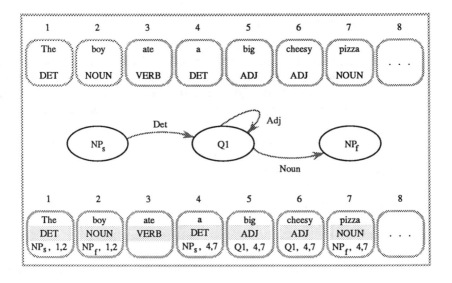

Figure 3-4:   Bulk processing of NL
in a parallel processor [Waltz 87, page 96]

Queries that can be answered positively based on these two facts and one rule include: *?married(pete).* "Is Pete married?" *?divorced(cindy).* "Is Cindy divorced?" *?relationship_stability(pete).* "Is Pete in a stable relationship?

If Prolog is used to parse NL input, the parsing procedure translates the NL query into a logical expression which, in turn, is evaluated as a Prolog program; then, the program's clauses, which constitute its knowledge base, are interpreted and the query is answered. Positive aspects of Prolog include (a) pattern-directed rule invocation, (b) automatic backtracking, (c) system-maintained database, and (d) rapid prototyping. Negative aspects include (a) no global variables, (b) poor control primitives, and (c) the small number of data types.

3.2.2 Production rules

Allen Newell proposed production rules within a theory of how humans reason [Newell 72]. Production rules, also known as IF-THEN rules or situation-action rules, consist of an antecedent, representing a pattern that is matched to input features by a simple procedure, and a consequent, which determines the action once the antecedent pattern is matched. For example: IF someone is married or the length of the relationship is greater than 2 years THEN the relationship is stable. The antecedent can consist of a number of conditions (AND/OR) that have to be met for the rule to "fire". In Newell's production rule formulation, the stipulation is that production rules are contained in short-term memory. The production rules are tried in an iterative control mechanism residing in short-term memory until the antecedent of the rule is matched, which, in turn, causes the rule to fire and the action on the consequent of the rule to take effect.

Production systems contain a set of production rules, an algorithm for pattern matching, and a working memory. The conditions on every production rule are matched against the current data in the working memory. If the conditions do not apply, a new rule is tried. If a condition matches the antecedent of a rule, the action proposed in the consequent changes the working memory, which then may cause further rules to match. The cycle of trying to match the production rules continues until all rules are tried.

The knowledge representation in production systems is modular because every production rule contains a separate piece of knowledge. Modularity is a useful feature for knowledge representation schemas because it facilitates the change, addition, and deletion of "knowledge" from the system. For larger systems, however, the modularity provided by production rules comes at a price: if all rules have to be matched against every single input the procedure is very inefficient.

Positive aspects of production systems include the uniformity of their
structure, the modularity of the independent elements of their knowledge
base, and their easy extensibility. The major disadvantage stems from the
potential of a combinatorial explosion if the rule set is large and unordered,
since every rule has to be considered as a potential candidate during each
cycle of pattern matching. Rule orderings, partitioning of the rules set, and
heuristics are ways of overcoming the performance issue.

3.2.3 Semantic networks

Semantic Networks are used to represent relations between members of a
class of objects. They consist of nodes that stand for concepts or events, and
links that show relationships between nodes. The relationships can be labelled
semantically and can be highly arbitrary. Interpreting the links as IS-A or
PART-OF is left to the designer of the specific implementation. Positive
aspects of semantic networks include (a) the explicit and efficient
representation of related objects and (b) a property inheritance hierarchy
whereby objects can inherit properties of objects higher up in the hierarchy.
Problems that arise mainly stem from the subjective decision regarding what
type of relations are expressed by links in any given system [Brachman 83].

3.2.4 Conceptual dependency

The central idea behind a conceptual dependency [CD] is to create a
canonical representation of a sentence, based on certain semantic primitives.
A canonical representation is simply a form of representing the meaning of
a sentence. Different sentences that mean the same thing will all have the
same canonical representation. For example, "Jean eats the candy" and "The
candy was eaten by Jean" both share the same canonical representation
"Jean<-->INGEST<--candy".

Starting in the late 1960s, Roger Schank began formulating the theory of
conceptual dependencies. His idea of representing the meaning of a sentence
such as "John threw a ball to Mary" is to postulate primitive actions to
represent semantic relationships. These primitive actions included PROPEL
("apply a force to") and ATRANS ("to change some abstract relationship
with respect to an object") [see Figure 3-5] Schank's original theory,
explicitly described in [Schank 75], postulated only seven primitives. Five of
these referred to physical actions: PROPEL, MOVE, INGEST, EXPEL, and
GRASP. The remaining two described state changes, e.g., PTRANS for a
physical transfer of location, and MTRANS for the mental transfer of
information.

In this theory, semantic primitives are the most basic entities used to describe the world. Individual words can always be analyzed further, but semantic primitives cannot. The most serious criticism, leveled mostly by linguists, addressed the nature of primitives being postulated and their increasing number. Many researchers that held opposing views to Schank argued that the number and the nature of the primitives were extremely arbitrary, a criticism borne out by the later development of the theory, in which Schank increased the number of primitives to 40, while encountering primitives that were very similar to actual word meanings, e.g., WANT as a primitive for "want".

The further development of his approach included scripts and higher level memory units that were said to abstract meanings of sentences, scenes, etc to form new concepts, learn and remember. In retrospect, Schank's theories have been viewed by the linguistic community and some critics within the AI community as erratic, too speculative, and theoretically less interesting than other linguistic theories [Dresher 76].

3.2.5 Frames

Frames/scripts are based on Minsky's theory [Minsky 76] of how to represent information in knowledge based systems. Scripts are framelike structures used to represent sequences – dynamic frames – of events [Schank 77]. In frame theory, the knowledge base is decomposed into "chunks" of knowledge, which are the data structures that represent stereotypical situations.

> When one encounters a new situation (or makes a substantial change in one's view of the present problem), one selects from memory a structure called a frame. This is a remembered framework to be adapted to fit reality by changing details as necessary. [Minsky 76]

In NLP systems, frames are used to represent linguistic as well as non-linguistic knowledge. A frame consists of "slots" and "fillers", which store the components of a particular concept. A frame contains slots, and slots are made up of fillers. The slot of one frame can point to another frame with slots of its own. The concept "room" can be represented by a frame consisting of the slots of "door", "window", "floor", etc. A noun phrase can be represented as a frame consisting of the lots "determiner", "adjective", and "noun". Each slot can have an arbitrary number of fillers.

If a particular concept is mentioned during NLP, the corresponding frame

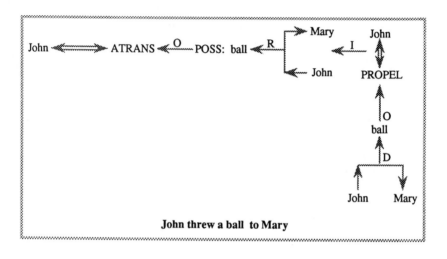

John threw a ball to Mary

Figure 3-5: Example of a conceptual dependency for
the sentence "John threw a ball to Mary"
including the two ACT primitives
ATRANS and PROPEL [Schank 75, page 51]

```
(INTERROGATIVE (PLAN ((ISA ACTION)
                      (PRED SEARCH)
                      (AGENT USER)
                      ARG ((NAME SYSTEM-FILE-SPACE)))
               (GOAL ((IS ACTION)
                      (PRED FIND)
                      (AGENT USER)
                      (ARG ((ISA FILE)
                            (NAME SPECIFIC))))))))

"Okay, how can I search the directory space to find a file?"
```

Figure 3-6:   Example of a frame for the
query type that searches
directories for files

for this data structure is activated. The retrieved information can then be used for processing the NL input. Frames can be interpreted as either a "static data structure about one stereotyped view" [Charniak 75] or "organizing the processes of retrieval and inference, which manipulate the stored representations" [Hayes-Roth 79]. The manipulation of data within a frame is done by "triggers" or "demons", which are procedures attached to the frame itself, the slots or their fillers. In Figure 3-6, the frame contains the structure for a typical interrogative used in interfacing to an operating system. Not surprisingly, one of the early attempts to build a transportable interface to DBMSs consisted of identifying four query types to be represented by individual frame structures. The combinatorial explosion of different queries for different databases made this approach infeasible for production systems.   In general, frames are stereotypical representations of objects that have the following characteristics [Minsky 76, Winograd 77, Roussopoulos 79]:

- Explicitness: objects, relations and attributes are made explicit; in the absence of disconfirming evidence, a default value is used.

- Triggering: procedures can be attached to a frame or its components and executed automatically (e.g., "IF-NEEDED", "IF-ADDED").

- Inheritance: frames are conceptually related, allowing attributes of objects to be "inherited" from objects higher up in the hierarchy.

- Modularity: the knowledge base is organized in clearly distinguished components.

The idea of having a "precompiled" knowledge structure as background information during NLP is theoretically very useful because a transparent and easy-to-manipulate representation gives insights into what information is necessary to process language. However, as a psychological theory for human information processing it is less plausible for two reasons: on the one hand, if we had indeed frame-like structures stored for easy retrieval, "a lot less human discourse should occur than actually occurs" [Brown 83], because most of the information would be present in "our" mental frame representation, and nobody would have to bother making the structures explicit. On the other hand, although stereotypical knowledge can be expected, it cannot be guaranteed.   Discourse producers "make their discourse reflect this fact and present the information in a format that serves as a reminder for those who already know and as an instruction for those who do not" [Brown 83].   Another important issue for frame based systems is the decision as to which frame should apply in a given context. If multiple frames are plausible, what criteria should be used to activate one, and which one should be the primary one?

3.3 CONCLUSION

Formalisms and knowledge representations do not contribute to the power of a selected theory. The implementation issues are separate from that of the theory behind an NLP system. While the theoretical approach is guided by criteria such as completeness and consistency, the focus of implementation issues is on optimization and efficiency.

The parsing formalisms developed over the past few decades have not produced any one clear winner. The drawback for most of the formalisms is that they consider mostly syntactic, i.e., structural, facts, generating descriptions of sentences that contain many dozens of alternative parses. It is interesting that parsing strategies do produce a different number of parses. "Plows changed the life in Europe" will produce eight parses for a top-down parser and additional parses for a bottom-up parser because a bottom-up parser has to consider multiple versions of the same phrase (e.g., "plows" as a verb and as a noun) [Tennant 81].

Knowledge representations are representationally equivalent when it comes to their "expressiveness": whatever can be represented in a frame based system can also be represented with logic or any other knowledge representation schema. While knowledge representations struggle with issues like inheritance, parsing formalisms in the past were in general too powerful, not allowing theoretical and principled constraints on the theory to be implemented. The recent trends in NL engineering give reason to be optimistic:

- Increased interest in the study of extending, inventing, and testing formalisms for constructing NLP systems.

- Emergence of a group of unification formalisms that provide a common denominator for different linguistic theories.

- Doyle's rational psychology allows a novel look at the question of how implicit knowledge can be derived from explicit knowledge.

- The trend towards syntactic and semantic interaction is supported by knowledge representation schemas.

3.4 SUGGESTED READING

A good overview of various formalisms of parsing is provided in the
anthology edited by Sparck Jones and Wilks [Sparck 83]. Much more
technical is Cullingford's "Natural Language Processing" [Cullingford 85] that
contains sample programs for building NLP systems as do the books [Schank
81, Mellish 85]. Tomita's book on efficient parsing for NL [Tomita 86]
provides both a thorough discussion of the debate concerning context-free
languages and a description of some "hands-on" applications of his algorithm.
The best and shortest summary of unification based formalisms is included
in [Shieber 85]. A "food-for-thought" article on selecting a parser is
Charniak's paper "Six Topics in Search of a Parser" [Charniak 81]. For the
topic of knowledge representation Brachman and Levesque's
reader [Brachman 85] spans the spectrum of the most recent approaches.
The fundamental issues of knowledge representation are discussed in Doyle's
writings, especially in his essay on "Implicit Knowledge and Rational
Representation" [Doyle 88], the best and shortest exposition on the problem
of how "implicit knowledge is derived from explicit knowledge via a logic".
Doyle's contention that implicit knowledge is based on a rational choice
amongst different interpretations of explicit knowledge is worth thinking
about.

PART II - APPLICATIONS

The times when people referred to NLP as a technology in search of an application are over. Too many products are already on the market or being readied for release. Also gone are the days when NLIs were the only linguistically oriented software. Talking cars were the thing of the 1980s, talking refrigerators will be the thing of the 1990s, beyond that, it is everybody's guess. In brief, NLP technology is for real. The marketplace for NLP technology is still heavily oriented towards NLIs. In the spring issue 1989 of *ORACLE. The SQL Database Journal*, four NL companies advertised their interfaces: Battelle, Natural Language Inc., Intelligent Business Systems, and Dynamics Research Corporation. Spell and grammar checkers are also among the favorite NLP products. Machine aided translation devices are gaining market presence. The real breakthrough application will be in the text database arena. NLP will not only provide easy access to but also consistent update for gigabytes of text.

NLP technologies are significant on three levels of maturity: (1) the off-the-shelf product level, (2) the one-of-a-kind system level, and (3), the R&D level. In the early 1980s it became fashionable for AI companies to be in the tool business. While the tool metaphor is still among us, the meaning of "tool" has become more specialized. No one is successfully selling NL tools without a clearly defined application (e.g., database interfaces, machine translation). There is no general NL processor available, nor will there ever be.

The off-the-shelf product level includes stand-alone and embedded NLP systems. Applications for stand-alone systems are spell and grammar checkers, hand-held translators and voice processing devices. In most other commercial NLP applications, the NL capabilities are either embedded or added on (e.g., NLIs, gisting programs). The one-of-a-kind system level includes large government and private industry installations that are designed for one application only. The R&D level includes exploratory programs and proof-of-concept systems which by the 1990s should include many thousand prototypes.

NLP measured by research activities and funding level can be divided into six major areas, quantified by level of effort[3]:

- Intelligent user interfaces which allow humans to communicate with the computer in natural language (40%).

- Machine translation and machine aided translation systems which allow for assistance by the NLP program in the pre-, or post-editing stage (20%).

- Text understanding systems which summarize, scan, and answer questions about texts (10%).

- Text generation which constructs texts from internal representations, or is based on linguistic theories (10%).

- Speech recognition and synthesis systems which allow the computer to interact with humans in speech mode (10%).

- Spell checkers and grammar checkers (10%).

NLP software packages, despite riding high on the wave of the AI boom, have not yet achieved anywhere near technical credibility nor market acceptance. Whereas ten years ago it was possible to describe all existing NLP systems in one journal article, recent surveys show that the number of functioning NLP programs at the prototype stage is now in the thousands, while off-the-shelf, mail order and public domain NLP software programs are in the hundreds. Consequently, the criteria for mentioning a program include either market presence or notoriety within the scientific community.

In the future, the impact of NLP technology on finding new applications will be market-driven for two reasons: on the one hand new applications, such as text understanding, full text database management, electronic publishing and groupware, will become necessary because the user needs NLP capabilities to cope with the information glut. On the other hand, classical applications such as machine translation and NLIs will be mature enough to become embedded into everyday computing software, especially in the office environment.

---

[3] Percentages given are based on Battelle's International Clearinghouse for NLP technology. The Clearinghouse was founded in 1985 and continues to grow. It contains many datapoints for each NLP project and product that has been reported.

CHAPTER 4

NATURAL LANGUAGE INTERFACES

I'll offer, on behalf of Artificial Intelligence Corporation, a $100 reward for a question that can't be asked in half as many keystrokes in English and a $200 reward for a question that can't be asked in fewer keystrokes. The example can be in any general-purpose query language, whether command or menu driven. Obviously, predefined queries invoked by PF keys don't count. [Larry R. Harris, Chairman and Founder of Artificial Intelligence Corporation, in: *Information Center*, October 1986]

The function of an interface is to mediate primarily between the user and the application program. For the user to access the computer applications, he must either rely on his programming skills, or the modes of interaction provided by the interface designer (e.g., fourth generation languages, NL, icons, menus). While commercially available NLIs traditionally have been used as front-end for database management systems, recent NLI products focus on interfacing to operating systems, allowing users to type English rather than DOS or Unix commands, and on spreadsheet interfaces. All of these applications allow access to computing resources without extensive training in query and command language protocols. Moreover, they alleviate the infrequent user's retention rate problems of cumbersome mnemonics. Still in the laboratories are dialog based interfaces that are suited as front-ends for advisory and expert systems. They may also be suitable for database access. The science of the interface has just begun. It is to be expected that further research in cognitive science will lead to specifications for sound implementation and application. NL will enter into this process as a major component. NL will by no means be the only factor; just as in human discourse, half of the information is exchanged non-verbally, and the use of visual languages is important [Shu 88].

Matching intelligent user interface techniques to computing tasks requires: (1) a clear understanding of the information processing task of a particular application program. The application programs require special scrutiny when it comes to tailoring interfaces to special needs for the application programmer/end-user. A word processing program requires as much of a task oriented interface as a DBMS; whereas the former is best served by a direct data manipulation interface, for the latter a NL interface is more apt to satisfy the user. (2) an analysis of the user groups. The role of the users is characterized not only by their varying degrees of sophistication, both computationally and domain-specifically, but also – what is of particular interest to IUI research – by differences in memory structure, behavioral patterns and performance measures. (3) thorough knowledge of what specific IUI techniques entail. The IUI itself consists of at least two dimensions: a "physical" and "cognitive dimension". The physical interface includes any conventional devices like keyboard, mouse, microphone, but also data gloves and touch sensitive devices that allow the user to get his ideas transmitted to the computer program. The cognitive side consists of the possible modes of interacting with the program based on the software that supports the interaction, e.g., menu, command languages, NL, direct manipulation. (4) a strategic integration into the computing infrastructure including computational platform, vendor orientation and long-term planning (e.g., an IBM shop will have different options for satisfying the same needs as a DEC/Apple environment).

An intelligent user interface actively assists the user in accomplishing a given task (e.g., word processing, database retrieval, medical diagnosis) with assistance ranging from providing contextual help messages to drawing inferences without explicit user input. In general, the function of an interface is to facilitate and enhance the communication process between man and machine. The human communication with a computer is different from that between humans. In the past, man-machine interaction was characterized by the term "command" language whereby the computer executed the user's instructions. In the future, the role of a genuine dialog with the computer becomes more important as the degree of complexity of the program increases and computers become more ubiquitous. Such a communication with machines rather than an operation of machines requires many sophisticated interface capabilities. For example, looking at a conversation whose subject is

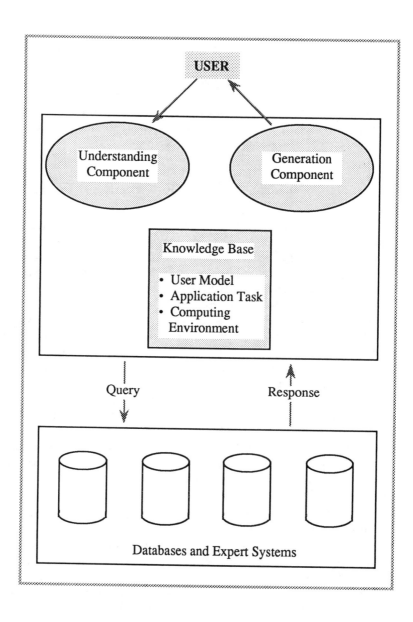

Figure 4-1:   Functionality of an NLI

the resolution of a problem or performance of a task, humans normally state the problem, provide alternatives and let the listener provide feed-back to make sure they understood. For an NLI to accommodate similar activities, the NLP system has to be able to synthesize utterances above the sentence level, and generate responses beyond mere fact retrieval. The NLI includes text understanding and language generation capabilities. These two subjects are discussed in chapters 6 and 7, respectively.

4.1 THE INFORMATION PROCESSING TASK

The central problem for NLIs is the transformation of potentially ambiguous English input into an unambiguous form that can be used internally by the system to instigate an operation on the backend system (e.g., database, spreadsheet). The mapping and accessing process of data structures varies in complexity depending on the particular application. Three types of NLIs have emerged: (1) the translation based NLIs that simply map English language input into command language output, (2) the transformation based NLIs that take the input string and map it into an intermediate logical form before translating it into a query language format, and (3) the dialog based user model NLIs that take the input string and determine what action to take next, based on their access to user, domain, and application model. Most of the existing NLIs fall into one of these three categories. In Figure 4-1 the functionality of an NLI is described. The function of an NLI is to assist the user to effectively issue a query to the backend database to retrieve the desired information. The task of an NLI [see Figure 4-2] is to translate the English question into the specific query syntax of the database management system and to display the appropriate answer.

Translation based NLIs for operating systems, spreadsheets, etc. perform a conversion of the English input to the command language the back-end system uses by identifying the relevant commands and their arguments. After translating the English input, the program sends the command to the system for processing. A many-to-one mapping of two separate languages is at the core of the processing. Since programming languages are normally designed not to have ambiguities, the many ways of expressing an operation in English are reduced to system level command. The same holds true for NLIs connected to spreadsheets. Besides the mere translation of the English into the command language, the NLI also has to determine in what order requests that are made up of more than one action have to be executed. For instance, the command "Move the last file into the new subdirectory labeled 'New'" requires the system to first create a subdirectory and then copy the file from the current directory into the newly created one.

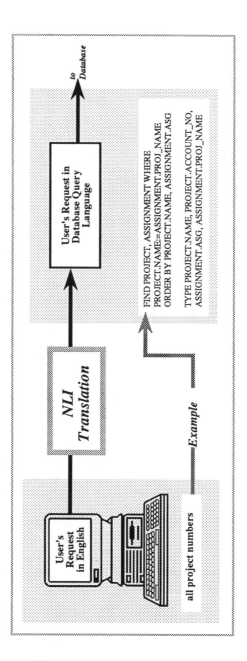

Figure 4-2:   Task of an NLI

Transformation based NLIs for relational DBMSs perform the following information processing (see Figure 4-3): on the one hand, the NLI has to provide a many-to-one mapping of English words for one particular database field (e.g., there are many words in English to refer to the database field "employee"); on the other hand, the NLI has to provide a one-to-many mapping from the same English word to many database fields (e.g., the English word "name" can refer to numerous data fields containing "name" as an element). For reasons of data integrity, some commercial NLIs allow only retrieval of data, and not updates.

Dialog based NLIs for knowledge based systems perform a multitude of tasks including accessing a user model and the existing knowledge base for it. While the knowledge base proper contains linguistic and conceptual information to facilitate inferences, the user model contains information on expectations, expertise, and habits a particular person might have who accesses a computing device. User modeling ranges from simple profiling of preferences, self-correcting spell checkers without user feed- back, to second-guessing what the user's real needs are.

4.2 APPROACHES

The clash between academic wisdom and commercial pragmatism has never been greater than in the area of NLIs. The designers of currently available NLIs typically subscribe, not always exclusively, to one of the following three schools of thought: (A) The pattern matcher is convinced that the regularities of language can be captured by a brute force algorithm that models language in a finite number of patterns by reducing NLP to stock phrases and token processing. (B) The linguist adheres to the notion that language makes infinite use of finite means and therefore builds a library of formalisms, preferably syntactic in nature, that exhaustively captures the very essence of language. (C) The AI researcher subscribes to the dominant role of knowledge in any act of intelligence, the use of NL included, and therefore opts for modeling a particular domain, preferably through "knowledge engineering".

After taking a first look at the approach to NL of these schools of thought, one is tempted to either agree with all of them and render NL processing an eternal undertaking, or pick one approach as the most pragmatic and declare all NL processing problems as solved in principle. Eternity and dogma have always provided a way out of dilemmas of all kinds, NL included. After taking a second look, however, a more realistic approach is at hand.   What if the three major drawbacks, robustness, memory and transportability, are not primarily a function of the complexities

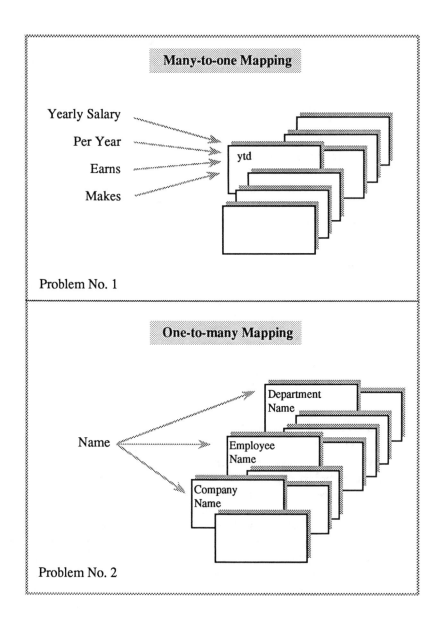

Figure 4-3:   Two problems for NLIs

of NL processing but a function of particular approaches? What if in removing the dogmatic edge of most current approaches a more appropriate paradigm of NL processing emerges?

While pattern matching systems are easy to set up and maintain, they afford the user a minimum of utility; for linguistic oriented systems, the customization involves the tagging of all the values in the database, effectively duplicating the databases for the NLI. Since they are mostly based on linguistic processing, ambiguities have to be resolved by the end-user. The AI approach goes even further than the linguistic one. In effect, within that approach, the domain of a particular data base is modeled around database values and relations. Setting up such a system requires a substantial investment.

The notion of NLI encompasses many more aspects of NLP than just translating English into command, query or knowledge representations. Ideally, any form of text should be understandable to the system. Questions about metaknowledge – knowledge about the content of the database – should be properly answered (e.g., Who makes more than 80K?" should have an answer like "The vice presidents", rather than a list of names). Question–answering systems have only just begun to address the deeper issues of question formation and question answering.

4.3 NLI APPLICATIONS

HAL, the cunningly righteous board computer in *2001 – A Space Odyssey* unfortunately has set the standard for what people expect from a NL interface. The misconception, that using English means being intelligent, backfires twice. On the one hand, people with severe retrieval problems look to these NLI to cope with issues which it normally takes a well-trained information specialist to handle. So, what they need is an expert system for information retrieval, not a code generator for SQL queries. On the other hand, the end-user, not knowing anything about how databases follow their own logical and physical view of the universe, experiences a clash with how he thinks the relational universe is structured. Disappointments abound; the reality is not HAL.

There are as many problems with the use of NLP technology as with the technology itself. Managing the expectations of the users, assessing their knowledge of computers, and considering their motor skills are the keys to successfully and effectively using a NLI for a specific application. High expectations almost always turn into disappointment and frustration. Frustration on the part of the user of NLI products comes in many forms.

Take the allegedly best, most successful PC package, in fact take almost any NLI, and you will find it annoying at times because of overcorrecting spell checkers [By "all" do you mean "Allen" in your dictionary, or "all" in mine?], frequent requests for clarifications ["List all the leads after 5/5/87" - Shall I do the following: "Select and view the forms on which the Last Call is after (the Last Call where the initial Contact is 5/5/87)?"], and finally, the response: "Please wait ... Your request is complex and will take a bit more time than usual to complete."

Frustration also comes on the part of the data processing person, who is stricken not only with an admiration for "computerese" but also often with poor command of his native tongue. He is called upon to install and maintain the NLIs while keeping the user happy. After going through a crash course on morpho-syntactic lexicography he is often ready to ask for demotion or assistance; but not to set up a system that is highly in demand - by everybody. A third area of discontent with NLIs is related to the level of reasoning power the system should have. At times, casual users of databases, after retrieving some piece of data, want to have elaborations and explanations of why and how the retrieved piece of data relates to the overall scheme of things (e.g., List the customers who paid their credit card debts after Christmas. Did they respond to our grace period offer? If so, how?). Without explicit preparation of the NLP system to explore causal relations, state of the art NLIs would be at a loss to come up with these answers.

NLIs are meant to be used by intelligent agents that know English on at least an elementary school level, and that know what tasks they have to perform. Anyone asking an interface to a shipping database to list all the lotharios over 40 years old is defeating the purpose of an NLI, while the same question may well be appropriate for a cautious female connected to the DBMS of a dating service. Idiot proofing NLIs is not only impossible and uneconomical - it takes away resources better spent elsewhere on improving the system. Moreover, as Edwin Hutchins pointed out, assuming mass idiocy will result in an artifact that is suitable for idiots.

The operational knowledge of computers is another factor that presents an obstacle for the success of NLIs. Some general remarks must be made about letting a casual, untrained user access major computing resources. Issues like security and cost lurk in the background. Given that it may save money if anyone can access corporate information resources, thus cutting James Martin's "invisible backlog" - everything you ever wanted to know but were afraid to do with a computing device - problems may arise if someone who issues complicated searches ties up the resources spending large sums on expensive retrieval operations. Another factor of productively making use of the technology is the typing skills the prospective user has. Motor skills for using a keyboard may be even more important than understanding the basics of a computer.

Unfortunately, many applications with big but short-term pay-offs for the developers are never considered primary targets since scientists are in the habit of targeting the hard problems for applications first. Thus, applications like NLIs for spreadsheets or operating system commands were brought to the market relatively late, although these applications are straightforward, albeit still fraught with problems. NLIs also have to be rejected for certain applications like word processing where a mouse or function key approach is much more effective and efficient. Different approaches are suited for different applications: if only a limited NL capability is desired or needed, a fixed number of patterns will suffice. The common wisdom with NLP systems in general and NLIs in particular is that there is no generic NL processor possible. Moreover, the fact that certain domains use a specific sublanguage, characterized by special syntactic, semantic and lexical choices, does not help alleviate the NLP problems: it simply reduces the number of tokens rather than the types of NL structures. The NLP system, no matter how simple its domain or application, still has to cope with all the hard problems, even though on a smaller scale.

4.3.1 Translation based NLIs

Interfaces for operating systems have to assist the user in executing commands that normally have to be translated into systems commands. The basic DOS or Unix concepts require extensive training without the constant update in capabilities. As with any application software, the mnemonics are often opaque, easily forgotten if not frequently used. Take for instance the Unix command for deleting blanks from a file – GREP – V $FILEA>FILER – and the utility of NLIs even for power users becomes obvious. The problem is augmented by the different protocols that different packages require. To exit out of different packages may require you to type "exit", "logout", or even "system". Different operating systems require different mnemonics which will also change over time. The same holds true for spreadsheets or any other software package.

4.3.2 Transformation based NLIs for database management systems

Interfaces for DBMS have to mediate between the view of the database developer and the database user. Three "views" enter into this process (see Figure 4-4): the physical view (how the data structures are implemented); the logical view (how the database developer has structured the data for a

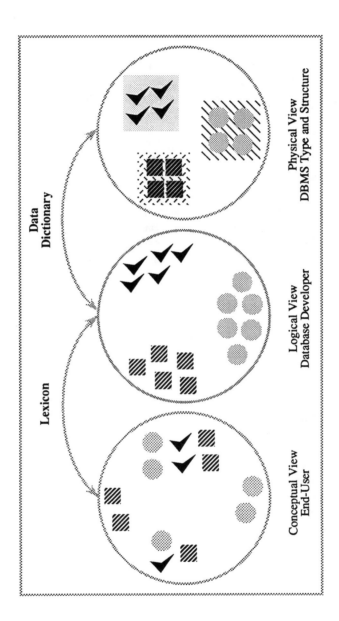

Figure 4-4:   Three views of the database

particular domain); and the conceptual view (how the end user can access the information of a particular domain). It is important to note that NL cannot assist the user in accessing information that lies outside of the logical view. For instance, if two tables in a relational DBMS are "joined" on one particular field, the NLI also has to follow this path, even if the intention of a user in a particular query may be different. In brief, the NLI has to function within the universe laid out by the database developer. The level of the accuracy and the quality of the retrieved data is hard enough to assess for third and fourth generation language access; NL adds another dimension to it because it transforms the English into a third or fourth generation language.

The various types of DBMSs (e.g., relational, network, hierarchical) provide a trade-off between efficient search and effective retrieval. Hierarchical DBMSs are fast to search but tedious to access, whereas relational DBMSs pose opposite problems. While hierarchical databases require a programmer to specify in a third generation language like Cobol how to get to the data, a relational database allows the user to specify what he wants in a fourth generation language like SQL. A relational database allows the user to get data from different files, called "tables" in relational terminology, which requires the user to understand the underlying structure of the data base. The two major problems for users of DBMSs are: (1) the hard-to-learn search protocols, including differences in the required fourth generation languages that differ from DBMS to DBMS in spite of the so-called ANSI standard SQL; and (2) the knowledge that the user is expected to have about the structure of the database itself, the "view" problem.   Considering an example of SQL, a fourth generation language query language (e.g., SELECT COUNT (*) FROM EMPLOYEE, DEPARTMENT WHERE DEPARTMENT.DNO=EMPLOYEE.DNO AND DEPARTMENT, BUILDING-NO=7), it is apparent that not only has the user to know what can be asked, but also how the information is distributed.   Moreover, the translation process requires of the user an acute sense of what exactly needs to be retrieved.

Advantages of NLIs include: (1) Flexibility for the user: NLIs effectively solve the ad hoc query problem. The user is not required to learn yet another computer language in order to retrieve information. Unlike menu-drive systems or fourth generation languages, NLIs ideally do not impose restrictions on the formulation of the queries. Even power users, knowledgeable SQL users, experience time savings. (2) Habitability: the time spent on learning how to access information stored in computers or make sense of computing devices is small. (3) Data structure and system independence: the user does not have to know the search protocols, mnemonics. or setup procedures of the database management system.

4.3.3 Dialog based NLIs

There is a significant difference between traditional, transformation based NLIs that require from the user a querying strategy to extract meaningful responses from databases, and dialog based user models that try to get at the intention of the user while trying to be cooperative during the interaction. Cooperation has to be reactive and proactive, correcting misconceptions and preventing errors.

For an NLI to enable a dialog with the user it has to have access to domain, task and user-models. Current systems are in an embryonic state. Their target applications include expert systems, CAD/CAM systems, CASE technology, and supercomputing. The complexity of these systems requires easier ways for the user to express his needs and wants; while at the same time and because of inherent ambiguities the NLI must be a vehicle for clarifying actions the user wants the system to perform

4.3.3.1 Expert Systems

Expert system research in the past has successfully eschewed the issue of effectively interfacing the user of the expert system.   Most expert systems are built to perform tasks requiring expertise in one particular area. The problem solving activity is emphasized, without making the reasoning process transparent to the user. Issues in interfaces to expert systems include (1) how to assure the user that his intentions are understood and that the problem is solved based on sound principles, (2) how to provide proper feedback and interaction between the user and the expert system, and (3) how to incorporate the knowledge base of the expert system into the interface.

4.3.3.2 CAD/CAM

The current computing technology in computer-assisted design and manufacturing has drastically changed the role of the human in the design and manufacturing process. IUIs have to reflect this change in which the computer controls the processes and the human operator has primarily a supervisory role. The supervisory role entails that the human operator has to make fewer low-level decisions but has to make more high-level decision at a greater speed. The complexity of computing tasks for process control applications, for instance, requires the operator to function in at least three modes: the planning mode including scheduling, inventory control; the monitoring mode of multiple processes and selective actions; and the trouble-shooting mode in which the operator determines spot checks and maintenance.

In brief, the function of IUIs for CAD/CAM systems lies primarily in assisting the operator in high-level decision making, while rendering the onslaught of information from multiple knowledge sources manageable. Rather than taking the human out of the loop, current CAD/CAM systems attribute even more importance to the human factor. The human skill for making fast and reliable decisions becomes more significant as the automation of processes increases.

4.3.3.3 CASE

The market share of CASE [Computer Assisted Software Engineering] technology will supercede that of DBMS by 1992, according to a major computer manufacturer. The sheer number of different software applications requires a way of integrating all the available computer resources at a level manageable for the application programmer. An emerging technology that breaks through this complexity barrier, which also exists in conventional programs, is CASE technology. While, in the short history of computing, the complexity barrier has been at least temporarily reduced by introducing higher level languages, the solution to managing future programs lies in an interface that "understands" what the program does by error-checking, debugging, and, possibly, providing answers to "why-questions".

4.4 PRODUCTS/PROTOTYPES

The lack of commercial success and user acceptance to some extent is based on a fundamental misconception of what an NLI should and should not be. An NLI should make it easier for the user to retrieve data without having to learn yet another computer language, and ideally should integrate various software programs (e.g., spreadsheets, graphics) into the data retrieval process. Ultimately, an NLI should be the "lingua franca" for all computer application programs. An NLI should be considered neither the panacea for all the retrieval problems, the magic wand against computer illiteracy, nor the pinnacle of AI research. NL should be the fifth generation language, possibly used in conjunction with other interface strategies (e.g., menus, icons).

4.4.1 Translation based interfaces

Traditionally, NLIs were primarily developed for database management front-ends. The NLP technology in the 1970s was still a technology looking for an application. This situation stemmed from the fact that many obvious applications were far too difficult for the available technology. While database access via English has turned out to be a much harder problem than anticipated, "easy" and "simple" applications – like allowing users to enter English rather than operating systems commands – have sprung up in the 1980s. The Unix Consultant developed at Berkeley by Wilensky and associates allows users to enter English commands to a Unix operating system [Wilensky 88]. Language Craft from CMU also allowed operating system commands to be entered in English. The most recent potential success story is DOSTALK, a Lisp based program whose kernel takes up 5K bytes of RAM. After typing the command in English, the system provides a translation and executes the command. The 5K kernel calls a 180 Kbyte program that contains the English conversion capability. If DOSTALK cannot process the English input, it engages in a dialog with the user. As with other programs that have NL capability (e.g., Q&A, HAL) serendipity makes the system shine. The feature to search for any file without changing directories is very appealing, even though it does not have anything to do with the NL capability. The NL capability, however, enables the user to go to files without having to know about subdirectories and other logistic intricacies. DOSTALK, which sells for under $100, is marketed through SAK Technologies. The company was able to align itself with major computer vendors that will include the package in their standard package. DOSTALK is already being used at Washington's National Airport and by the FBI.

Natural Access, a product by Texas Instruments, is an interface builder that lets you define interfaces for spreadsheets and databases. It originated as NL-Menu for the TI Explorer Lisp machine and does not provide any NL capability by itself. Rather, the developer setting up Natural Access defines the various options for the vocabulary the user can use. Ultimately, Natural Access provides choices for completing requests and commands via pop-up menus. This interface strategy eliminates the worst problem that NLIs face: ambiguities. The user can only select what is unambiguously understood by the system. By the same token, Natural Access limits the freedom of the user just like a menu does. Menu driven NLIs do not even come close to the versatility of free form NL access. MBNLQ for IBM's S/36, S/38 and AS/400 databases is based on the same technology as Natural Access. IBM markets this product for their line of databases.

4.4.2 Transformation based NLIs

The product spectrum of transformation based NLIs begins with systems that do simple keyword (pattern) matching operation to systems that perform intricate inferencing operations. While, in the early stages of development and productization, the NLIs were very much tied to a specific application, the first somewhat widely used systems were domain and application

Vendor	Product	Hardware Required
Artificial Intelligence Corp.	Intellect	IBM Mainframes DEC VAX, VMS
Battelle	Natural Language Query (NLQ)	IBM PC and Compatibles (For Most Mainframes)
Bolt, Beranek and Newman	Parlance	VAX, SUN LISPmachines, SUN
Carnegie Group, Inc.	Language Craft	DEC VAXstation, TEXAS Instruments EXPLORER, Symbolics 3600
Dynamics Research	SPOCK	SUN, VAX
IBM	MBNLQ	IBM PC and Compatibles
Intelligent Business Systems, Inc.	EasyTalk	DEC MicroVAXII, VAX
McDonnell Douglas Computer Systems, Co.	Natural Language	Minicomputers
Natural Language, Inc.	Natural Language (DataTalker)	SUN, VAX
Online Software	English (Works with RAMISII)	IBM Mainframes
Programmed Intelligence, Corp.	Intelligent Query	IBM, SUN
Stanford Research Institute	TEAM (only licensed to universities)	Symbolics

Figure 4-5:   NLIs for DBMSs

independent. A large group of current products can perform inferences that the structure of the DBMS and the contents of the database could not support by themselves [see Figure 4–5]. Here is why.

The problems with relational technologies as well as with the older DBMS paradigms have forced certain complexities onto NL interfaces that want to appear very intelligent. In general, the information stored in the relational system is very limited even for translating English requests into SQL statements. What most NLIs resort to is the creation of an outer layer of intelligence around the DBMS and its specific applications, thus in effect re-creating and re-tooling the database for want of doing up–front inferencing. The restructuring of the database universe accounts for the high costs of NLIs that strive to be more informative than the database itself. For general use however, this overkill in performance does not benefit the everyday user. The added capability often requires much more effort than that for the needed base capability. While powerful, these NLP systems still do not have the capability of information retrieval experts. Without modeling the user, the task and the specific application domain, outside of what is provided in the database, the NLI cannot deliver what some users expect – a system that can actively manipulate data and turn that data into real information.

Few people see that by changing the DBMS paradigms many interface issues could be solved. Thus companies leapfrog by embracing object–oriented database technology, e.g., NCR and Control Data Corporation exploring Orion, an MCC sponsored project, or start–up companies like Neuron Data with their Nexpert product. Object–oriented databases are much more amenable to inferencing on the data objects themselves without going through intermediate data structures. Once the object–oriented DBMS is firmly established, the currently used, very intricate processing algorithms will be superseded by a more appropriate knowledge structure and control mechanism that will directly tie into the knowledge representation provided by the database. The knowledge manipulation mechanisms of the near future used for database access will no longer look at linguistic structures, rather it will look at conceptual structures, just as keyword thesauri are turned into conceptual thesauri.

The distinction between domain dependent or special purpose systems and domain independent or general purpose systems has been conveniently used to separate NLIs on grounds of performance, and surreptitiously of cost. While in the 1970s, NLIs were sometimes built for one application only (e.g., Lunar), handcrafted systems using domain specific semantic grammars were built and later adapted to another domain requiring major redesign, this method no longer applies to current systems. Current products do require setup procedures that range from intricate to cumbersome. Underlying all the current systems is the notion that within a certain approach to NLIs, the NLI administrator has to follow a technique that is inherent in the NLI shell. There are three dimensions that are useful in classifying current NLIs: (1) the hardware dimension distinguishing personal computer based systems from mainframe or workstation based systems; (2) the structural dimension distinguishing pattern based systems, including those that bear a resemblance to neurally inspired algorithms, from syntactic and (semantic) knowledge based systems; and, most importantly, (3) the functional dimension distinguishing inference capabilities limited to what is explicit in the database from capabilities that are embedded in the outsider interface layer created through the shell. While a list of the majority of available systems is given in Figure 4-1, the following discussion focuses on the impact each dimension has on performance, productivity, and feasibility. This general product review will address issues that are specific to each group.

The hardware dimension helps classify three types of systems: (A) personal computer based systems [see Figure4-6] that are tied into the personal computer based database (e.g., DBase, R:Base); (B) mainframe or workstation based systems; and (C) micro-to-mainframe linkages that allow access to mainframe based databases while having the NLI portion of the program resident on the PC. Three major characteristics that distinguish types (A)-(C) from each other are their size or memory requirements, their linguistic and conceptual coverage, and the cost of bringing the system up.

A PC based NLI co-hosted on the same machine as the database is limited in memory. Its customization effort, often done by the end-user himself, is commensurate with the productivity gain. The setting up of an interface by the same person who set up the database is extremely straightforward since this person has a good grasp of what questions to ask and what vocabulary to use. More often than not, the person who sets up his own database will seldom resort to the NL capability. However, for the large user group who pays consultants to set up their databases, NL capability will be extremely helpful.

Unfortunately, current systems are often based on outdated and inefficient algorithms, that are time-consuming and require frequent clarifications. The problem with clarification stems often from an over-correcting spell-checker. A mainframe or workstation based system normally is designed to download most information from the database into the NL processor. First generation systems labeled the values in the database in the lexicon of the NLI to perform mostly syntactic parsing on nouns, verbs, etc. Second generation systems construct a representation of the domain more powerful than the data in the database to increase utility of the NLI. Both generations are based on the assumption that the setup of the NLI will demand a major customization effort and investment. The new era of PC-to-mainframe NLI

Vendor	Product	Hardware
Battelle	MicroNLQ	IBM PC and Compatibles
Information Builders Inc.	EQL (English Query Language)	IBM XT, AT, and PS/2
Microrim, Inc.	Clout (Works with R-Base)	IBM PC and Compatibles
Programmed Intelligence Corp.	Intelligent Query	IBM PC and Compatibles
Savvy Corp.	Savvy Database (DBMS)	IBM PC and Compatibles
Symantec Corp.	Q&A Intelligent Assistant (DBMS/Word Processing)	IBM PC and Compatibles
Texas Instruments	Natural Access	TI Explorer

Figure 4-6:   NLIs for PC-based DBMSs

links brought about numerous advantages: the increase in speed as a result of separating the processing tasks; the increase in utility since users could now use their favorite spreadsheets and report writers in conjunction with mainframe DBMSs; the overall integration of mainframe and PC based software; the alleviation of computer anxiety. The cost factor has always been an issue. With the prices of DBMS systems for mainframe starting at $15,000 and up, NLIs in the price range of upper $50,000 are not destined to become commercial successes. NLIs as a commodity are.

The structural dimension helps classify the NLIs according to their approach and architecture into pattern based, primarily syntactic or knowledge based processors [see Figure 4-7]. We already discussed the approaches in section 4.2. In brief, a simple pattern matching program reduces the language to a number of stock phrases, a syntactic oriented NLP system requires an elaborate grammatical analysis and knowledge based program accrues a large overhead for modeling the domain. The higher investment for knowledge based NLIs may pay off later if sophisticated inferencing capabilities are expected.

The functional dimension divides the NLIs into two groups: on the one hand, systems that concern themselves with the information provided by the database and data dictionary; on the other hand, systems that create their own outer layer of data representation which lets the interface reason by itself without accessing the databases. However trivial the example, the question "What color is Fred's white horse?" would not invoke an SQL query but could be handled within the interface module. And then again – who would ask such redundant questions in the first place? It is debatable if the gain in coverage and robustness is worth the effort. While linguists gloat over the slick package that handles backward and forward anaphora, quantifier scoping, etc., the question from the end-user perspective is: who needs it? The critical factor with most of the sophisticated system is the setup time and the maintainability. For the majority of these "outer layer" interfaces, many applications are simply not worth the effort. Moreover, the computing infrastructure becoming more and more based on personal computers still experiences a bottleneck when it comes to the memory that is available. Economy of scale is another factor that has to be considered. While a multi-purpose shell can be sold at a reasonable price, the shells requiring customization often have to be marketed with a lead time of up to one year. The common trend in the software industry is certainly moving away from using outside consultants especially with the increased availability of CASE technology. Another factor is the habitability of NLIs. Most users become familiar with their NLIs within one month while getting to know the subset of English the system will process.

Multi-purpose shells have to ensure that they are transportable and easy to

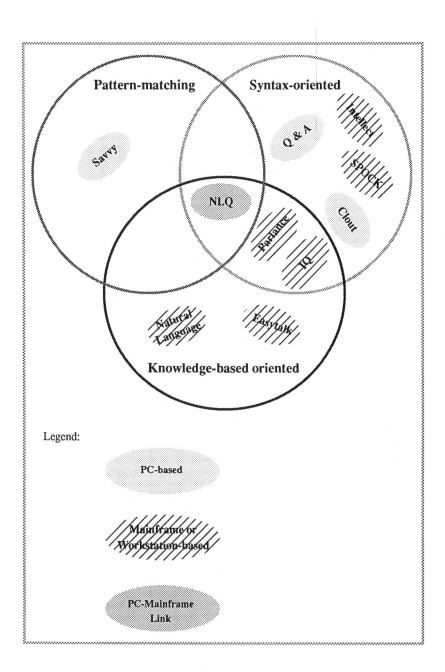

Figure 4-7:   NLIs according to their hardware
and structural dimensions

set up. One example of a multi–purpose shell that not only fits on the personal computer but also accesses mainframe databases is a product called NLQ, Battelle's PC based NL query system for relational databases combines essential characteristics of all three approaches [see section 4.2]: it links the limited number of patterns for querying any database with the knowledge already provided in the structure and content of the existing database to parse an infinite number of NL queries. NLIs strive for exhaustive coverage of the two ways of mapping without being sure that users actually require the many possible constructions [see Figure 4–3. Such attempts at exhaustive coverage require an exorbitant amount of memory and processing time while often not handling one user's admittedly idiosyncratic query. NLQ's answer to overkill and user idiosyncrasies is a processing model that determines which structural and lexical information is necessary at any given stage of processing to complete the retrieval process. The user model allows a particular user to fine–tune NLQ for his special needs and dialect. NLQ is built on the principle that every user has his own style of querying a database. Therefore, rather than providing an NLI that gives the user the illusion of being able to deal with every possible English construction and to do magic with interpreting ambiguous and vague queries, NLQ is a powerful tool that makes querying a complex relational database easier.

Many NLIs produce mappings from English to one particular DBMS or mainframe. Currently, there are at least 50 (relational) DBMSs commercially available, all with their own idiosyncrasies when it comes to their query language and their mainframe specific access protocol. NLQ, residing on a PC, allows access to virtually any mainframe over a modem. NLQ's open architecture allows hook–ups to most commonly available relational DBMSs. Because NLQ transforms the English query into a logical representation which in turn will be converted to a specific query syntax, NLQ can interface to multiple databases from the same PC. NLQ consists of two modules: the NLQ setup module that provides a fully automated link to any relational mainframe database allowing the NLQ administrator to customize NLQ for a particular application and the main NLQ end–user module that translates queries, keeps track of anaphoric references during a dialog and helps the user along if his query is ambiguous or too vague for processing. NLQ provides many options to view various stages of the query process, thus leaving the user in control of what is being processed and when.

Processing the English query in NLQ is done in three steps [Figure 4–8]. The input string is first labeled in the linguistic analyzer module according to word categories and syntactic markers for complex sentences. The result of the string analysis is then put into the pattern matcher component. The pattern matcher contains a grammar based on the relations in the particular database. Information about relations and contents of the database structure is previously loaded by the automated NLQ administration procedure. The

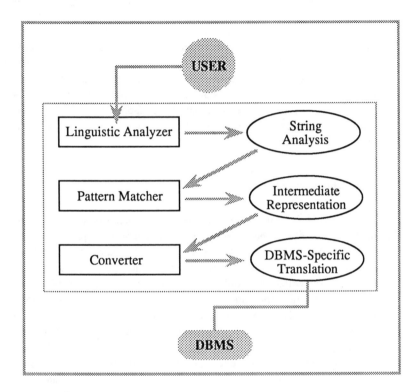

Figure 4-8:   NLQ's NLP steps

output of the pattern matcher consists of an intermediate representation. Depending on what fourth generation query syntax is required, the appropriate converter module translates the intermediate representation of the query into the DBMS specific format. NLQ's modular architecture is proof that NLIs can be useable and economic. NLQ, originally designed on a Lisp machine, requires in its [compiled C] product version only 640K of memory, and thus is able to run on any IBM or compatible while communicating over a modem link to the mainframe based DBMS. NLQ lends credence to the conclusion drawn by *Computerworld* [December 1, 1986] that "from a user's perspective, especially a micro user's, a NL interface is an ease-of-use product. It does not have to be perfect, it just has to make computing easier".

4.4.3 Dialog based NLIs

Today's NLIs cannot "make conversation" which extends over more than one or two utterances. The apparent lack of discourse capabilities of commercial NLIs, coupled with overdrawn expectations, has contributed to the frustration of the user. If the buyers and the users had been properly instructed and educated, the situation would have never arisen. The man-machine interface which allows the computer program to converse with the user in English requires knowledge about (1) proper turn-taking, (2) appropriate topic-shifts, and (3) conversational rules, to name just a few. It is much easier to capture syntactic rules than conversational rules. Thus, most existing NLIs rely primarily on syntactic and semantic knowledge to process NL. The unsatisfactory responses of such a system can be labeled uncooperative [Kaplan 79] as in the response to the question "Which female makes more than 50K in department 302?" Responses like "None", "Does not compute" are unacceptable; the response "There are no females in the department" is cooperative since the capability of the program to do more tells the user the whole story. In a cooperative response, the specific point of failure in the attempted retrieval process is returned to the user for possibly rephrasing the question. Metacommunication expressed in clue words like "but first" as in "Which of the employees in department 601 were promoted in 88, but first, tell me who was over quota", exceeds the capability of the current NLI systems. The two examples illustrate that NLIs have to do more than process isolated utterances. The NLI has to know the rules of conversation that underlie the discourse. The problem is compounded by the fact that different domains use specialized sublanguages, characterized by syntactic, semantic and lexical idiosyncrasies.

Dialog based NLIs are still in the laboratories. They are often built around very specific research topics that include modeling beliefs, goals, and plans. Some of the projects include: modeling (1) an expert assisting an apprentice who repairs an air compressor [Appelt 82], (2) a tax advisor assisting people in completing the income tax [Wahlster 86], (3) an UNIX/SINIX consultant [Wilensky 88], and (4) a hotel manager renting his rooms [Jameson 80], to name just a few.

4.4.4 Generic tool kits

In the early 1980s it became fashionable in the AI arena to provide tools and tool kits for certain problem solving activities. In lieu of a generic NL processor, many companies tried to please various markets, mostly database and expert systems markets. Since many of the tools required either expertise in knowledge engineering or databases in addition to linguistics, NL companies made hefty sums on the customization effort. In a sense, NLIs for DBMSs are tools or shells that need to be customized, or, as is the case with HAL, can only be used for one particular application package. What we call generic tool kits in this section are products that can be used for many different retrieval applications, not just DBMS. The drawback with general purpose shells – in close analogy to expert systems shells – is that a lot of time has to be invested to customize them, while special purpose shells give developers a "head-start", thus saving money in indirect costs, e.g., salary.

In 1988, many new shells were advertised. Gopher, a multiple database access retriever is a personal computer based, "simultaneous multiple database access interface in NL that automatically combines information from disparate sources in responding to user queries". Jake is an application independent NL user interface that allows an application programmer to design an interface within 64K RAM and 100K of disk space for the built-in dictionary of 3,000 entries. The currently available NLIs for expert system shells on the PC normally work in conjunction with the expert system shell. The listing in Figure 4-9 contains some of the popular products currently available.

4.5 HISTORY

At the Oracle International User Group meeting in Orlando, Florida, in October 1988, it became obvious that NLIs have staged a comeback: four companies were offering as their main product line NLIs for relational DBMS, emphasizing in particular their Oracle connections: NLQ, Natural Language (previously "Datatalker"), Easytalk, Spock.

NLIs used as front-ends to DBMSs "translate" the English input either into an intermediate form and then into the DBMS specific query language, or

Vendor	Product	Hardware Required
American Expertech, Inc.	Xi Plus	IBM PC, XT, AT, PS/2 and Compatibles
Micro Database Systems	Guru (SpreadSheet/ DBMS/Expert System Tool)	IBM PC and Compatibles
Micro Database Systems	K-Chat (Works with Knowledgeman-2	IBM PC and Compatibles
Programming Logic Systems, Inc.	APES (Augmented Prolog for Expert Systems)	Requires Micro-Prolog IBM PC, XT, AT and Compatibles
Softwync, Inc.	SuperExpert	IBM PC, XT, AT and Compatibles

Figure 4-9:   NLIs for personal computer
based expert systems

directly into the query language of the back-end **DBMS**. One of the earlier NL interfaces was based on the idea that the processing algorithm could be directly tied to a particular domain. The so-called domain dependent NL interfaces used semantic grammars that had to be changed for each application. With the advent of a technology that could make the NL interface more transportable, the domain dependent systems disappeared. Another innovation was the creation of intermediate forms to construct the correct queries. In general, the NLIs of the 1970s, the first generation systems, contained at the most three types of knowledge: "linguistic knowledge, domain and discourse (i.e., what types of questions) knowledge" [Boguraev 82]. The domain dependent systems were characterized by either merging discourse with database knowledge (e.g., Lunar [Woods 72]), or merging linguistic with domain knowledge in their (semantic) grammars (e.g., LADDER [Hendrix 78], PLANES [Waltz 78]). The domain independent systems separated various levels of structure and were based on a generic syntactic analyzer with added domain semantics (e.g., TQA [Damerau 80], PHILQA 1 [Bronnenberg 80]). In many domain independent systems, semantic routines are either interleaved with syntactic processing (e.g., DIALOGIC [Grosz 82]) or bundled after the syntactic processing is completed (e.g., TDUS [Robinson 80]).

Transformation based NLIs to DBMSs have a brief history in the commercial market place: INTELLECT, based on first generation technology and theories dating back into the late 1960s (e.g., ATN), was commercially introduced in 1980. Q&A, a PC based product, was released in 1985 after major investments, reorganization of staff, and change of application. Q&A now features an NLI as part of an integrated package including DBMS and word processor. NLQ, the first PC to mainframe link NLI, was released in 1988. NL Inc. started in 1984, and released their first product in 1986.

The new era of PC-to-mainframe NLI links began with NLQ after Intellect had announced a PC-resident product for many years. It is interesting to note that both DBMS technology and NLI technology got started on the same project, the analysis of lunar rocks. While NLIs for DBMS were considered the cutting edge technology, many NLI opportunities to other software packages were not deemed appropriate in the early stages of NLI development because of limited market share. The trend to capitalize on the limited use of limited NL capability opened the mass market for NL products.

4.6 TRENDS

The trend in NLP software is to provide the capability at a reasonable cost for a wide audience of computer neophytes that need to access computers but do not want or find the time to learn all the intricate access protocols.

With the advent of object–oriented and semantic databases, the task of adapting an NLI to a particular application will be facilitated. Current commercial NLIs in effect create a dummy knowledge base out of the given relations and data structures.   What current NLIs also have to do is to build the smarts into the system that would enable it to answer queries that are outside of the database domain, yet within a certain reasonableness of coverage. Much has been written about linguistic and conceptual coverage of a system. On the one hand it is impossible to benchmark NLIs since the way they are constructed and set up for particular applications is so different. On the other hand, the inferencing bells and whistles often are not used because they require much handcrafting and overheads. The everyday user will want to build queries that are not taxing, either in SQL or in NL. The complexities of actual database queries is much overstated. The tendency of rather intricate systems such as NLIs is that they do not deliver the basic capabilities while they ironically shine in tough situations.

In the short term (1995), domain modeling will be possible in a much more straightforward fashion than in the 1980s. In the mid term (2000), user–modeling and parallel processing will be areas of some success in consolidating the NLI market. In the long term (2010), the object–oriented programming language paradigm will have made it possible to turn English into the lingua franca of software.   The technology will be based on reasonable tasks and thus provide a higher degree of customer satisfaction than in the past.

4.7 CONCLUSION

While databases grow larger and the user population increases, [relational] DBMSs are still built for retrieval efficiency and not user effectiveness. The interface has become increasingly important for catering to casual computer users. The multitude of application packages, ranging from spreadsheets to "courseware" make an integration of mainframe DBMS and PC utilities more and more attractive. NL capabilities of an interface significantly enhance user productivity by providing a universal language, a "lingua franca", that is ready-made for solving the hitherto cumbersome DBMS access problem and also provides a gateway to multiple software packages to manipulate data more effectively. NL rather than being the pinnacle of AI research may well turn into the pinnacle for data manipulation per se.

Just as Fortran was touted the eliminator of programming (over Assembly programming) in 1957, NL will be the ultimate programming language, allowing users to write specifications of programs in English. Even better, such a programming language will provide the ultimate form of interaction, a dialog between the user and the program.

For the 1980s, the bad news was:

- Mainframe or workstation based NLIs that followed any of the three approaches to NLP – engineering, linguistic, and AI – suffered from excessive memory requirements [4–8 megabytes) and costly customization,

- the initial hype and the failure to harness user expectations made the user community at large very sceptical with respect to NLIs, and

- the infrastructure of everyday computing was not set up to accommodate the infrequent ("casual") user,

The good news, however, is that

- The new generation of NLIs that provide personal computer to mainframe links reduces the overhead considerably,

- better and faster ways to set up an NLI are already integrated in the new product releases, and

- the real needs of the user are better understood than a decade ago.

NLIs, some of which not too long ago embodied parlor tricks and snake oil slogans, are starting to make an impact on the proverbial "ever growing computer market". As the complexities of the computing environment and the programs themselves increase, the "intelligence" contained in the interface has to increase: NL is the logical way to do this. NL, if used appropriately in the interface, for fast, friendly, and effective access to the computer, is leading the way.

4.8 SUGGESTED READING

The most recent study on the subject of NLIs in the commercial arena is Shwartz' book "Applied NL Processing". It is promoting the Schankian knowledge based approach and arguing against multi-purpose and domain independent NLIs. A somewhat dated discussion is found in [Johnson 85]. Both publications also contain information on NLP in general. Two excellent overview articles are [Lehnert 88, Perrault 88]. Lehnert discusses knowledge based NLP, while Perrault et al. focus on NLIs. Two classic books on the issues of question answering and cooperative query systems are [Lehnert 78] and [Kaplan 79], respectively. The most recent discussion on the topic of "User Modeling" is published in [Kobsa 88].

4.9 USEFUL CONTACTS

The following five major software companies provide NLIs: *Natural Language Query - Battelle*, 505 King Avenue, Columbus, Ohio 43201; *AICORP*, 100 Fifth Avenue, Waltham, Massachusetts 02254; *Natural Language Inc.*, 1802 Fifth Street, Berkeley, California 94710; *Intelligent Business Systems, Inc.*, 185 Plains Road, Mail Stop 120, Milford, Connecticut 06460; *Dynamics Research Corp.*, Dept. 948, 60 Frontage Road, Andover, Massachusetts 01810.

CHAPTER 5

MACHINE TRANSLATION

The U.S. National Academy of Science has disputed the 1966 ALPAC Report's assertions regarding machine translation potentialities. Mainly Japan and European countries, however, have continued research on machine translation. As a result, computers are gradually becoming scientifically sophisticated to handle translation [quoted from the Prospectus for the *International Forum For Translation Technology*, held in Japan on April 26–28, 1989].

5.1 INFORMATION PROCESSING TASK

Machine translation [MT] systems perform the transformation of linguistic input from a source language into a target language. The transformation process takes place on the lexical, syntactic, semantic and – ideally – the pragmatic level. The complexity of the transformation process increases on every level. On the lexical level, the most appropriate word sense of the source language is mapped into the target language whereby one out of many word senses is mapped into one word sense in the target language. On the syntactic level, differences in word order and special constructions are considered. Subtleties expressed in certain syntactic constructions have to be handled by pragmatic rules, e.g., the passive constructions in English are mostly used for emphasis, while in Japanese other constructions are used for emphasis. On the semantic level, word sense nuances and idioms create some of the hardest problems for translations.

For the "ideal" MT system, a relation of equivalence between source and target language exists, whereby sets of correct sentences of the source language are mapped into sets of sentences in the target language. The MT system accomplishes this task by either directly mapping the elements of the source into those of the target language, or by first mapping the source language into an intermediate format which then gets mapped into the target language.

For the "real" MT systems, consider the translation of the German equivalent for random access memory, *Direktzugriffspeicher*, or imagine a translation of the French noun phrase *Analyse d'une methode dynamique specifique d'etablissement de balance materiel d'une instalation de retraitement de combustion nucleaire par simulation* [Wilks 87, page 15], or just think about an English compound like *main fuel system drain valve* in which *main* modifies *fuel system* and not *drain valve*. The task of an MT system is thus to reconstruct functionally in addition to structurally the sense and meaning in the target language. The task, once proclaimed impossible by Bar-Hillel [Bar-Hillel 60] because he believed that world knowledge could not be embedded in computer programs, is now the bread and butter of AI research.

5.2 APPROACHES

The task of MT is orders of magnitude larger than ordinary NLP for one language. Given the initial unrealistic goal that true MT was to be 95% accurate, the eventually dwindling enthusiasm for MT research was inevitable. The current state of the art shows three approaches to MT, direct and indirect (including transfer and interlingua). The direct approach differs from indirect approaches (i.e., transfer and interlingua) in that, in the direct approach, the analysis of the source and the synthesis of the target language is one interdependent process, while for the latter the analysis and synthesis are two independent processes. In general, indirect approaches require more intermediate processing.

The direct approach consists of a mapping from source to target language without an intermediate representation. Only minimal and source language specific disambiguation is performed. The direct approach does not contain a meaning processing component. The direct approach brings up an interesting point: "Is translation possible without understanding?" While it is possible to achieve some performance in direct translation systems (e.g., GAT), their capability is limited to one target language for each source language.

For the transfer approach the source language is mapped into a structural representation of itself and from that into an abstract meaning representation of the target language before getting mapped into the target language. The transfer approach requires different representations of meaning for every source/target language pair because the meaning representation is dependent on the target language. The approach requires the construction of two grammar pairs for two languages. The directionality of this approach promotes ad hoc extensions of systems because any problem can be delegated to lexical or syntactic exceptions. Moreover, the number of transfer systems for 70 languages would be about 5000. Current commercial systems are still solely based on the transfer approach, absolutely requiring pre-, or post-editing. Transfer systems for restricted domains can be very successful, e.g., TAUM, METAL.

In interlingua approaches the meaning representation of the source language is independent of the target or any other natural language. In turn, the interlingua representation is the basis for generating the target language. The principle of interlinguas is very attractive for two reasons: (1) it makes the translation procedures modular, requiring only one translation and one generation module per language; and (2) it constrains the required theory to produce a representation that is language independent. It also gives raise to speculations about possible language universals. The significant drawbacks are: (1) the mapping process from source language to interlingua can generate a subset of interlingua interpretations not shared by that of the target language (e.g., the interlingua receives a particular interpretation, while the generated target language interpretation may be different); (2) the lexical and syntactic make-up of the target language generated is most likely very different from that of the source language, thus rendering the approach not feasible for poetry or other forms of text which require the preservation of structure.

The interlingua approach for MT is yet another battlefield of linguistics versus AI. Two quotes regarding interlinguas and their significance for the study of language suffice to show the sharp and polemic contrast between the two disciplines. Jonathan Slocum, the leading linguist in the METAL project at the Linguistic Research Center in Texas sponsored by Siemens, remarked in a survey article on MT that "the linguistic universals searched for and debated about by linguists and philosophers is the notion that underlies the interlingua" [Slocum 85, page 4]. In sharp contrast, Rod Johnson, a linguist from the University of Manchester, England, stated that the interlingua view "tends to be the way that non-linguists see translation.

By non-linguists I mean people who do not have good familiarity with more than one language" [Johnson 87,page 264]. Interlinguas are another target for the dyed-in-the-wool linguist's disdain for considering anything but purely linguistic information in the analysis of language. These ideological differences make it very hard for the commercial market to get an unbiased, performance based assessment of the technology. The proposed nature of interlinguas ranges from using well-known knowledge representations used in AI to using Esperanto as the intermediate language.

The methodology of MT has taken advantage of the growing field of sublanguage research. In fact, METEO, allegedly the only fully automated MT system, that translates weather reports from English to French in Canada, is built around a sublanguage grammar. Sublanguage grammars are built around the notion of having application and domain specific language that is characterized by limited vocabulary, syntactic, and semantic idiosyncrasies. Sublanguage systems eventually reach a stable state that cannot be extended. The METEO system reached that state in 1981 after being operational for four years, with a throughput of about 25,000 words a day and an error margin of 10% mostly due to garbled input. Canada is the focal point of sublanguage research for MT.

5.3 APPLICATIONS

Just as writing is 90% perspiration and 10% inspiration, MT is, as Albert LaMothe, a freelance translator, puts it, 90% bullwork and 10% creativity. In his opinion, the pay-off in computerized MT is not in achieving any lofty intellectual goals that academics propound, but in increased quality and productivity. Quality in terms of consistency of translation, especially on large projects with many different translators. Productivity in terms of faster dictionary look-ups and initial-pass translations especially on technical documents. MT capabilities are becoming more important because English is no longer the lingua franca of science, and the onslaught of information on a global level is on the increase. The closer ties with Japan and Europe based on the interdependence of economies is another factor that requires an increase in MT technology to keep up with the demand. The major areas of interest in applying MT technology commercially are (1) technical translation, (2) business correspondences, and (3) foreign language training devices.

The three areas of much of the activities in MT include: (1) translation aides including hand-held devices for the general public, on-line dictionaries, and terminology databases; (2) machine aided translation (MAT) including interactive MT; and (3) MT per se including systems that require either pre-, or post-editing. The initial dichotomy between stand-alone MT systems and MT tools has been bridged by systems referred to as machine assisted translation systems [MAT]

Translation aides range from on-line dictionaries and thesauri to terminology databases. For technical translations the ranges of domain require the availability of up-to-date terminology. A standard look-up capability ensures consistency in word usage. Machine aided translation is performed by interactive computer systems. The role of the human translator is either limited to helping the computer system to perform the translation, or making use of that system to produce it. In brief, MAT is a matter of degree. A first type of interactive system is application specific. It allows the user without knowledge of the target language to produce brief documents on-line and have them translated without need for post-editing. As Kay pointed out [Kay 82], this method is desirable if the same document has to be translated into several languages, or if the document is so technical that domain experts have to be consulted to translate it. A second type of interactive system possible is that without source text at all. For a small well-defined class of documents (e.g., business letter, memo), the system can prompt the user for the minimal information necessary to construct the text immediately in the source language. Stand-alone MT systems are responsible for the translation with pre-or post-editing being part of the translation cycle. It is important to note here, that every translation, even when performed solely by humans, includes a post-editing phase.

5.4 PRODUCTS AND PROGRAMS

Currently available off-the-shelf MT software is at the stage of intelligent translation aids. Most output of the commercial systems requires heavy post-editing, less so for highly structured technical texts. Commercial systems are based on the transfer approach, use chart parser techniques and phrase structure grammars and are limited to sentence level processing. These systems are grounded in linguistic, mostly syntactic-oriented theories with semantic extensions [see Figure 5-1]. While it is true that MT without semantic considerations are not effective, the redesign of older systems is only a temporary solution. An exception to this statement is Systran, the Russian-English translation system that appeared on the scene in the early 1970s and is in constant use at the USAF Foreign Technology Division at Wright Patterson AFB.

The embryonic nature of MT technology explains the scarcity of viable quality measures of the products. Attempts at establishing yardsticks have produced quality dimensions along lexical, syntactic, semantic, and pragmatic invariance measures. As the state of the art advances, new systems still

Name	Techniques	Linguistic Theory	Languages	Application	Status
Georgetown Automatic Translation	Wordbased Transfer Grammar	None	Russian-English	Information Acquisition	Defunct 1960
Centre d'Etudes pour la Traduction Automatique	Grammatical Interlingura Semantic Transfer Grammar	Dependency Grammar	Russian-French	Mathematics Physics Text	Defunct 1971
Traduction Automatique de l'Université de Montréal	Syntactic, Semantic, Analysis	---	English-French	Weather Forecast, Aviation Manuals	Defunct 1981
Automated Language Processing Systems	Transfer Grammar with Human Assistance	Junction Grammar	French, German, Portuguese, Spanish	(ALP) Ecclesiastical Texts; (ALPS) Translation Aid	(ALP) Defunct 1980; (ALPS) Production System
Systran	Wordbased Transfer Grammar	Ad hoc Semantic Features	Russian, English, French, Italian	Military, NASA, GM Manuals	Production System
Logos	Transfer Grammar	Case Grammar Valency Theory	Vietnamese, German-English	Military	Production System
TAUM-Meteo	Transfer Grammar		English-French	Weather Forecasts	Production System
Weidner	Wordbased Transfer Grammar	Phrase-level Syntax	Spanish, Japanese, Arabic, German French	Translation Aid	Production System
Spanam	Transfer Grammar	Phrase/Clause Syntax ATN [ENGSPAN]	English, Spanish, French, Portuguese	Health Organization Documents	Production system
METAL [LITRAS]	Transfer Grammar via Transformations	Context-free Phrase Structure Grammar	English	Manuals	Production System R&D
GETA	Transfer Grammar	Grammar Is a Graph of Subgrammar	English, French	Generic Translation	R&D
SUSY	Transfer Grammar (Interlingual SUSY II)	Dependency Grammar	Russian, German, English	Patent Description	R&D
EUROTRA	Transfer Grammar	Dependency Grammar	EEC Languages	EEC	R&D

Figure 5-1:   The MT programs/products

contain escape hatches in case the systems produce substandard translations. Good translation aids are commercially available in the form of technical machine–readable multilingual dictionaries. The current state of the art of stand–alone MT systems shows three types of systems: (1) mostly defunct, first generation systems following the direct approach, based on word level translation with minimal syntactic processing; (2) current production systems (e.g., METAL), based on grammatical and computational theories within the transfer approach including some semantic processing; and (3) future interlingua systems which are still in the laboratory.

Research and development systems include AI techniques, and mostly deal with investigating interlingua (knowledge) representations. There is a wide choice of interlinguas including formalized languages, artificial languages, or symbolic representations. Esperanto is the adopted interlingua for the distributed language translation [DLT] system, a multilingual system that is expected to translate non–literary English into French by 1990. The DLT system uses system–initiated dialogs requiring the user to be fluent only in the source language. DLT uses dependency grammar to express the necessary rules going from the source language into the interlingua (i.e., Esperanto). The interlingua contains all the knowledge of the world necessary to perform the translation from source to interlingua, and interlingua to target language. Since the interlingua solves every language independent problem, any new source language should be accommodated by adding stylistic rules in addition to syntactic and morphological information. While the approach of DLT is intriguing, as are many other non–mainstream approaches, the notion of Esperanto being able to encode all necessary knowledge is doubtful considering languages like Japanese with their extensive honorific system. Furthermore, the claim that Esperanto is free of word ambiguities applies only if all ambiguities are listed in canonical form. Finally, the claim that DLT's metarepresentation is a human language still does not ensure that the problems of knowledge representation are solved; on the contrary, in DLT there is still no workable intermediate representation of the knowledge necessary to truly understand what is meant in the source language and then truly translate into the target language. The knowledge base of the interlingua contains for the most part the canonical forms of the lexicon.

5.5 HISTORY

The first prediction of the impact of MT appeared around the turn of the century in an article in *Popular Mechanics*. The article predicted that at some point in the future people would be able to dial up a central switchboard that would give callers the ability to dial up any number world wide and have the messages automatically translated. While French and Russian scientists in the 1920s tackled some of the theoretical problems of

MT, it was not until the 1940s that enough excitement was generated, especially in the intelligence community, for funding of MT research begin. In 1946, Warren Weaver and A. Donald Booth, basing their research on their use of computers for breaking encryptions, began work on computerized translation. In their understanding, MT consisted of the mapping between two dictionaries, leaving aside problems such as ambiguities, word order and idioms. In 1948, Weaver drafted his famous "Translation" memorandum [Weaver 55] in which he made two pivotal observations: (1) limited look-ahead would allow a translation system to translate the words correctly most of the time; and (2) a universal language or interlingua exists that links source and target language.

In 1955, A.G. Oettinger [Oettinger 55] designed a system for word matching translation from the Russian into English. As many Russian words have multiple translation, the disambiguation would be left to the post-editor, a common practice even for translation done entirely by a human translator. Thus, a sentence like "In recent times Boolean algebra has been successfully employed in the analysis of relay networks of the series-parallel type" [Oettinger 55, page 58] would be derived from the following computer output:

> (In, at, into, for, on) (last, latter, new, latest, lowest, worst) (time, tense) for analysis and synthesis relay-contact electrical (circuit, diagram, scheme) parallel-(series, successive, consecutive, consistent) (connection, conjunction, combination) (with, from) (success, luck) (to be utilize, to be take advantage of) apparatus Boolean algebra. [Oettinger 55, page 55]

After increased research activity and the launch of the journal *MT* in 1954, Bar-Hillel in the early 1960s shed some doubt on the feasibility of MT if it could not at the same time model the world of a native speaker. Bar-Hillel's doubts regarding high quality MT were echoed in the famous ALPAC report delivered to the National Research Council in 1966. After the Automatic Language Processing Advisory Council issued the report, funding for most MT projects stopped. Nevertheless, long-term funding for the field of computational linguistics increased. In 1973, only a handful of government funded MT projects remained; two years later, all of them were terminated. Curiously enough, many systems (e.g., Systran) that were developed around the ALPAC report still remain operational for translating Russian documents into English for intelligence organizations in the US.

"95% FAHQT" ["95% accurate, fully automatic high quality translation"] has been an MT promise and goal of researchers from day one [Bar-Hillel 60]. Besides the severe limitations of 1950s computing technology and the lack of sound linguistic theories, adequate measures for quality have been slow in developing, apart from attempts to at least qualitatively assess the dimensions of the translation process along the different levels of invariance between texts [Carbonell 81]. Moreover, depending on severity, even a 5% error rate may prove to be disastrous. With hindsight, the initial excitement for the very idea of MT is understandable – if realizable, MT programs would be proof of intelligent behavior of computer programs. Leading AI figures proclaimed quite justly that an operational quality MT program could serve as a proof for whatever AI stood for. With hindsight, the initial excitement for the very implementation of MT is beyond comprehension – neither technological nor theoretical prerequisites were in place. The first MT systems were not based on any syntactic theories; in fact, the prevalent theory of structuralism proposed strictly linear processing between the stratified model of linguistic analysis. Once lexical processing was finished, the syntactic analysis would be performed, then the semantic one, etc. Many classical issues of word sense ambiguity (e.g., the pen is large) and pronoun reference made it clear that without viable semantic theory, MT was a futile undertaking.

As with any new technology, the initial funding spree by government and R&D projects ended after the first failure, the cause of this development being, as usual, having promised too much too soon. The field of MT became a dormant area of research and development, with some systems still in use from the heyday of MT (e.g., Systran). Contemporary ones are being developed more realistically as translation aids rather than stand-alone systems. MT profited from developments in AI, especially in the area of knowledge representation, and from new linguistic theories and computational paradigms.

The current state of the art of MT is characterized by commercial systems based on the transfer approach requiring post-editing and the emergence of translation aids. While, in the laboratory, knowledge based approaches are being directed towards the explorations of interlinguas, the latest development in machine interfaces and MT theories allows for interactive MT with good results. Another important development is the increased use of machine aided translation aids and systems. In 1984, about half a million pages of text were translated by MT programs [Slocum 85, page 1]. The establishment of MT centers at Carnegie Mellon University and New Mexico State University, the increased involvement of major publishers (e.g., Berlitz) and high technology companies (e.g., Siemens), and the international involvement in MT by Japan (who founded a world translation center in the late 1980s) and Europe are indications for a new wave of MT research. Very few MT companies have survived the resurgence of demand and interest of the past 10 years after the lull in the 1960s triggered by blatant failure of the systems. Overall, the too ambitious goals of academic MT research influenced the productization.

MT became another example of underestimation of the difficulties, overselling to obtain funds, and premature introduction into the marketplace.

5.6 TRENDS

Applications of MT technology for the distant future will lie in the on-line translation of languages without necessary human intervention. In as much as this has been and will be the elusive goal of any NLP system – the complete automation of NLP tasks – intermediate stages become clearer. MT technology is not highly valued in the US, with the exception of the obvious interest of the US government in obtaining fast and reliable Russian translations. Consequently, translators are in general poorly paid and not as well trained as their European colleagues, who are required to pursue extensive college-level degrees in translation. While, in the US, academic debates about lofty goals and theories about automation and quality of MT smothered with AI terminology are rampant, these issues matter little when it comes to MT technology in the marketplace where performance and cost-effectiveness is what matters.

In the near term [1995], translation aids profit from advances in speech technology that will make it feasible to have hand-held translators that have embedded speech recognition and synthesis capabilities. Sublanguage translation will enable almost stand-alone MT systems, especially for the area of highly structured manuals and scientific texts. In the mid term [2000], world-wide electronic information services will be accessible in major natural languages without human translators. Limited in their retrieval capabilities, they will become more sophisticated as the state of the art of intelligent database retrieval advances. In the long term [2010], fully automated, simultaneous translation will become possible. Large corporations in the US will mostly be responsible for technological breakthroughs, while government-sponsored long-term programs in Europe and Japan will finally pay off.

The technology will advance in two parallel developments: the interaction of MT systems and user will improve and carry the weight in the near term for enhancing existing MT aids. While research in the knowledge based MT approach will be promising in the 20th century, its impact on production systems will have to wait until the next century. Theoretical advances in the short term will be in step with the development of knowledge representation schemes, especially in the form of interlingua research. While parallel processing may speed up full-scale production systems, true breakthroughs can be expected from neural network technologies. Just as neural network approaches produced one of the first laboratory speech translators, neurocomputing will lead MT in particular and NLP in general into the 21st century.

It will not be surprising that Europe and Japan will eventually corner the MT market. The sharp contrast between Japanese and European endeavors and funding and that available in the US was observed by Mark Fox after returning from a study mission to Japan in March 1988. According to Fox, numerous MT products are widely available, however low their performances and high the percentage of human intervention required may be.

5.7 CONCLUSION

MT remains a desirable and desired capability that should be automated to the limit. The global marketplace, the coming together of the idea of a unified Europe, the growing role of Asiatic economies, foremost Japan, all are factors for increasing the demand for MT that is both practical and profitable. Advances in technology resulting in the shrinking of computing technology to the ultimate supercomputing technologies, along with theoretical advances in knowledge representation, are to bear fruit in the near, but much more so in the distant, future. The following factors will promote the needed improvement in the development of MT technology:

- Japanese and European successes,

- improved input devices (e.g., optical character readers, speech recognition),

- innovative linguistic theories and formalisms, and

- realistic sublanguage–specific MT systems.

5.8 SUGGESTED READING

William J. Hutchins in his book *Machine Translation: Past, Present, Future* [Hutchins 86] provides a readable and thorough overview of the field of MT. The well–balanced account of historical facts, the concise rendition of linguistic and computational issues, and the references make it stand out as a landmark amongst the few books on MT. A more contemporary book is [Nirenburg 87], a selection of 17 papers from the MT conference at Colgate in 1985. The selection reflects the mood that the participants projected during their talks. Far less attention was paid to practical issues than to the outerbounds of interlinguas. Machine aided translation or M(a)T took the backseat. The book does reflect the current state of the art.

5.9 USEFUL CONTACTS

In the US, the following companies are in the MT market: *Automated Language Processing Systems, ALPS*, 190 West 800 North, Provo, Utah 84604; *Logos Corporation*, One Dedham Place, Dedham, Massachusetts 02026; *Smart Communications*, Box 963, FDR Station, 655 Third Avenue, New York, New York 10150; *AWA Translation Systems, Inc*, 4331 Reno Road, Washington, D.C. 20008.

CHAPTER 6

TEXT PROCESSING/UNDERSTANDING

World Shaken – Pope shot = Earthquake in Italy – One Dead.

The rendition of the newspaper headlines "World shaken – Pope shot" as "Earthquake in Italy – One dead," lets one appreciate the necessary cognitive processes involved in understanding NL. These processes include word recognition, syntactic integration, and semantic selection. The complexity of modeling text understanding [TU] became fully understood when for processing one page of text about a divorce, more than 20 complex knowledge structures had to be created and controlled [Dyer 83].

The fact that in Turkey high government officials receive urgent newswire reports selectively in their homes around the clock depending on what priorities they put into the computer system lets one appreciate the practical implications of such systems. While current systems are far from being able to process and understand unconstrained text, the biggest pay-off for NLP technology lies in producing special purpose TU systems. TU systems as viable technology to combat the "information glut" will help solve the general massive update problems of text databases and the selective retrieval of information from electronic information services. TU systems will also support international business, such as summarizing and translating telexes from foreign banks.

6.1 INFORMATION PROCESSING TASK

The information processing task of a TU is to integrate the new information that is in the text with the old information that is already in the knowledge base.   A TU system processes the literal form of a text to get to the intended meaning.   In Figure 6-1 the representation of intentional information is necessary to adequately process the different perspectives of a story (e.g., divorce proceedings).   Psychological theories support the way experiences and intentions are represented in the computer program. Consequently, AI theories of TU often use empirical studies, i.e., reaction time experiments, to support their claims:

> Currently, people are the only examples of systems capable of understanding complicated narrative text. Therefore, BORIS tries to mimic the behavior exhibited by people who have performed the task of reading various narratives. Specifically, subjects were asked to read a given narrative. Two weeks later they were asked to recall the narrative in as much detail as possible. Others were given the opposite task of first recalling the narrative and then two weeks later answering questions about the narrative.This data was then used to guide the program design decision. [Dyer 83, page 19]

Just as humans have built up expectations from previous experiences, the TU must have a set of knowledge structures to base its inferences on.   The inferential process requires a certain amount of time for humans as common experience and psychological tests indicate.   Similarly, during the understanding process, the NLP system establishes "missing links" [Brown 83, page 257] that require additional processing time [Haviland 74] in the form of "bridging assumptions". Missing links that require no additional processing time are part of the knowledge representation and automatically activated − a reflex response, as Schank puts it [Schank 74]. The distinction between automatic associations and non-automatic inferences depends on the individuals.   Their point of view determines what is automatic and what is not, e.g., the processing time for the sentences "Mary got some picnic supplies out of the car. The beer was warm." varies depending on people's assumptions about picnic supplies [Haviland 74]. Inferences depend on the context, text type and the predisposition of the listener. TU programs will therefore have to develop mental models of their own to interpret texts realistically.

TU is the process of transforming linguistic information into data structures that allow the reconstruction of information contained in the text to (1) answer question about the text, (2) summarize it (gisting), or (3), index it. Understanding is a matter of degree: it ranges from in-depth

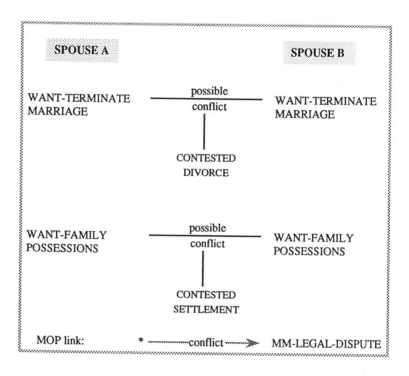

Figure 6-1:   Knowledge representation of
a text understander [Lehnert 83, page 27]

understanding for being able to answer questions to shallow understanding to index documents. TU requires the analysis of information on many levels of linguistic and extra-linguistic structure. TU has a great deal of subjectivity to contend with. Depending on a person's prior experiences, current expectations and intentions, the same story or text may be interpreted from vastly differing perspectives. The task of a computer based TU is to reconstruct the content of a text based on a mental model [see section 1.4]. The significance of creating these mental models lies "not in their phenomenal or subjective content, but their structure and the fact that we possess procedures for constructing, manipulating and interrogating them" [Johnson-Laird 81]. TU systems are built around models that selectively process text and put the extracted information into data structures the computer program can then use.

6.2 APPROACHES

Approaches to TU are either structure-driven ("bottom-up") or expectation-driven ("top-down"). Structure-driven approaches analyze the syntax and semantics of a text based on grammars or, most commonly, based on a subgrammar that contains the specialized syntax and vocabulary of a specific domain. Expectation-driven strategies perform limited syntactic processing and are restricted to processing only that type of knowledge that is expected in a given domain. While structure-driven approaches consider primarily the sentence and word level, expectation-driven approaches try to analyze each text as a token of a particular situation type the program has to recognize. Some situation types are difficult to recognize. In this case, an expectation-driven TU system encounters problems in analyzing the text. Empirical studies have shown that for humans TU is a phenomenon exhibiting regularities. It is these regularities which must be modelled in a program in order to even begin to claim that it "understands".

While structure-driven approaches focus on the extensibility and robustness of their linguistic coverage, expectation-driven approaches deal with constraints imposed by their conceptual coverage for a given domain. The success of both approaches depends on how well they can capture the essential linguistic and conceptual structures for each domain, respectively. Structure-driven approaches for TU are based on the notion of sublanguages whereby the system only recognizes predefined and domain specific words and syntactic constructs:

> We define sublanguage here as the particular language used in a body of texts dealing with a circumscribed subject area (often reports or articles on a technical speciality or science subfield) in

which the authors of the documents share a common vocabulary and common habits of word usage. As a result, the documents display recurrent patterns of word co-occurrence that characterize discourse in this area and justify the term sublanguage. [Hirschman 83, page 26]

The syntactic component of a sublanguage system is somewhat better defined than that of language at large. Rather than making infinite use of finite means, within a sublanguage, one makes finite use of finite means. The constraints on the semantic component make it easier to construct a comprehensive knowledge representation of a particular domain. Sublanguage systems are more manageable; they are on the whole not easier to build when it comes to the classic language problem that NLP systems encounter. There are still many ambiguities left. The TU system still has to determine modifier-host relations (e.g., "had fever one day prior to admission" versus "had one day fever prior to admission"). In general, the quantitative complexity of the modeling environment is reduced, the qualitative complexity of the model remains.

Expectation-driven systems for TU are mostly based on Schank's theories of conceptual dependencies, scripts, and memory organization. These TU systems exhibit different levels of understanding ranging from skimming of stories to in-depth understanding. Top-down approaches include: (1) script based systems which developed out of the need to capture episodes and situations beyond the "acts" level. Scripts are based on the notion that the world is made up of (stereo-typical) action sequences and situations that can be embedded into the discourse structure. (2) Memory based, systems including TOPs and TAUs which derived from the need to go beyond a shallow understanding of what a particular text was all about. These Thematic Organization Packages and Thematic Abstraction Units refer to the higher order of abstraction used to comprehend and later recall stories and their significance.

From the current research in TU it becomes clear that in order for a program to comprehend a story, even superficially, it has to be able to abstract from what is explicitly stated in the sentence and integrate the information into what is present in its current knowledge base. In practice, the understanding process consists of two steps, a bottom-up parsing and top-down or expectation-driven processing. In the past, most systems have relied on either one of these steps as their primary strategy, thus missing, usually deliberately, pieces of information in the analysis of texts. These one-dimensional approaches were greatly aided by the fact that they operated on texts of well-defined sublanguages (e.g., medicine) or clearly defined situations (e.g., divorce proceedings). The structure-driven approach could employ the limited vocabulary and syntax for TU, whereas the expectation-driven approach was constrained by what pieces of knowledge could be recognized and stored, based on the predefined structures in the knowledge base.

6.3 APPLICATIONS

Automated text analysis/understanding is important for three types of applications:

- Text segmentation and classification, also known as automated indexing. The growth of information that electronic information services provide has created a serious bottleneck which frustrates the on-line searcher's need for timely and accurate information. Studies have indicated that about 67% of retrieval from a library database that was judged relevant by the user population was in fact not relevant for the subject under search. Thus, quantitative and qualitative pay-offs would be achieved by a faster and better TU system that could assist in text database management, including retrieval and update.

- Text skimming ("gisting") to produce summaries of newspaper articles, stories, etc. The nature of the skimming process ranges from superficial to in-depth understanding of the text. Primary areas of application here are summaries of on-line newspapers that are produced based on a user's interest. Areas like information arbitrage, bank telexes, and other dated information stand to gain a competitive edge by employing this technology.

- Text skimming to generate databases for retrieving data in a structured format. Medical diagnostic systems and financial services are but two examples of vertical applications. For medical expert systems, it becomes important to have an automated front-end processor that can transform the English input into data structures that are easily retrievable by humans or expert systems. Recent applications of generating such representations are found in CAD/CAM systems, used to derive formal design models from specifications and requirements written in English. The area of software engineering using CASE technology could also profit from NL input specification as the starting point of man-machine interaction.

Most of these applications assume either a question answering system, a text generation component, or both. Since both components are not immediately related to TU programs, we only consider the first step of transforming the text into data structures that other processing modules can then use, e.g., question answering.

6.4 PROGRAMS/PRODUCTS

The few commercially available products have a very narrowly defined application domain. Most systems are still in the laboratory. The funding levels are substantial because in contrast to NLIs there is widespread agreement that TU systems do fill a real market need (e.g., text database management).

6.4.1 Indexing

Gerald Salton [Salton 85], one of the leading figures in developing indexing schemes, only recently embraced the idea of having a syntactic analysis support the automated indexing schemes. While inverted indexes are very much used for text databases, their effective creation and update is a major step in fully automating the indexing process. In section 3.1.5, I discussed an indexing program hosted on the *Connection Machine* that uses syntactic parsing to create inverted indexes [Waltz 87]. In the UK, the *Tome* system is widely used. The Medsort project at Carnegie Mellon University [Carbonell 85] addressed the update issue by stipulating that, as a first step, the linguistic analysis of headlines of incoming journal articles would help curb the update problems.

Besides the linguistic oriented approach to TU for text retrieval purposes, the following two, more statistically oriented approaches are viable. The *Savvy/TRS* text recognition system is based on neural network technology. Each new document requires a "learn time" to identify the unique recognition patterns within a text. When a query is issued it is linked to these previously "learned" patterns. The 1988 brochure of Excalibur Technologies for *Savvy/TRS* gives a retrieval time of 00:00:03 seconds for searching the Bible on a MicroVax II for the search clue "Samson Philistines Delilah". During the *IEEE International Conference on Neural Networks 1988*, I could verify what the brochure claimed concerning *Savvy/TRS*. *Savvy/TRS* was one of the most impressive products at the show.

Another revolutionary program for text databases is *The Intelligent Text Management System* from Information Access Systems, Inc. Proprietary

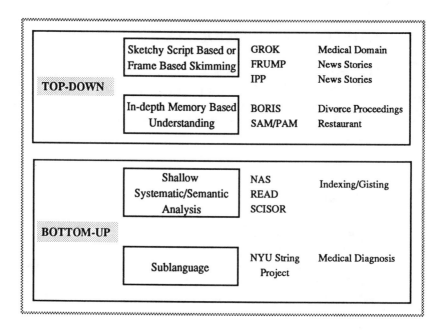

Figure 6-2: Text understanding programs

software called *Judgment Space*, abbreviated as *J−Space* allows the
construction of the judgment of individuals that are experts in a particular
area (e.g., medicine, finance). Because a particular judgment space is
automatically constructed after the expert determines the rank order of
terms, no rule maintenance is required. The *ITMS* software accepts English,
Japanese, French, and German as its query language.

6.4.2 Skimmers

Skimming programs have a great deal of latitude as to how much
information of a given text they can process. Skimming programs are domain
specific and flounder if texts from outside their domain of expertise are
introduced. Current programs that perform any degree of understanding rely
extensively on the expectation−driven, top−down strategy or on a
sublanguage−oriented bottom−up strategy [see Figure 6−2]. Skimming
programs produce a representation of the text in a format that the language
generator can use to provide a summary. The following four programs,
FRUMP, IPP, BORIS, and ATRANS are based on Schankian theories of
script and memory based TU.

FRUMP is a program that skims news stories taken from UPI wire
services. FRUMP consist of two modules: the predictor, which generates top−
down predictions on what is relevant in a story, and the substantiator, which
tries to confirm the generated predictions. FRUMP first analyzes the text in
terms of conceptual dependencies and then combines these into "sketchy"
scripts. The sketchy script format allows FRUMP to ignore information that
does not fit into the script. IPP (integrated partial parser) is a program to
process and generalize from news stories. IPP uses predictions from memory
structures, creates top−down context, and lets the text drive the analysis.
While FRUMP uses sketchy scripts and consequently ignores information that
cannot be processed, IPP invokes other processing modules to fit the initially
incomprehensible item into a knowledge structure. BORIS is a program that
tries to process everything that it reads as deeply as possible. BORIS reads in
a story on a divorce and is able to answer questions that can be asked about
the story, including those requiring an understanding of causal and temporal
relations in the story. ATRANS is a commercial TU system that summarizes
bank telexes from Belgian banks and translates them into English. The
major differences between FRUMP, IPP, BORIS, and ATRANS is their depth
of understanding. BORIS is also able to answer questions about the text,
whereas FRUMP and IPP only summarize the stories they process, while
ATRANS structures the summaries in a format that is the input to a
translation system.

6.4.3 Database generation

The ultimate prototype for this application is the most ambitious one: it would be to simulate the reader of a newspaper who while reading can create his own clipfile that is used for selecting only pieces of information of interest for the reader. While currently available newspaper article TU systems are limited in their conceptual coverage, some prototypes exist: *READ* from Battelle is a TU system that processes newswire reports from the *New York Times* and analyzes each sentence as to "who did what to whom, when, and where" [Obermeier 84]. A similar system called *NAS* from A.D. Little is also at the prototype stage [Kuhns 88].

The NYU String Project [Sager 81] was a landmark research undertaking for demonstrating the significance of sublanguages. Sager and her associates studied the syntax and semantics of medical case histories. Based on their investigation they could construct a grammar that captured the linguistic essence of the domain. Her research also showed that only a limited subset of English was needed to computationally model the domain.

Another approach to TU is to define a domain in terms of its event structure. A TU system that analyzed domain specific information together with temporal information is *GROK* [Obermeier 85a]. The input to *GROK* consisted of patient case histories that served as input to a medical expert system. The program performed the following operations: (1) parse a text from a medical journal using linguistic and extralinguistic knowledge, (2) map the parsed linguistic structure into an event representation, (3) draw temporal and factual inferences within the domain of liver diseases, and (4) create and update a database containing the pertinent information about a patient.

GROK is interesting for two reasons: on the one hand it showed that domains may be structured in terms of their temporal relations which in turn would facilitate further processing (e.g., question answering, gisting). On the other hand, *GROK* demonstrated that such a domain specific knowledge representation can drive the parsing process in conjunction with a phrase level syntactic analyzer. Unfortunately, *GROK* never made it beyond the prototype stage, thus leaving the contention that any domain is defined by its stereotypical events unproven.

The *SCISOR* system [Rau 88] is important for two reasons: (1) it combines top-down and bottom-up strategies, and (2) it is the a fully developed functional system that scans naturally occurring texts in a given domain (e.g., corporate mergers and acquisitions). *SCISOR* integrates syntactic, semantic and domain-specific knowledge to extract information from texts and to answer questions.

6.5　HISTORY

Text analysis in the 1950s and 1960s was limited to indexing procedures for text which in turn was based on statistical methods. This line of research is nowadays augmented through syntactic parsing programs and shallow semantic analysis.　With the advent of semantic–oriented NLP, started in the AI arena, the focus of understanding centered around deeper levels of structure than syntactic analyses could provide. As problems were delineated and the complexity of the underlying psychological models grew, the levels of abstraction postulated for deeper understanding increased dramatically.

The first major TU systems in the early 1970s were designed by Charniak and Rieger for their Ph.D. theses. Charniak's program analyzed children's stories [Charniak 72], especially under the aspect of what kind of inferences can be generated when reading a story. The knowledge structure mechanism of choice in the 1970s was the script [Schank 77]. Soon scripts required extensions in the form of plans and goals that would be the motivation behind inferences. Dyer's work on BORIS [Dyer 83] became the milestone for the development of TU system in terms of complexities of its knowledge representation. In the late 1980s the dichotomy between episodic and semantic memory surfaced.　Episodic memory refers to the anecdotal evidence that makes us remember things, whereas semantic memory refers to the process of accessing semantically connected links in an orderly fashion.

In the 1970s, linguists started exploring the notion of sublanguages that provided a rationale for pursuing a syntactically oriented processing approach for TU.　In the 1980s, the update of text databases and their access became a commercial issue for NLP applications.　Robust systems such as *SCISOR* [Rau 88] will make TU a commercial success in the long term.

6.6　TRENDS

Application of TU technology extends to the pre–processing of all written material, the ever–increasing volume of which makes it necessary for humans to rely on filtering devices to obtain a reasonable amount of daily reading. In the short term (1995), TU programs will be useful for limited domains that include text that can be clearly defined as to its characteristics and ultimate use, e.g., bank telexes, stock reports, patients' case histories.　In the mid term (2000), it will become desirable to extend the text analysis program to semi–automate the update of text databases.　TU programs will be a factor for introducing data into expert systems.　In the long term (2010 and beyond), the fully automated update of databases from raw text will become reality.

The technology will provide automation of all processes through intelligent software programs, integration of hardware starting with OCRs to CD-ROM and desk top workstations, and increased functionality based on innovations in telecommunications. Theoretical advances will include cluster analysis of documents based on neural network technology and statistical models. Knowledge management will make unified update and retrieval mechanisms possible.

6.7 CONCLUSION

Text understanding has been one of the most complicated areas of research due to the many aspects of language involved. Most text understanding systems of the future will share the following characteristics:

- reliance on semantic and pragmatic information processing,

- use of structural and semantic redundancy by matching the text into predetermined knowledge structures,

- focus on interaction of the available knowledge sources, and

- predominance of memory research for determining knowledge representation.

The TU systems of the future will theoretically be based on psychological theories of human TU and practically be grounded in robust knowledge representation methods. Coupled with hypertext functionality for the retrieval process, TU will allow you, among other things, to read all the newspapers you want within a reasonable time frame and get summaries of complex areas of interest.

6.8 SUGGESTED READING

Dyer's book on "In-Depth Understanding" [Dyer 83] has already become a classic. Apart from giving a quick overview of the field of TU the book contains a detailed description of the program BORIS. A thorough 50-page overview of NL understanding from the point of view of Yale is presented in [Lehnert 88].

6.9 USEFUL CONTACTS

Excalibur Technologies, 122 Tulane SE, Albuquerque, New Mexico;
Information Access Systems, Inc., 3340 Mitchell Lane, 2nd Floor,
Boulder, Colorado, 80301;

CHAPTER 7

TEXT GENERATION

The freckles were tattoed, the girl his mistress; called, on account of some associate mind, Irvin. [Thomas Pynchon, *V*]

Imagine hearing the sentence for the first time: you can see her now, Irvin, a luscious red hair. Imagine having to describe Irvin to your best friend. Could you just take the image that you conjured up and, without having memorized the original sentence, reproduce exactly Pynchon's rendition of Irvin? What would you say instead, and how would you say it? These are the three central questions for text generation [TG] research: (1) is there a bidirectional grammar for both understanding and generation of language? (2) how is the knowledge represented? and (3) what are the processes that transform such a representation into a sentence or whole text?

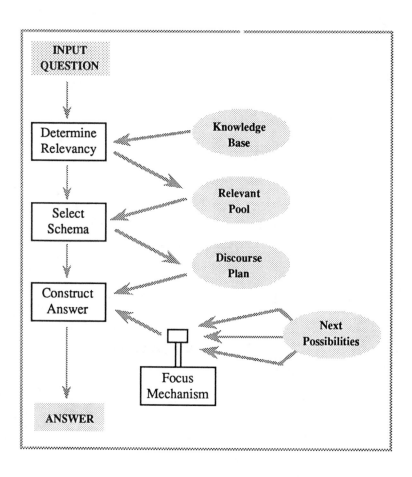

Figure 7-1:   Flowdiagram of a text generation
program [McKeown 85, page 12]

7.1 INFORMATION PROCESSING TASK

The task of a TG program is to determine what to say and how to say it. A general processing model for text generation has two phases: during the first phase, the content and structure of the discourse is determined by means of a "strategic" component; during the second phase, the message is transposed into NL via a "tactical" component. Much of the previous work in TG has been centered around the tactical component, that is, generating grammatical sentences. TG programs construct the text based on a communicative goal. The strategic level is the level where all the planning takes place, i.e., the selection of concepts and their relationship. On the strategic level, the problem solving of the program includes also the planning of utterances with respect to what the informative content of the utterance is and the level of communication with the user of a particular system. On the tactical level, the program has to fine-tune the utterance depending on context, length, and stylistic variations. Again, a choice in terms of qualitative and quantitative responses has to be made.

Information processing tasks for TG differ from those required for language understanding programs. While some research suggests that linguistic and extra-linguistic mechanisms are the same for interpretation and generation [Winograd 83], the majority of systems separate the processes for each task [McKeown 85]. Whereas in language understanding programs, a given text is analyzed by selecting options presented in the text, language generation programs must be able to determine the best possible option at any given time. The task of planning enters into the generation process at least during the strategic phase: (1) when the program needs to decide what information to communicate, (2) when the program needs to determine what goes into a single sentences and, (3) how the single sentence fit together into a coherent and cohesive paragraph. A further distinction separates TG systems from dialog systems. For the former, the text generation process requires a considerable amount of planning of what lies ahead; for the latter, the generator needs to react to questions asked and perceived changes in the intention of the receiver of the messages.

7.2 APPROACHES

The dichotomy between strategic and tactical components reflects the different approaches for TG: the tactical component is commonly thought of as the linguistic component, and the strategic component is viewed as being in the realm of AI. The majority of TG systems sharply distinguish the generation from the understanding task. The dichotomy is based on the preconception of being able to separate linguistic from extra-linguistic knowledge. For reasons of modularity the knowledge sources should be separated along the lines of their functionality. But the claim in the strategic/tactical distinction is that processes responsible for planning the utterance or text do not interact with the processes responsible for generating syntactic and semantic output. This widely adopted view is grounded in the autonomy of syntax paradigm discussed in section 2.1 and is especially used in MIT research, e.g., McDonald [McDonald 81].

Linguistically oriented and AI based approaches to language generation differ in terms of the structure and interaction between the tactical and strategic components. The linearity of processing and the stipulated autonomy of both components has polarized TG research along strategic/tactical lines. AI being more interested in the strategic component whose major problem solving area is planning. While linguists see the tactic component as their major research interest.

Two areas attracted AI attention for language generation, planning, and explanation based reasoning. Since one stereotype of language generation is that planning precedes speaking – a somewhat dubious assumption considering some statements people make – AI based planning strategies can be adopted without modification. D. Appelt's KAMP system [Appelt 82] is based in its strategic planning capability on Sacerdoti's hierarchical planning mechanism [Sacerdoti 77], in which each goal is divided into subgoals. Once the system has determined what the overall plan should be, linguistic and non-linguistic subgoals are established that lead to the desired result. In the area of generating explanations for expert systems, the mere listing of the invoked rules was inadequate for explaining the reasoning process and therefore replaced by "meta-explanations" that could summarize and substantiate the drawn conclusions.

A methodological difference in language generation exists between proponents of the declarative approach to knowledge representation and the proponents of the procedural approach. Procedural systems that use, for instance, ATNs for generation purposes are so powerful that they allow any kind of operation within their mechanism. The declarative approach promotes more discipline because its power lies in the knowledge representation per se. As a consequence this makes for systems suited to bi-directional processing, that is language generation and understanding.

The issue of bi-directionality of NLP systems has been under discussion from day one of NLP. Proponents of the view that different mechanisms have to be postulated for recognition and production systems cite the many differences in information processing tasks. To assess the possibilities of having bi-directional processing, three criteria become relevant: (1) procedural versus declarative knowledge representation, (2) degree of similarity between concepts in the strategic and the tactical component, and (3) types of applications.

7.3 APPLICATIONS

The three major areas of TG programs in the field of NLP are: (1) NL interfaces to operating systems, databases, and expert systems; (2) in language understanding programs that produce summaries or answer questions concerning a processed text; and (3) MT systems, especially those based on the interlingua approach, which employ a TG system for a particular target language. The common denominator for these applications is that the TG takes a given data structure and transforms the information into linguistic utterances or text.

NLIs are often viewed as one-directional systems that allow the user to command ("command language") what he wants from a particular computer system. NLIs, however, have a much more important task when it comes to the actual interaction between the user and the computing system: NLP systems instruct, summarize, and explain when used as interfaces to operating systems, databases and expert systems, respectively. The instruction task of an NLI for an operating system has to take into account the user's plan or goal. The simple question "How can I delete a file?" contains multiple tasks that the translating program has to recognize. If necessary, the TG program has to be able to instruct the user at the right level of expertise. If the user does not have any concept of what a file is, the program should explain the setup of files and incidental characteristics, e.g., version number, file extensions. If there are, for example, multiple copies of the same file, maybe the user knowing about wildcards could save himself considerable time if he is suitably informed. TG programs have the task of formulating responses at the appropriate level.

The task of summarizing information of a DBMS for an NLI can take many forms: it can mean providing meta-information of what the database is all about, or it can mean summarizing the retrieved data after a request is issued, e.g., rather than bringing back all the names that fit the following query "Who makes more than 5K per month?", the NLI may just answer "All the vice-presidents".

The explanation task of an NLI for an expert system may require a step-by-step rendition of how the expert system arrived at a conclusion, e.g., simply stringing together the rules that have applied, a "concrete" explanation as opposed to an "abstract" explanation that addresses the overall strategy of problem solving. Current TG for interfaces does not provide a very detailed user model to help the system to determine what information should be presented to the end–user without being redundant and uninteresting. Given the prospect that eventually all human–machine interaction will be based on NL, generation programs are at the forefront of research, and will be, into the 21st century.

7.4 PROGRAMS/PRODUCTS

In the late 1980s, there are no commercial TG systems available. TG capabilities are either sold in conjunction with other products that are used for database access, expert systems, etc., or still in the laboratory. In general, TG systems are embedded in applications and product–oriented, or stand-alone R&D endeavors.

Commercial programs that contain language generation capabilities are natural language interfaces to databases. In particular, *Natural Language* [previously *Datatalker*] from Natural Language Incorporated answers questions put to the database by giving a meta–explanation. If, for instance, in the query a user asks who works with the systems analysts, the appropriate response may be "the programmers", and not a list of all the programmers. The mostly exploratory programs fall into three categories [see Figure 7–2]: (1) predominantly tactically oriented, (2) predominantly strategically oriented, and (3) integrated systems that combine both components.

Tactical generators deal primarily with the grammatical well–formedness of the generated sentences. *BABEL* is the language generator for Schank's *MARGIE* program [Schank 75]. *BABEL* uses a semantic discrimination net and a conceptual representation to determine the appropriate word choice. *NIGEL* is part of Mann's *PENMAN* system [Mann 83] and most recently has been included in *JANUS*, Bolt Beranek and Newman's contribution to the DARPA project mentioned in section 11.3 [see Figure 11–2]. Jacobs focuses his TG research on extensive knowledge representation, rather than procedurally heavy programming. Over the past decade, Jacobs has done extensive work in knowledge intensive TG. Systems like *ACE*, *PHRED*, *KING*, and *SCISOR* [Jacobs 87] fall into this category.

Strategic generators concentrate on the conceptual aspect of TG. The *TEXT* system [McKeown 85] generates English text in response to database queries. The strategic component creates the propositions which in turn are translated into English by an unification based formalism. *BLAH* [Weiner 80] provides an explanation facility for an expert system. The focus of

Weiner's research is on a step-by-step explanation with emphasis on the focus of attention. Swartout's *GIST* system [Swartout 83] also deals with explanation facilities in expert systems. In particular, *GIST* tries to take traces of programs and turns them into logical explanations by summarizing and reformulating the content of the traces.

The integrated systems include tactical and strategic components. *ERMA* [Clippinger 75] was the first system that modelled linguistic discourse planning. Clippinger's goal was to show how linguistic planning and discourse goals often conflict, become modified, and ultimately result in an acceptable utterance. The *PENMAN* system [Mann 83] consists of a text planning and TG system (*NIGEL*). *KAMP* [Appelt 82] integrates hierarchical planning, possible world semantics, and knowledge logic. In *KAMP* a robot instructs a human to remove a pump from a platform. Wilensky's *UNIX CONSULTANT* [Wilensky 88] allows access to the UNIX operating system using English by inferring the user's goals from his requests and plan the program's response accordingly. *PROTEUS* [Davey 78], a tic-tac-toe commentator, uses Halliday's systemic grammar [Halliday 85] that is also the basis for *NIGEL*. *PROTEUS* explained its moves and compared a best and an actual move. A number of other TG programs are under development [Sondheimer 86, page 243-245]. Many systems are application oriented and domain specific. The majority of these programs requires extensive knowledge of the domain it works in.

7.5 HISTORY

The linguistic approach to language generation, much in contrast to the AI approach, is focused around the processes that are necessary to turn a given knowledge representation into grammatical, linguistic output. Yngve [Yngve 61], as early as 1962, and Friedman [Friedman 71] in 1969, built random language generators around models of transformational grammar. Later attempts used case grammar, and more recently systemic or functional grammar. Interestingly enough, most of these theories are more successful in language generation than in language analysis. Because transformations, by definition, can move, delete and insert things, no one can ever be sure what part of the sentence has undergone any of these operations. The same reason holds for many theories, thus requiring explicit and differing theories for both generation and recognition.

Projects in the 1970s included the use of ATN's and primary mappings between semantic and syntactic structures. Simmons and Slocum [Simmons 72] were amongst the first to employ ATNs for language generation that mapped semantic information into syntactic structure. Running an ATN "in

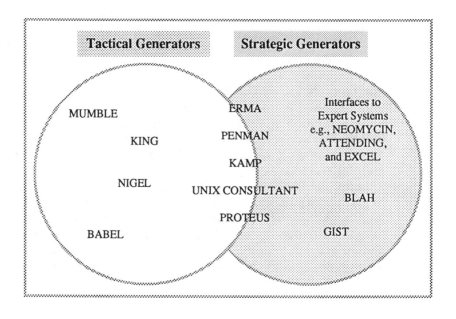

Figure 7-2:   Text generation programs

reverse" required a reassignment of the functionality for the nodes and arcs. Projects in the 1980s were dominated by systemic grammar theory and discourse modeling. In AI, early generation systems were implemented based on ATN grammars and on conceptual dependencies in the 1970s. Later research focused on planning and discourse coherence. Very few systems address both the strategic and tactic side of language generation with equal importance. The Penman system, for one, was conceptualized with both components in mind. To this day, Nigel, the part of Penman responsible for tactical decisions, is the more developed part. Erma, a program developed to model the hesitations of a psychoanalytic patient, was the first to model discourse planning. More importantly, Erma provided links between linguistic structures and the discourse goals.

7.6 TRENDS

In the short term (1995), TG programs will become useful for database access and surface explanations for expert systems. In the mid term (2000), explanation based reasoning, boosted in particular by the need for explanation components in expert systems, will dominate the research and application domains. In the long term (2010), TG programs will be integrated into any major computer application as a form of feed-back of what the program is about to do. As supercomputers will become part of the common computer infrastructure, knowing what the program is about to do may prove very economical indeed, considering the resources spent on searches and tasks the user may not have intended.

The most important developments for TG research will be:

- Theoretical advances needed for the strategic component to be made more powerful, and

- user-modeling needed for high quality responses and providing communicative interaction.

7.7 CONCLUSION

A text generation program must decide what information to communicate, when to say what, and which words and syntactic structures best express its intent. Early research has addressed the problems of lexical and syntactic choice; future research has to deal with the internal representation and discourse coherence of the text to be generated. The underlying problem of separating the strategic from the tactical components, superficially positive for reasons of modularity, is somewhat unrealistic when it comes to actually generating conceptual structures.

The technology of text generation is not mature enough to have a major impact on the NLP market. As add-on capabilities in well-defined applications (e.g., data base access), they provide a useful additional capability. Coupled with speech synthesis, text generation programs could make a dream come true, after 2001.

7.8 SUGGESTED READING

Besides MIT [McDonald 81], SRI [Appelt 87], Paul Jacobs at the GE AI laboratory has a strong influence on the field [Jacobs 87].   Jacobs' contention is that NL generation requires a large amount of knowledge. Consequently, his systems derive their power from the knowledge representation itself. McKeown's book *Text Generation* [McKeown 85] provides a good historical perspective and an insightful discussion on her own system.

7.9 USEFUL CONTACTS

General Electric Company, Corporate Research and Development, Schenectady, New York 12345; *Cognitive Systems*, 234 Church Street, New Haven, Connecticut 06510.

CHAPTER 8

SPEECH

The hottest voice recognition product research is in the area of continuous speech. Clearly, vendors see the corporate office and voice dictation as prime targets. [*Computerworld*, December 1986]

Speech technology is one of hottest topics in NLP, and will remain so for years to come. NLP systems of the future will be able to recognize and produce speech. We distinguish two different applications of speech technology: speech recognition/speech understanding, and speech synthesis/digitized speech. Speech recognition is the process of detecting and identifying the individual sound signal, while speech understanding subsumes the recognition and cognition aspect of the sounds. Speech synthesis is the process of transforming ASCII text into human speech, while digitized speech is the the process in which human speech is converted into digitized format for later playback. While speech recognition/understanding technology is judged by its ability to analyze speaker dependent and continuous speech, speech synthesis is evaluated by its naturalness.

Before discussing the computational side of speech, we will briefly summarize the process of human speech. In order for us to produce sounds, the airstream coming up from the lungs is modified at various parts of the

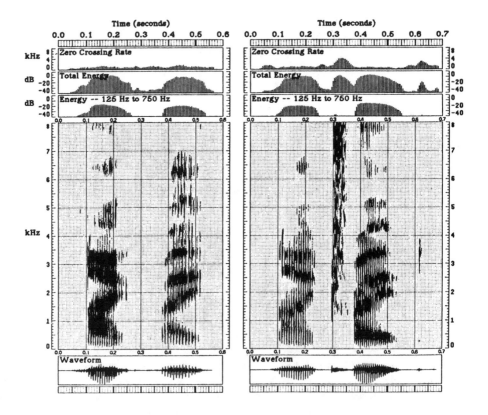

Figure 8-1:   Spectogram of the utterances
"night rate" versus "nitrate".
[Church 87, page 47]

vocal tract, starting at the vocal cords situated in the back of the mouth. The vocal chords together with the throat resonator, the mouth and nasal resonators, and the positioning of the lips give linguistic sounds their characteristic qualities. The three primary resonators, throat, nasal, and oral, correspond to frequency distribution that can be captured in a three-dimensional plot called a spectrogram that is used to show the formant frequencies as bandwidth over time, and as the amplitude being the third axis. The three formants correspond to the three resonators. While it would be rather straightforward to analyze sounds according to their formant frequencies, continuous speech introduces many confusing factors into the analysis process. The influences from adjacent sounds, stress and pitch, in brief the intonation patterns over and above the invariant formant frequencies make the speech recognition process difficult. Ambient noise, fatigue, and other temporary factors add to the arduous task of determining which sounds or words are to be recognized. On the synthesis task of speech technology, similar problems apply "in reverse". Producing natural-sounding speech is impeded by the need to program proper intonation into the speech synthesizer.

8.1 SPEECH RECOGNITION SYSTEMS

8.1.1 Information processing task

The task for speech recognition systems is to separate the signals and classify them into groups of sounds that make up individual words. The speech recognition system transforms the analog acoustic data into a discrete digital format. To convert the acoustic data into electronic data, the waveform is encoded either via processes such as waveform encoding or delta modulation. Direct waveform encoding refers to the process of transforming an analog signal into an ASCII string by means of an analog-to-digital converter. Delta modulation is similar to direct waveform encoding except that it only stores the changes of the signal over time. Delta modulation records the value of the signal only relative to the previous one.

Many physiological and psychological processes play a role in the production process and have to be accounted for in the speech recognition [SR] system. On the surface, speech recognition research is based on three different viewpoints. Speech can be analyzed in terms of its (1) acoustic signal, (2) production mechanism, (3) sensory perception.

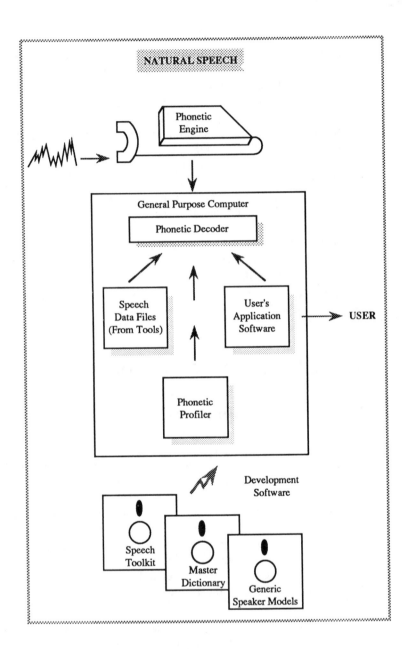

Figure 8-2:   Flowdiagram for the Phonetic Engine, a
speech recognition system from Speech Systems

8.1.2 Approaches

Speech recognition systems are based on three different approaches: (1) a template matching approach in which speech is reduced to a number of stock tokens that need to be identified, (2) an acoustic feature identification approach, and (3) a multi-level approach in which syntactic and semantic information drives the analysis. Approaches (1) and (2) deal with speech recognition whereas (3) is used for speech understanding programs.

The template matching approach is based on the idea that the same utterances share some basic invariant characteristics. These may vary minimally every time we pronounce the same word or sound. Thus, storing the stereotypical pattern in memory, every new token of the same type can be identified by comparing current utterance and template. For the person uttering "night rate" the program would simply look up the characteristics of the spectrogram and compare them with the input. Template matching is very attractive because of its technical and theoretical simplicity. The major drawbacks, however, include on the one hand the exorbitant requirements on storage of patterns, and on the other hand the retrieval time required for comparing templates to current input. Given a sampling of a signal at 8 kHz per second at a rate of two words per second, 4,000 samples per word have to be compared which requires 4 million comparisons for each word for a 1,000 word vocabulary. The speaker independent system DECvoice requires 75 templates for 13 words, while a speaker dependent version of the system could accommodate a vocabulary five times that size. The template searching process is often optimized by using another form of template matching called chain code matching in which the matching algorithm scans the spectrogram starting at a central point and by comparing nearest neighbors identifies the underlying template.   While template matching is useful for speaker dependent isolated word recognition systems, it is not feasible for continuous speaker independent recognition systems because the number of templates needed to reside in memory would rise beyond practicality.

Speech recognition systems [see Figure 8-2] utilizing feature analysis generally involve acoustic waveform input, acoustic analysis, a feature extracter, and a pattern matcher that operates on the extracted features. Features for speech recognition include pitch, timing, and formant frequencies. While the ways of extracting the features may differ, once they are extracted they are compared to the stored reference set. The most salient features are the formant frequencies that remain constant no matter how loud or how clearly the sounds are enunciated. A feature based algorithm looks at the typical formants, an area of dominant frequencies for a given sound, and deduces what sound has been pronounced. In Figure 8-1, the spectrogram, a three-dimensional plot showing the sound frequencies, amplitude and time line, allows the person familiar with spectrograms to identify what sounds have been produced.

Many previous attempts at continuous speech recognition involved taking in a string of acoustic information and piecing together possible combinations at each linguistic level until, by a process of elimination, a complete representation of an utterance would appear. This is a very time–consuming process for one reason: no one level is in control. To counteract the thrashing between levels, an explicit control structure, the so–called "blackboard" has been introduced. The function of the blackboard is to help determine what level of structure (i.e., knowledge source) has the best solution for the current identification problem. The blackboard strategy is in direct contrast to the stratificational linear strategy in which information is passed from one level of structure to the next without ever being able to go back to a previous level of structure. While feature detection and template matching are approaches viable for isolated speech recognition, the multi-level approach tries to bring to bear syntactic and semantic information on the recognition process. The common dogma has been that syntactic and semantic information is necessary for a continuous speech recognition system. In fact, many systems were designed to have syntactic and semantic processors determine what the utterance was. Only recently has this position been challenged [Church 87] based on the following phenomenon.

A factor in the analysis of speech is the phenomenon of allophonic variations – the sound variations based on the context (e.g., a [t] will be aspirated in word–initial position as in "tick", but not as the second sound in "stick") – which provides viable information for SR. Allophonic variation is ubiquitous and the processes are almost innumerable. Thus, the common wisdom is that allophonic processes are at best noise that distract the speech recognition system, making it next to impossible to identify the word boundaries. It can be argued, however, that allophonic variation is information, rather than noise and, if appropriately used, can contribute a tremendous amount to the speech recognition tasks. While the common wisdom on the structure of SR systems is that syntax and semantics do in fact drive the analysis process, recent work implies that semantic/syntactic information is at best secondary to analyzing speech: it is necessary to identify the sound segments before understanding the word.

8.1.3 Applications

Speech recognition systems can be classified according to two distinctions: speaker dependent versus independent, and continuous versus isolated speech recognition. Speaker dependent systems require from the individual a training session in which the system establishes templates for the idiosyncrasies in his own speech. Continuous speech recognition systems are hard to develop because of many unresolved research issues. The majority of systems are based on isolated speech input. Isolated speech recognition systems require a pause before and after the utterance to isolate tokens. Because isolated speech recognition systems rely on a fixed number of such templates, their effectiveness depends on the size of the vocabulary. Isolated speech recognition systems require the digitization of a template for a given speech token, a pattern-matching technique to match unknown matrix against template matrix, and a scoring and decision method. These work well for experienced users. A remaining problem is the time length of the utterance.

Advantages of speech recognition systems include the elimination of user inhibition in front of the keyboard, easy access via telephone, low training period, usefulness in hands-free environments and tasks. Disadvantages include the constrained use of normal speech patterns and the training required. Applications for isolated speaker dependent speech recognition include television, cockpit emergencies, quadriplegics and speech impaired, robotic safety, security voice verification, and the talk writer.

8.1.4 Products/prototypes

Speech recognition products fall into one of three classes: chips, boards, and, most commonly, stand-alone systems [see Figure 8-3]. While there was a slump in 1984 in getting into the speech technology business, recent offerings by IBM and DEC seemed to have legitimized the technology. Concurrently, there has been an increase in quality and robustness of the systems on the market in 1989. The majority of speech recognition prototypes currently under development in the laboratories are based on hidden Markov models. These models are based on the assumption that every word is made up of a sequence of phonemes – the abstract sound elements of a language that are modified in the context of neighboring sound elements. The abstract sound elements are said to be realized as allophones. Because every phoneme can have a multitude of allophonic variants, the combinatorial explosion of possible allophones increases the search space of the intended phoneme. To constrain this search space grammatical and other linguistic knowledge sources are employed.

8.1.5 History

The groundwork for computerized speech recognition was laid by Jean B.J. Fourier (1768–1830) in his book from 1822 *The Analytical Theory of Heat* when he showed that complex waveforms like speech signals can be analyzed

Company	Product	Vocabulary
Speech Systems	DS100 PE200	20K
Dragon	Voiceable 1,000 2,000	1,000 20K
IBM		5K
Kurzweil	KWV	7,5-20K
Votan	VPC2140	

Figure 8-3:   Speech recognition system products

as the sum of a series of simple sine waves. Georg Ohm, in discovering his acoustical law, showed that the human ear itself performs like a Fourier analyzer while processing speech. After the development of sound spectrography in the 1940s, few attempts to build speech recognizers were made. In 1971, the "biggest event in speech recognition history", a five-year, $15 million speech understanding project, was launched by the Advanced Research Projects Agency [ARPA]. The ARPA project charged five principal contractors with producing separately a complete speech recognition system that could understand continuous speech from a wide range of speakers within a general American dialect. The system was to perform within a restricted domain and with a 1,000 word vocabulary, and not in real time. The conditions for the final test would be optimal, e.g., quiet room, good quality microphone. In 1976, four systems were tested: (1) Systems Development Corporation dealt with facts about ships; (2) Bolt Beranek and Newman's HWIM [Hear what I mean] system answered questions about travel budget management; and (3) two systems by Carnegie Mellon University, Harpy and Hearsay II, chose document retrieval as their domain. Harpy was the only system that fully met the original specifications. After the ARPA project, funding for speech recognition systems became scarce, and sales of commercial tools have only recently picked up.

8.1.6 Trends

Although many strategies have been employed to analyze continuous, speaker independent speech, all have suffered from limited accuracy and excessive computational requirements. In general, attempts at continuous speech recognition have been orders of magnitude away from real time analysis and suffer from poor accuracy (60% range). The current focus of research into speaker and even dialect independent continuous speech recognition systems is on real time processing without exorbitant expenditures of resources. Such a system depends primarily on two factors: some form of parallelism and the software configuration. Parallel processing allows the software to calculate independent pieces of data simultaneously without wasting time by having to wait for important information such as acoustic features. The technologies for continuous speech exist, and the solution lies in the way these technologies (both in hardware and software) are organized. On March 6, 1989, *Voice Processing Corporation* of Cambridge, Massachusetts, announced a development agreement to provide speaker independent, continuous voice recognition for *DECvoice* that understands the speech of callers regardless of dialect variations. *Natural MicroSystems* of Santa Clara, California, is expected to provide voice capabilities for Sun workstations.

Applications are predominantly in areas where isolated and even speaker dependent systems are sufficient. Many mundane applications, e.g., data entry, voice activated appliances, are beginning to become generally accepted. In the short term (1995), these systems will provide ample opportunity to be cost-effective and entertaining. In the mid term (2000), speaker independent systems will emerge. Advances in telecommunications will provide a wide open market. In the long term (2010), conversational systems will become a reality. The technology, especially chips and better audio equipment, will enhance the quality of the products. Theoretical advances, especially in neural networks and general parallel processing, will advance speech technology to a viable product category.

8.1.7 Conclusion

Speech recognition is the transformation of analog sound data to digital format. Approaches to speech recognition come in three forms: (1) the pattern or template matching approach stipulates that for each sound or word there is a stereotypical sample that the input can be compared to. Template matching works fine for limited and well-defined applications that do not require an exorbitant number of templates. (2) the feature extraction approach in which acoustic features are being extracted. (3) the multi-level approach in which syntactic or semantic levels interact and evaluate the output of the acoustic analyzer.

Common problems with speech recognition systems are in general the issues for a program that is based on an algorithm to resolve regularities from noisy input. In particular, homonyms, slurs, dialects, stress factors and, above all, the changing characteristics of sounds due to allophonic variation make it very hard to determine the word or utterance. Speech recognition systems have two types of applications: applications that require only isolated and mostly speaker dependent capabilities, e.g., appliances, cars; and applications that require continuous speech to conduct conversations with human counterparts.

In the future, we will see

- an integration of speech recognition in the computing environment, i.e., allowing voice annotations of computer files via "Etherphone",

- an integration into everyday life especially with the advent of voice mailboxes, and

- a reduction in cost of the speech capability will come down as a function of the mass market and the development in chip technology.

8.1.8 Suggested Reading

There are many good introductory books on SR [Fallside 85]. Larger endeavors at research institutions are described in [Allen 87b, Young 89]. My favorite book on the subject is [Church 87]. Besides the theoretical contribution regarding the allophonic processes in SR, Church demonstrates originality in the implementation as well. He opts for the implementation of his theory in the form of phrase structure rules, as opposed to rewrite rules. Phrase structure rules allow him to capture contextual dependencies by expressing them in non-terminal symbols. The intermediate representation produced by the phrase structure rules is then matched against the lexicon. While his contention is plausible, it begs the question of what syntax or semantics contributes to the process of SR. It is unfortunately true, as Church points out, that "speech recognition has progressed to the point that no one person can do it all".

8.1.9 Useful Contacts

Speech Systems, 18356 Oxnard Street, Tarzana, California 91356; *The Voice Connection*, 17835 Skypark Circle, Suite C., Irvine, California 92714.

8.2 SPEECH SYNTHESIS

8.2.1 Information processing task

Speech synthesis is the emulation of human speech by a machine. The input to the speech synthesis program is in the form of ASCII text which is then transformed to human-like speech sounds.

8.2.2 Approaches

Speech synthesizers are either based on the process of synthesis-by-analysis, or synthesis-by-rule. The major difference between these two approaches is that synthesis-by-analysis uses input from a human speaker, while the input to a synthesis-by-rule program is an ASCII text file.

Text-to-speech synthesis programs normally identify the sentence boundaries, and analyze individual words by comparing them to the built-in dictionary of less than 10,000 words. Words not found in the dictionary are pronounced based on rules that are built around the invariant sound features

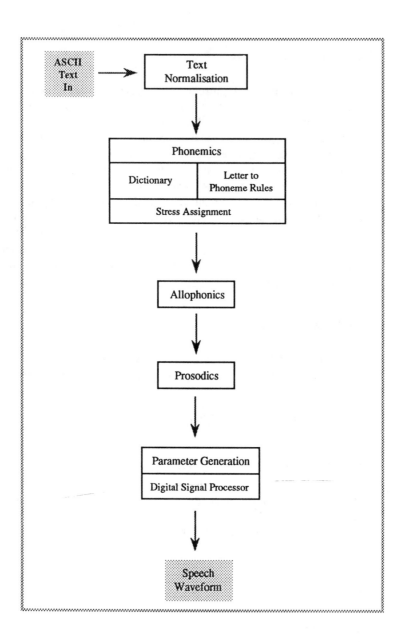

Figure 8-4:   Model of a text-to-speech
synthesizer [Waterworth 87, page 18].

and their suprasegmentals. The trade-off between table look-up and rule based computation of speech is that irregular words stored in the look-up tables are pronounced adequately if the built-in dictionary has priority, while regular words are pronounced more adequately if the rule-to-phoneme portion has a large enough number of rules.

The four classical approaches to speech synthesis are: (1) phoneme synthesis, (2) linear predictive coding [LPC], (3) Fast Fourier Transform [FFT], and (4) waveform digitization. For phoneme synthesis the individual sounds are combined to form a word. Linear-predictive coding uses the method of storing filter coefficients and excitation frequencies. The FFT uses as input values for intensity, pitch, and formant frequencies to compute the digital output. Klatt built a FFT synthesizer that allows 40 variables, at a 5 msec interval and a sample rate of 20kHz stored in 12 bits. The best quality synthesis results from waveform digitization at an uncompressed pulse code modulation rate of 50kHz at 16 bits.

8.2.3 Applications

Voice response systems using digitized speech have become commonplace. At Carleton University in Ottawa, the voice response system for student registration activated via touch tone phones has been so successful that it now replaces in-person registration for their 15,000 undergraduate students. It has also eliminated lining up at 3 a.m. in the morning to get a guaranteed spot in certain classes.

Speech synthesis lends itself for information services that have frequent changes in the data, e.g., weather forecasts, electronic mail and banking. Voice mail is the fastest growing sector of voice response systems. For internal applications, many companies use synthesized speech systems whereas for customer services high quality speech is a prerequisite. *DECvoice*, according to Paul Gilmartin, DEC's group manager of voice applications marketing, indicated in an interview for *Digital Review* on April 3, 1989 that the five key industries are: banking and financial services applications, insurance, distribution, health care and government.

8.2.4 Programs/Products

The market in 1989 of voice response systems is characterized by a major exodus of companies. The high end systems requiring mini- or mainframe computers are often too expensive to compete with the low-end system hosted on PCs. The best known and very effective *DECtalk* provides speech synthesis at an affordable rate. With *DECtalk* you can vary the speaking rate (150-400 words per minute), the intonation and the pitch.

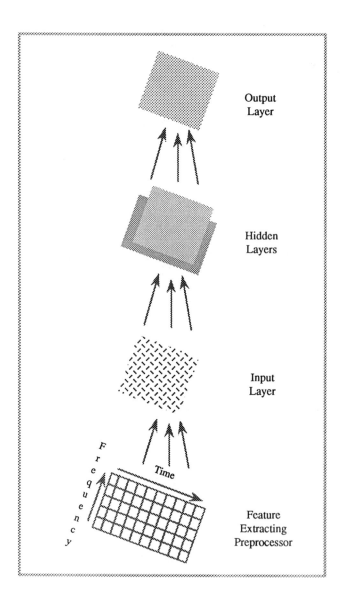

Output
Layer

Hidden
Layers

Input
Layer

Feature
Extracting
Preprocessor

Figure 8-5:   Flowdiagram for NETtalk

At the low end off the market, the phonemic synthesizer SSI263 for Apple computers, the *Echo General Purpose Speech Synthesizer* from Street Electronics of Carpintera, California and a host of similar devices sell for about $100 at the low-end and with poorer quality than the Cadillacs' of the industry. The more expensive systems, however, are often not successful: Engineered Systems of Omaha, Nebraska, could not sell enough of their *TCS/500 Transaction Communication*, ranging in price from $20,000 to $240,000.

Cullinet Software, Inc.'s product *Enterprise: Expert* works in conjunction with *Decvoice* to function as an interface between the DECvoice hardware and applications software on the VAX. While *Enterprise:Expert* was designed as a stand-alone expert system it will function as an intelligent dialog expert that instructs *DECvoice* only to ask the user pertinent questions during the conversation.

In the laboratories in the meantime, neural network technology is taking hold. Terence Sejnowski and Charles Rosenberg designed NETtalk, a neural network that performs text-to-speech conversion [see Figure 8-5]. The input to the network consists of a five-sound sequence at a time. The system learns how to pronounce the middle sound using the surrounding sounds as contextual clues for the correct pronunciation. Connected to a speech synthesizer, NETtalk pronounces the new words that are not in the initial training set with 95% accuracy.

8.2.5 History

Voice response systems have been commercially available since the 1960s, Recent technological improvements and reduction in costs have made them more affordable. The market for synthesis systems is extremely volatile. In a *Computerworld* article from January 1983, the author comes to the conclusion that although the market is "poised for huge growth" no company was commercially successful. Even in the 1990s the volatility remains, and companies leave the voice systems arena.

8.2.6 Trends

The change in the user population, the increase in quality, and the reduction in price are major factors for foreseeing a renaissance of speech products. The projected revenues of $800 millions for 1989 back up this optimism.

New applications gave the market a needed boost.   Voice mail and voice
message systems provided the impetus for many companies to enter the
marketplace, only to find out that the technology was too expensive for mass
marketing.

8.2.7 Conclusion

Speech synthesis in general and speech response systems in particular can
expect a hefty growth over the next decade. It becomes obvious that
commercial success will only be achieved for the following reasons:

- major computer vendors support the marketing (e.g., DEC, Cullinet),

- there is a real need for the product (e.g., voice response systems), and

- the technology is mature enough to keep the costs reasonable.

8.2.8 Suggested Reading

A good introduction into the subject of voice processing and speech
synthesis is [Waterworth 87]. Trade publications such as *Computerworld,
Digital News* contain many articles on recent developments.

8.2.9 Useful Contacts

Cullinet Software, Incorporated, 400 Blue Hill Drive, Westwood,
Massachusetts 02090.

CHAPTER 9

WRITING AIDS

> Your word processor gives you the power. Rightwriter gives you the clarity. Not a spelling checker – Rightwriter is a sophisticated expert system that applies the rules of good writing directly to your documents. [Quotes from the sales literature]

Just think how annoying misspelled words, garbled syntax, and missing subject-verb agreements are. The necessary corrections of the text according to the rules of a given language are a natural application for NLP. Considered in the past to be mundane and scientifically less challenging applications, writing aids, including spelling and grammar checkers, are now the leading money makers in all of NLP technology. As the need in the US for better desk top publishing programs and interfaces to databases arises, and world-wide the demand for machine translation of business correspondence increases, writing aids in one, or, even better, in multiple languages, are gaining market shares.

NLIs profit from the spelling checkers that have been developed because they require typing English to the keyboard. On-line dictionaries offered in many forms, hand-held spelling checkers and translators, integrated linguistic systems (e.g., Proximity linguistic system) and new storage media (e.g., NeXT's magneto-optical drive allowing 256 megabytes per cartridge) that allow you to take "the world with you", will make NLP on a large scale and at different levels of complexities part of the everyday computing environment. Peripherally related to writing aids are integration capabilities that let you pull in data into your text file from different programs (e.g., spreadsheets and DBMS). The wave of the future for writing aids will be a combination of current technology with future character and handwriting recognition.

9.1 INFORMATION PROCESSING TASK/PURPOSE

The information processing task of writing aids ranges from spelling correction to stylistic and grammar evaluation. Spelling correction programs are based on various algorithms that deal with the two basic error types that occur: orthographic and typographical errors. While orthographic errors are cognitive in nature – the writer simply misconstrues the orthography and would not be able to correct it himself – typographical errors are of motoric nature. Typographical errors include deletion, insertion, substitution, transposition, and other more complex forms of errors [Peterson 80]. Characteristically, misspellings in word–initial position are rare, doubling and transposition very common. The task of correcting typographical errors is a mechanical checking of commonly occurring mistakes. Orthographical errors are more cumbersome and embarrassing. They occur usually in the form of homophones and are therefore less obvious. The task of the spelling checker is to determine what other homophone is close enough to be substituted. Even then, the writer may not recognize the right spelling because he does not know it.

Grammar or style checking programs try to analyze the sentence structure of text. They perform minimally a keyword match of patterns contained in the program. Maximally, grammar checkers contain expert knowledge of how to construct the sentence and text properly. Grammar checking programs determine structural and stylistic errors [see Figure 9–1]. Their task is to recognize word, sentence and paragraph boundaries, determine well–formedness of the sentence, compile statistics on word usage, and identify stylistically ill–formed constructions (e.g., split infinitives). The common denominator for the information processing task is search. While comparing input strings with a large number of possibilities, the programs have to be able to do intelligent searches on their databases, preferably on a personal computer.

Just think how annoying misspelled words, gargled syntax, and missing subject-verb agreements are. The necessary corrections of the text according to the rules of a given language are a natural application for NLP. Considered in the past to be mundane and scientifically less challenging applications, writing aids, including spelling and grammar checkers, are now the leading money makers inall of NLP technology.<<*_G3. SPLIT INTO 2 SENTENCES? *>>
<<*_S3. LONG SENTENCE: 29 WORDS *>> and interfaces to databases arises, and world-wide the demand for machine translation of business correspondence increases, writing aids in one, or, even better, in multiple languages, are gaining market shares.<<*_G3. SPLIT INTO 2 SENTENCES? *>>

<<** SUMMARY **>>

Overall critique for: C::\WP\rite.wri
Output document name: C:\WP\rite.OUT

READABILITY INDEX: 15.34

```
        4th       6th       8th       10th      12th      14th
     |****|****|****|****|****|****|****|****|****|****|
     SIMPLE      |- - - -GOOD- - - - -|              COMPLEX
     Readers need a 15th grade level of education.
     The writing is complex and may be difficult to read.
```

STRENGTH INDEX: 0.38

```
     0.0                      0.5                      1.0
     |****|****|****|****|    |      |      |      |      |
     WEAK                                             STRONG
     The writing can be made more direct by using:
                  - shorter sentences
```

DESCRIPTIVE INDEX: 0.47

```
     0.1                 0.5                 0.9       1.1
     |****|****|****|**   |      |      |      |      |    |
     TERSE    |- - - - - - - -NORMAL- - - - - - - -|    WORDY
     The use of adjectives and adverbs is normal.
```

JARGON INDEX: 0.28

SENTENCE STRUCTURE RECOMMENDATIONS:

1. Most sentences contain multiple clauses.
   Try to use more simple sentences.

<< WORDS TO REVIEW >>

Review this list for negative words (N), jargon (J), colloquial words (C), misused words (M), misspellings (?), or words which your reader may not understand (?).

according (M) 1	annoying (N) 1
demand (M) 1	garbled (?) 1
inall (?) 1	interfaces (J) 1
mundane (?) 1	nlp (?) 1
nlp. (?) 1	scientifically (J) 1
syntax (?) 1	

<< END OF WORDS TO REVIEW LIST >>
<<** END OF SUMMARY **>>

Figure 9-1:   A sample output
from *RightWriter*

9.2 APPROACHES

The effectiveness of a writing aid is measured by how well it maximizes the number of probable corrections and minimizes the number of unlikely ones. Approaches to the construction of writing aids are two-fold: on the one hand, there are programs based on statistical strategies; on the other hand, there are programs based on linguistic strategies. For spelling checkers, the common typographical errors, coupled with the positions they normally occur in, can be the basis for the statistically oriented spelling checking program. Linguistically, the program has to know something about the sound structure of the intended and actually spelled word. This phonemic analysis is not suited for detecting typographical errors. Consequently, a spelling checker has to consist of both types of processing.

The underlying formula for calculating the allowed number of errors per word for many spelling checkers depends on the word length. For instance, the number of allowed errors per word equals word length times (1 − percent/100), where percent is the degree of correctness. According to this formula, a word length of three letters or fewer allows for 0 errors, 4–6 letters allow for 1 error and so forth. To check for the various typographical error types (e.g., substitution, transposition, deletion, insertion), the program then applies a certain method, using hash tables of significant words, digrams or trigrams and often the third letter to start corrections. For each typographical error, the program then tries to undo transpositions, deletions, insertions, etc. While soundex methodology (i.e., the spelling is based on an impressionistic rendition of the sounds that make up a search term), is useful for DBMS access, it can deal only with orthographical and not typographical errors. Therefore, a combination for correcting phonological and motoric based errors is the most effective solution to the problem.

The situation is similar for grammar and style–checkers. Because of the memory constraint of personal computers in the past, a typical program for checking grammar and style such as *Grammatik* or *Writer's Workbench* contains a limited number of patterns, usually less than 1,000, that cause replacement of stylistically inferior constructions (e.g., "in view of the fact that" is replaced by "since"). In contrast to this statistically oriented approach, linguistically based programs analyze the words and the syntax of the sentences before the stylistic rules are applied.

Product Name	Approach	Method
Acute	Typographic	Trigrams
Fuzzie	Typographic	Trigrams
Proximity [PF-474 chip]	Integrated	Proximity Value
Speedcop	Typographic	Similarity Keys to Speed Up Search
Spell	Typographic	Generate-and-Test Variants of Input String
Spell Therapist	Orthographic	Phonological Encoding into Grafon System
Triphone analysis	Integrated	Split Phonological Variants into Triphones

Figure 9-2:   Available Spelling Checkers

Product Name	Approach	Method
Critique	Linguistic	Full Parse Trees
Grammatik	Statistic	Stock Phrases
Right Writer	Linguistic	Heuristic Rules
Style and Punctuation	Statistic	Stock Phrases
Writer's Workbench	Statistic	Stock Phrases Compiles Usage Statistics

Figure 9-3:   Available Grammar Checking Programs

9.3 APPLICATIONS

The prime applications for writing aids now and in the future are education, publishing houses, and office automation. Besides ensuring conformity with the English grammar, automated writing aids also provide consistency in terminology and in spellings that may have legitimate variations. Stylistically, writing aids will help people to adopt a more concise and consistent style. The function of these programs is both reactive and proactive: reactive in the sense of correcting current mistakes, proactive in the sense of preventing them in the future.

Consistency of writing is an important aspect for written communication in the office. Publishing houses develop style sheets to encourage conformity to their self-imposed norm. For students, especially those studying foreign languages, writing aids will yield cost savings and more efficient training.

9.4 PROGRAMS/PRODUCTS

The commonly available spelling checkers fall into three major categories: (1) typographically oriented spelling checkers, (2) orthographically oriented programs, and (3) integrated approaches [see Figure 9-2]. Spelling checkers are incorporated in word processing software and in text oriented on-line storage and retrieval services.

The commonly available grammar checkers fall into two major categories: (1) statistical, and (2) linguistic oriented approaches [see Figure 9-3]. The largest and most ambitious system is *CRITIQUE*, an extension of the *EPISTLE* project which began 1980 at IBM [Richardson 88]. *CRITIQUE* combines morphological, syntactic and stylistic analyses based on an on-line dictionary of over 100,000 words. It is designed for multiple user groups (e.g., students, editors, office workers) and three levels of on-line help. While *CRITIQUE* is still being tested, *RightWriter* is already available for most word processing packages for about $100.

9.5 TRENDS

In the short term (1995), writing aids will improve their stylistic power and the user interface. In the mid term (2000), desk top publishing will have advanced the state of the art in the area of writing aids. In the long term (2010), the recognition of handwriting will have been integrated into the writing and editing process.

The technology is taking advantage of the cheaper memory and higher storage capacity of the personal computer and workstation environment. In the light of the increasing internationalization and the decreasing importance of English as a lingua franca for business, companies that offer multi-lingual software (e.g., Proximity, Digital Linguistix) are positioned to reap the benefits of commercial globalization. Theoretical advances that will provide better algorithms will be based on neural network technology. Since the search space is large and the problem of spelling and grammar checking is one of pattern matching, neural networks are ideally suited for this task.

9.6 CONCLUSION

While methods to improve the editing tools have been widely used, the technology is just now beginning to have an impact in the marketplace. Two factors have contributed to this trend: on the one hand more casual, not keyboard trained, users access computers; and on the other hand, there has been a great increase in desk top publishing activities, including mark-up languages. Writing tools are either linguistic or statistic based. While many currently available systems are based on either one or the other approach, future products will· have to contain both capabilities to stay in the marketplace.

The more sophisticated writing aids will become, the more impact they will have on the written language:

- The most popular style checker will determine the "unwritten" rules of the language.

- The human will rely too much on writing aids and loose the ability to form proper sentences, similar to people no longer being able to add numbers because they rely on calculators too much.

- The standard for document production will be measured on the performance of the tools available, thus forcing business people to purchase the latest writing aids.

9.7 SUGGESTED READING

Articles like [Peterson 80] can be found in few computer magazines and journals. Because this segment of the NLP market is not very intriguing, the number of publications is limited. Many computer magazines have articles on specific products.

9.8 USEFUL CONTACTS

Proximity Technology, Inc., 3511 N.E. 22nd Avenue, Fort Lauderdale, Florida 33308; *RightSoft, Inc.*, 4545 Samual Street, Sarasota, Florida 34233.

PART III - BOTTOM LINE

In general, there is a lot more to a technology than "gee-whiz" and "whiz-bang". There are the people that will use it, the businessman who will sell it, and the academic who will think about it. The infrastructure of a technology and its place within an even bigger infrastructure ("the bigger picture") determines what will come of it.

The people that will use NL technology have to overcome three barriers: (1) the technology barrier by understanding – in general – what NLP systems can do and cannot do; (2) the utility barrier by realizing – in particular – what part of a specific information processing task NLP systems are useful and appropriate for; and (3) the psychology barrier by appreciating the enhanced productivity rather than expecting job displacement. Unfortunately, the salesman and the professor will not aid in this process: hype helps to sell and science stops short of hypocrisy.

The businessman who will sell NL technology will have to know what sells and which aspect of the technology is profitable now and in the future. In "high tech/high touch" environments it is often the metaphor that sells for lack of a complete understanding of the technology itself. A case in point: the notion of a rule based expert system is intuitive, it accords with the human instincts for causality, simplicity, and generality. The use of NL for computer interaction is intuitive, at first glance. It is so intuitive that everybody expects it, at almost no cost. Yet NLP systems are far from becoming a commodity in the near future. Selling a product that everybody almost takes for granted at a level of sophistication only seen in the movies (e.g., 2001 and thereafter) without a fair price is more than a challenge for even the most adroit salesman. Successful NLP products are definitely a matter of packaging the technology for the right group of people. A case in point: NLIs require a top-down sell. It is at the level of the CEO that the technology has to be marketed because the MIS people will initially defend their SQL territory.

The academic who will think about NL theories faces two challenges: how to delimit scientifically the do-able and interesting problems of NLP, and how rationally to obtain funding for tackling them without selling himself short on the expected results. Now, everybody agrees that NL is a vital part of human existence and therefore warrants research. More importantly, being able to talk to the computer would increase the user population by orders of magnitude, apart from the sheer expediency of being able to access computational devices easily. However, the what, when, and how of this endeavor are still a matter of dispute. The question "What is language?" is still an academic one, a bad one at that, because it seduces scientists into thinking of paradigms rather than practical solutions.

NLP has been a controversial issue for academia and business. In academia, AI research was said to be practical but untheoretical, whereas research within linguistics was said to be theoretical but impractical. In the business sector, marketing and market penetration lagged behind the seeming superiority of the NLP technology; NLP software has turned out to be not cost-effective. What can be done about this situation?

The eclectic nature of NLP research has to give way to a more autonomous discipline dealing exclusively with the issue of NL understanding by biological and electronic organisms. Current NLP research is caught between the ideologies of the various academic disciplines. NLP systems of the future have to be based on more innovative linguistic and conceptual models if they are to become useful and acceptable on a large scale. The removal of the costly setup and maintenance of NLP systems along with a redefinition of cost-effectiveness for new software will open up a marketplace that is aptly characterized as being skeptical. Skeptical of the alleged increase in productivity, and skeptical in fulfillment of user expectations. Ultimately, NLP technology will open up a man-machine intercourse of bionic proportions.

CHAPTER 10

CURRENT ISSUES

> We're an information economy. They teach you that in school.
> What they don't tell you is that it's impossible to move, to live, to
> operate at any level without leaving traces, bits, seemingly
> meaningless fragments of personal information. Fragments that can
> be retrieved, amplified... [W. Gibson, *Johnny Mnemonic*]

For the comprehensive DARPA study on neural networks in 1988, the late
Richard Feynman asked three questions about the new technology: what is it
good for? How do you know that? What are the alternatives? – questions
very apropos for evaluating the state of the art of NLP technologies,
academic, commercial, and otherwise. For the following discussion we will
not consider any technological impediments: we will rather assume for
argument's sake that NLP is perfectly possible and does exactly what
everybody expects it to do.

What is NLP good for? NLP provides a natural way for people to
communicate and process information. In our day-to-day activities, we use
language to read, tell stories, ask questions, and take notes. The natural
modes of language use are processing spoken, and written input. Each mode
corresponds to a primary activity: we normally ask questions using speech,
we take notes using our writing ability. Looking at NLP from the view

point of functionality, there are some lessons to be learned as to where it makes sense to have NLP capability simply by observing human habits. Typing inquiries to databases is not one of the most obvious choices for making NLP a commercial success because, on the one hand, we are not in the habit of asking questions by typing them, and on the other hand, the computing infrastructure includes as a prerequisite for its players that they be able to use a keyboard. The misconception arises from the misleading assumption that all users have to learn how to use keyboards. The use of NLP in conjunction with database access, advisory systems or other applications requiring a layperson to access computers makes sense only if the user can speak to the system, thus eschewing the awkwardness of typing.

A second, especially lucrative and natural, opportunity of exploiting NLP is in recognizing handwritten input. With the advent of neural network technology, the capability is ready for large scale and commercial applications no later than by the year 2000. In a competition for the design of the personal computer in the year 2000 sponsored by Apple Inc., the underlying idea of the winning team for the personal computer of the future consisted of having the machine ideally integrated and designed for our day-to-day activities [Mel 88]. The most important goal, obviously, is the use of the computing device as a personal secretary and media switchboard. The computer's capability of recognizing our handwriting, and subsequently put the information into a retrievable format, does not fit into our preconceived and skewed notion of what NLP is. Contrary to the misleading notions perpetuated by linguists and academics in general, NLP is not primarily a matter of sentences and paragraphs. In fact, in person-to-person interaction very rarely do we finish sentences, nor do we take notes in perfect prose. The notion "language equals sentences equals nouns and verbs" has indeed lead to a wrong thrust of NLP.

The third, and in my opinion real, application where NLP has the biggest pay-off is the processing of text, either for storing, summarizing, or skimming information. Our natural way of reading newspapers, journals, and books would be greatly enhanced if we had an automatic processor available that would allow us to "sift through" our information resources and making the residue available. Currently, large text databases would benefit from a better indexing scheme, which in turn would be greatly enhanced by an automatic updating capability. The projected exponential increase of information which slowly turns us into, as the psychologist George Miller terms it, "informavores", would be easier to manage if aided by computing devices and programs. Incidentally, it seems only fair that the same technology that supports the causes of this onslaught, electronic publishing, etc., should also provide a cure for the problem it has created.

In summary: NLP is good for applications that exhibit a natural fit with our habits and our computing environments.   Because NL is a natural way to transfer information and knowledge, business opportunities for NLP arise whenever information exchange takes place. This opportunistic motivation for employing NLP is in sharp contrast to the academic notion.   The academic notion of what NLP is good for is mostly predicated on the idealistic assumption that NLP primarily deals with sentences, well-defined structures in the first place. Mundane applications such as recognition of handwriting, spell checking, and voice identification, are ordinarily not included in NLP proper. These applications, commercially very promising and profitable, tell the story of many high technology ventures: they are practical, feasible and above all, do-able with the current technology and therefore will generate enough revenue to become a commercial success.

How do you know that?   People use NL from their very early life onwards to communicate and learn.   Empirical evidence for this comes in two forms: on the one hand, by observing our natural inclination to do things in a certain way with NL that we could not do without it (e.g., reading a book); on the other hand, by looking at the market place for NLP technology itself, small as it may be. The current reluctance of some user groups to embrace NLIs is a symptom that although the interface capabilities may be on target, the applications are certainly not.

Ease of use, for instance, is not a technology problem but a people problem. If someone has to access a database but is at a loss to know what it contains, NL capabilities only help if he knows already what to ask for. Because NLIs are not yet omniscient, they are not the right tool to familiarize the novice with the contents of a database without prior training. No matter how powerful the NLI is, its sophistication will not be appreciated.

What are the alternatives?   Some areas of NLP applications allow for alternatives to process information, many do not.   Graphic interfaces, touch screens and menus are certainly in competition with NLIs, the most visible application of NLP thus far.   These are sometimes alternatives, simply because pointing and clicking are easier and more natural skills than using a keyboard. Speech would make a comparable interface from the standpoint of basic skill requirements. Once there are no prerequisites imposed on the user other than natural skills, the proof of effectiveness and user-friendliness is only in the specific technology itself.   While there are alternatives to interface applications, there are simply no alternatives for processing text. For processing text there is no other way but NLP proper.   It is in the area of text processing ("understanding" is too ominous) that NLP power, if properly developed can really shine.   Other areas like machine translation, text generation, etc., are also prime contenders for making NLP successful, both commercially and from a user perspective.

The success of NLP heavily depends on selecting applications and domains where there is a natural fit with the way we do things. In brief, NLP is useful for spoken interaction and general linguistic information text processing. It is of limited usefulness for typed interaction because it requires an additional motor skill and there are viable alternatives for some aspects of the interactive process. Unfortunately, academic wisdom has not helped in defining what NLP is good for, or worse, what it is. Even worse, the technical issues related to the NLP technology give us reason to pause and seriously consider what is do-able at this point in time when we look at the state of the art and on-going future-oriented research.

Current NLP systems encounter three major barriers before being fully accepted and successfully integrated into the software arena: a technology barrier brought about by linguistic and computational shortcomings, a utility barrier consisting of the limited applicability and usability of first generation NLP systems, and a psychological barrier created by unrealistic user expectations and anthropocentricity.

10.1 NLP - THE TECHNOLOGY BARRIER

Currently available NLP products and systems are too expensive and not user-friendly for two reasons: (1) basic research problems in understanding language and languages remain unsolved, and - somewhat as a consequence - (2) brute force algorithms prevail that have implicit limits that have been reached. Looked at it from another vantage point: what the blueprint of an NLP system can't provide, the final product has to make up for by an increase in overall cost due to customization. The underlying cause of the poor quality of NLP technology is the lack of proven theories, the unfounded support of 30-year-old formalisms that have never produced any viable results (e.g., ATN), and the ill-defined area of NLP in the first place.

NLP has also fallen into the AI trap [see section 12.4]: the AI trap is a phenomenon whereby prototype systems are elevated to production systems, either because of pressure for results or simply because it is not realized that scalability is a serious issue. The AI trap is especially far-reaching in an area like linguistics where the pressure is on finding "cute theories" based on "cute facts". On the one hand, linguists are not good with algorithms and linguists-turned-high-tech-grammarians will hack up systems to account for cute facts while leaving the real, "easy" problems for the masses. On the other hand, computer scientists accustomed to compiler theories and parsers for computer languages are not well equipped to tackle ambiguities and hard linguistic issues. Two examples will illustrate these statements.

NLIs of the first generation suffered from a lack of scientific understanding of how ambiguities on various levels can be explained, described, and handled. Disambiguation procedures start in the lexicon; as the lexicon, and consequently the computer memory, increases, the setup procedures become more expensive. As a result, natural language interfaces were not frequently used. Compound these problems with those of setting up databases with the appropriate structures for relational algebra and you understand the problems with current commercial natural language interfaces on a large scale – the bigger picture.

Machine translation systems suffer from the lack of scientific understanding how differences on various levels of language structures can be resolved for translation purposes. Again, for want of higher level, i.e., syntactic, semantic, pragmatic, solutions, most effort and cost goes into the lexicon. Satisfied customers that prefer to work through native language garble rather than starting with the source language? Perhaps, but what gets lost in the process? Current MT systems requiring pre- and post-editing are fine for saving some time, but they are a far cry from production systems that deliver what people envision when they hear the term automated/computerized MT.

The problems with current NLP systems are of linguistic and computational nature. While some researchers devote the better part of their careers to delving into the linguistic issues of how to analyze prepositional phrase attachments, e.g., "I saw the man on the hill with the telescope", others worry about the computational tractability of parsing algorithms. The general problem with NLP is that there is no good way to scale down the problem. Looking at a subset of English reduces the number of analyses from infinity to thousands. Every time someone starts building an NLP system, "the" natural language problem is tackled.

10.1.1 Linguistic factors.

A host of factors contribute to the current state of the art in NLP. There are the factors related to the macrocosm, the infrastructure of computing and linguistics; the lack of good theories, good techniques; the factors of language analysis and use themselves. While the infrastructure will be discussed in detail in chapter 12, this sections deals primarily with the data, the actual phenomena encountered when tackling NLP problems. The reader should come away from this section with a deep appreciation of what it would really take for a computer to process our natural language, as much as an appreciation of what cognitive feats we perform every day.

The most dominant problems for NLP research include ambiguities, anaphora, and ellipsis. These problems arise owing to the many forms a particular utterance can have while still expressing the same meaning. These problems are independent of the NLP application, but are often dealt with on different levels, e.g., a domain specific NLI can resolve ambiguities by relying on its knowledge representation rather than its syntactic processing module. By the same token, having a precise account of a sublanguage, the subset of a language used in a particular domain, e.g., medical, that is characterized by specialized words and their usage and idiosyncratic syntax, does not really allow an NLP system to avoid many of these problems, they are just reduced by an order of magnitude.

Ambiguity arises if a word or sentence can have more than one plausible interpretation. Note that for the native speaker of a language, his linguistic and extra-linguistic knowledge usually allows him to assign one interpretation to an utterance even though there might be an alternative interpretation present. The most important factor for assigning a particular interpretation is the context. If, for instance, the utterance "he was knocked out by the punch" is heard in the context of attending a party, its interpretation will be different from the context of discussing a boxing match. Hidden ambiguities, e.g., "The new boss couldn't decide whether to lay Mary or Jack off", will seldom be detected for reasons of psychological plausibility, or social propriety.

Ambiguities occur on at least three levels: the lexical level (e.g., "The pen is large"), the phrasal level (e.g., "old men and women"), and the sentential level (e.g., "I saw the man on the hill with the telescope"). Research into these ambiguities and their resolution by humans is divided into two camps. On the one hand, researchers believe that humans process one interpretation after another. If humans realize that a certain interpretation does not fit into the context of the sentence or utterance, the mistake is corrected by consciously backtracking to the point of analysis where the current, erroneous interpretation started out from. Research results that suggested these findings supported the popularity of ATNs, which do indeed backtrack if one alternative fails. On the other hand, deterministic parsers pushed the notion that whatever we do with syntax can be done in a parser that considers syntactic information up to a point and then hands over the processing to another, preferably semantic component. A host of other approaches to solving the ambiguity problem, psychologically real or otherwise, also lead into the two classic dead-ends of NLP processing: the assumption that the computer processes NL like a human, or the assumption that humans process NL like a computer, neither approach showing any results on the NLP side.

Anaphora requires the identification of a referent for a given pronoun whereby the pronoun can precede (e.g., "The woman that he loves despises Otto") or follow the object it refers to (e.g., "I took the box out of the refrigerator and closed it"). Even more problematic is the anaphoric reference across sentence boundaries. Ellipsis requires the insertion of a deleted element either within a sentence (e.g., "Joe left in a Porsche, John in a VW"), or within a dialog (e.g, "Give me all the employees in department 13. <.....> In 10).

The common denominator of these most dominant problems is their property of preventing a clear understanding of a particular utterance. While using language, native speakers are accustomed to a trade-off between efficiency, to be brief, and effectiveness, to be concise. In other words, the interplay between expressiveness and redundancy creates the problem. Because a native speaker knows all the ground rules of language use, he automatically balances these two characteristics of NL. Quite the contrary happens with NLP systems that have to be equipped with all the knowledge that goes into language use. The crux, therefore, is either to require the user to be intelligent enough to enter "straight talk" by trying to filter out the assumptions, or to require the system to detect hidden presuppositions. As humans are getting more accustomed to dealing with machines and machines are getting more responsive, some form of cooperation will alleviate the problem in the near future. Recent studies [Hauptmann 87] have shown that humans interact differently with NLP systems than with their fellow men. Their syntax and the amount of presupposed knowledge is decidedly different.

10.1.2 Computational factors.

Different programming paradigms have their inherent benefits that should be utilized when constructing NLP systems: functional Lisp programming embodies an explicit control structure with its own higher order computation; logic programming (e.g., Prolog) uses its declarative style for automatic deduction; object-oriented programming (e.g., Smalltalk) allows for inheritance, data abstraction and generalization. Resource management is the key to success for application programs. Unfortunately, large memory requirements for representing the required knowledge, and lack of robustness make NLP systems less attractive. Moreover, cost-effectiveness is a factor. As to large memory requirements, NLP systems require a large knowledge base since the interpretation of NL discourse can require arbitrarily detailed world knowledge [Hobbs 84]. Robustness is an important requirement for an NLP that should be able to interpret ill-formed input. Strategies for handling ill-formed input range from designing two separate NLP systems, one for well-formed and the other for ill-formed input, to using metrics, meta rules, or preference semantics [Weischedel 83].

Many of these problems with NLP technology arise from the absence of good algorithms for NLP itself. The fact that ATNs are as powerful, as Turing machines, because of their way of using registers, subnetworks and other fancy ad hoc mechanisms does not contribute to the stringent approach needed to make an NLP algorithm tractable. Chart parsers, with their "byzantine" complexities, only pass the underlying problems to the next level of analysis. AI people usually try to accommodate many issues by pointing to a different knowledge representation. Unfortunately, the greater ease of use of one representation over another is simply a practical issue. Granted frames may be easier to manipulate than logic or production rules, all these mechanisms are simply there to implement the theory. The "implementation equals theory" trap, in fact, "the implementation equals anything" fallacy is in full force.

10.2 NLP - THE UTILITY BARRIER

The adage "easy to use is easy to say" applies to NLP systems designed to access computing devices. Considering man's natural inclination to communicate, speech is the preferred way to use language, followed by the learned skill of writing, followed by the motor skill of typing. Oddly enough man's least favorite and most cumbersome way to use natural language is at the same time the most touted and promoted way to interact with computers using natural language – via typing on the keyboard. Naturally, any interaction that presupposes a skill not readily available to everybody will face an uphill battle. It comes as no surprise that NLP systems, however powerful they are, lack ease of use because of their sheer requirement of having to learn how to type. The dilemma with NLP systems used for computer interaction unfolds as follows: the user group – novice to casual – that stands to gain most from NL capabilities is at the greatest disadvantage to profit, by the very fact that most of its members lack proficient typing skills; while, for the user group – expert – that could experience productivity gains, current NL capabilities are not sophisticated enough to do away with specialized computer languages or other forms of interaction (e.g., graphics).

The most "natural" NL interaction with computer systems is thus the spoken word, the written word and lastly the typed word. The state of the art of speech systems currently does not support any large scale application of the technology; character recognition and handwriting analysis is off to a promising start but still in its infancy; the analysis of typed input is hampered by open research problems. Apart from users' different skill and expertise levels, individuals require different interface functionality based on their personalities. An individual who firmly believes in controlling himself and his environment requires an interface that allows for more initiative and intervention by the user than a person who thinks of himself as being at the mercy of outside forces.   Without going into the psychographics, differences in personalities a priori determine if and how NL interaction is appropriate.

Leaving aside all the social and psychological reasons for NL interaction problems, the sub-second response time postulate that computational resources cannot obey, create a profile for the optimal user that only very few people fit. On the one hand, there is frustration because the system is too meticulously helping the user along, second-guessing his input, while preventing disaster by being idiot proof. On the other hand, there is disenchantment because the system does not "understand" the idiosyncracies of the individual user.

10.3 NLP - THE PSYCHOLOGICAL BARRIER

10.3.1 User expectations

Hype raises expectations and lowers appreciation of the actual achievements of innovations - not just of NLI technology. "Computer understands you", "Good-bye keyboards". Movie-goers are no longer fazed by Hal the talker and Sally the walker. Consequently, users approach modern technologies with too many expectations, unwilling to be patient enough to optimize the computer.

Apart from suffering the media pitfalls as part of our cultural orientation towards sensationalism, NL interaction suffers from a behavioral aspect often neglected. In common language use, the speaker says what he thinks, rather than thinks about what to say. There is an immediacy in using language that precludes the user of a computing device analyzing beforehand what to say and how to say it. Consequently, the instruction issued to the computer in plain English may be totally obvious within the user's mind, while requiring an enormous amount of reasoning on the part of the NL program. Let's take an example from querying a database about car accidents. The information is stored according to type of accident, age of driver, model of car, etc. For the information specialist, the retrieval process in a specialized computer language would require an understanding of how the data is structured and what pieces need to be retrieved for the analysis. The pieces of information would then be analyzed by the appraiser. Imagine an NL system that allows the appraiser to retrieve the data directly without the intervention of the information specialist. It does not take very much for the NLP system to answer the appraiser's English questions about straight facts (e.g., what are the colors of cars involved in accidents after 5 p.m.?). It is next to impossible for the NLP system, however, to answer why-questions that require causal reasoning of generic or expert nature. And yet, isn't it difficult to delineate which questions can be answered, without confusing the native speaker?

10.3.2 Social issues

Humans like to think of themselves as the crown of creation. Anything similar in intelligence and capabilities is a priori suspect. NLP systems are no exception. In my experience of marketing an NLI for DBMs I have run across many people who take pleasure in "crashing" the system. Why? No one takes pains to render a spreadsheet inoperable, or lock up the keyboard on purpose.

The answer lies in the perceived threat to some individuals that do not want to concede any intelligence to non-human beings. Moreover, the Dreyfus phenomenon has shown that philosophers of a special ilk take pride in arguing against "artificial intelligence", using phenomenological arguments, dealing with understanding from a biological rather than a functional perspective.

Whereas in the past, knowledge of one of the computer languages elevated the individual to the ranks of a high tech priest and secured a high paying job, the present trend to open up the cast to ordinary users certainly is abhorrent and troubling to many DP professionals concerned about job security. For many system programmers, however, the existing backlog for writing code would definitely shrink, if only they could provide the end user with easy access to the databases. NL is not yet at a point where it can replace programming languages.

On a wider scale, automating certain menial tasks certainly means eliminating positions. But only at the expense of retraining the individual for a more meaningful, better position. Just as data entry changed from keypunching to optical character readers, progress in NLP will change our current understanding of how to program a computer. Enabling NL interaction with computers does not entail letting computers run our lives.

10.4 CONCLUSION

Martians, after a brief visit to our planet would depart with at least two misconceptions about human life: first, that diet drinks make people gain weight, and second, that only the elite of computer literate users are capable of teaching their programs to speak in English. Most humans believe the first misconception is wrong, but seem to have difficulty with rejecting the second. In this chapter, I have presented three barriers to explain why NLP products are not widely used, yet:

- the technology barrier compounded by language–related and computational problems,

- the utility barrier consisting of the limited applicability and usability of first–generation NLP technology,

- the psychological barrier erected by unrealistic user expectations and job displacement fears.

The change from the "instrumental" to the "subjective" computer has had a profound impact on society [Turkle 84, page 13]. The computer has become a metaphor for how our mind operates. It is explicit in language where "mind" jargon is used to refer to computer phenomena (e.g., "intelligent programs"), and vice versa (e.g., "my next lecture is hardwired") [Turkle 84, page 17]. It is implicit in the area of AI research where programs no longer just execute instructions, but instigate them. The changing functionality and role of computers in society brought about radically new requirements for computer interfaces and overall capabilities: the human is no longer on the outside of the program giving instructions but inside of the computing environment interacting with the computer in a common language. The issue remains what this common language will be.

10.5 SUGGESTED READING

The three references deal primarily with the topic of computers and society. The article on the personal computer in the year 2000 shows how many possibilities even the currently available technology already has with respect to character recognition and telecommunications. Sponsored by Apple Inc., the rules of the contest included the stipulation that only already available pieces of technology could be used for designing the PC of the future [Mel 88]. Turkle's book *The Second Self* addresses the already beginning changes in our society due to the integration of computers into our everyday lives. As the title suggests, the computer has become a close companion, and functions for some even as an alter ego [Turkle 84]. Unger's book entitled *The Fifth Generation Fallacy: Why Japan is Betting its Future on Artificial Intelligence* [Unger 87] advances the hypothesis that Japan is more interested in solving the problems inherent in its writing system(s) than in attaining economic or scientific supremacy. Albeit its sensationalist thesis the book is interesting more because of its cultural information (in particular, how a different culture plans to overcome an inherent social barrier by employing tomorrow's computer technology) than because of the accuracy of the author's claims.

CHAPTER 11

THE NLP BUSINESS

On a Million Machines By 1990 – Natural Language Processing Market 1984–1985 Growth Will Top 200%. In various forms, commercially available natural language processing products have been on the market since at least 1975. Grandfather rights notwithstanding, however, natural language processing – both products and concepts – remains, in 1985, a missionary sell. [*Artificial Intelligence Markets*, August 1985]

A myth is something that is true on the inside, but not true on the outside. Thus, the commercial viability of natural language products falls into the category of myths, because on the outside these products do not appear to be a factor in the business world of everyday computing – yet, on the inside, they will become necessary in the future computing environment. But, more importantly, who says you can't make money with myths? Here's how.

  By the year 2000, it is expected that everybody will know at least a modicum about computers, at least how to use one. Yet, computer literacy is decreasing proportionally to the number of people currently expected to know how to access computing devices, especially accessing databases. It is in the areas of NLP where there is a natural fit that commercial successes will be found. In the past, the NLP business suffered from productizing too early, promising too much, and tackling the wrong applications in the first place. A case in point is all the NL interfaces marketed by the end of the 1970s. They created a wave of enthusiastic followers, but disappointed the majority of the people taking a hard look at what was being offered. NLP in general had to endure setbacks first in machine translation, then in NL interfaces, soon to be followed by speech processing. History repeats itself certainly in terms of disasters related to high tech promises. This chapter will introduce the factors that determine the marketplace in general. There is the question of quality and delivery, in brief, what is technologically possible. The secondary question is to determine what applications are commercially viable, in brief the market orientation of certain products. Unfortunately, in the past, the market orientation was tainted by the academic perception of what should be interesting research endeavors. It is here where the technology–looking–for–an–application phenomenon started.

11.1 THE MARKETING OF NLP

It is difficult to sell NLP products. The primary reason being that there is a gap between the state of the technology and the user expectation. The user wants more for less money.   Marketing NLP is thus a major effort in educating people that will use the technology and carefully managing their expectation. Anything that makes life easier for personal computer users should be welcome. What people don't realize is that just because a system can respond to, not "understand", a subset of English, does not mean the system has the wherewithal to solve major retrieval problems or is able to perform intricate problem solving tasks. Often customers, dissatisfied with expert system performance in making access to their database easier, see NLIs as an alternative, whereas they are not. Current NLIs only do translations. Recently introduced products are only as informative as the information stored in the database and as powerful as the interface layer created during the setup procedure. NLIs amortize over longer periods of time. The crux of cost–effectiveness is the setup, during which the NLI administrator effectively recreates the database to allow the NLI to draw inferences that are not there in the first place.

NLIs are not the only NLP products that do not get a stronghold in the market because of quality and price. Take response systems as another example. According to an article in *Digital Review* on April 3, 1989, no fewer than half of the two dozen companies offering DEC–compatible voice products closed down within the previous nine months. The reasons cited for this development were (1) that the price for larger systems was one order of magnitude too high, especially when compared to PC–based systems, (2) the quality for synthesized voice is generally poor, and (3) that while developers are retooling at the low end of the market, the bigger companies like IBM, DEC, and Wang are vying for the large and more profitable accounts.

For an NL product/company to succeed, the following conditions apply: (1) the timing of introducing the product into the market place must be right; (2) the product must have a large enough linguistic and conceptual coverage to satisfy most of the user's need; (3) the product must have a champion within the company to support it, (4) the company must be strategically aligned with either an appropriate hardware or software vendor (e.g., for interfaces, a close relationship to a database vendor) to introduce the product into the infrastructure of current computing which, by and large, still has a "one-vendor" mentality; and (5) the marketing of the product must be forceful enough to counter the negative image NL products, especially NLIs, have acquired and at the same time show the benefits of NL versus pick-and-point interfaces. With the current technology, NLP products should be treated as a commodity and priced accordingly (low).

Market surveys have shown that introducing a software product as the first of its kind is more important for market shares than having a product that has the most power in terms of features. "Bad coverage is worse than no coverage" is an adage that people like to apply to NLP software. While limited coverage has its drawbacks, as long as the limitations can be clearly stated, the consumer will decide. Unfortunately, many NLIs, for instance, encompass coverage at a high cost in the following sense. While any NLP system can be brought up to about 70% of performance, no matter what the application itself is, an increase of another 25% will severely tax the performance, cost and maintainability. You may liken it to the experience people had with rule based, inference engine oriented expert systems. The quick and easy applications were cost-effective, the ones requiring more coverage blew the budget up out of all proportion. A trade-off has to be realized, a hard task for died-in-the-wool NLP aficionados.

As a technology still looking for more applications, NLP software does need supporters from within companies willing to install the software, use it and help to improve it. As with any product, experience and personal bias will determine whether a large number of NLIs is acquired. The biggest problem is the attempt of NLP companies to market stand-alone systems. The result: no one will buy them. It is hard enough for a software company to wean away the customer from a one-vendor mentality. It is even harder to instil in a customer the desire to try out a new product. The bad reputation that NLP systems created, especially in the late 1970s and early 1980s, has to be countered by educating the user, clearly summarizing the capabilities, and delineating the nature of cost savings for the customer.

On the whole, the marketing and designing of NLP products is much too oriented around what muscle the technology can flex. Furthermore, the proverbial consumer-orientation, much touted in other marketing arenas, definitely does not apply to a technology that is looking for showcases, and that also has potential applications that no one has even dreamed of. Just as spreadsheets were definitely not produced because of demand on the part of the customer, many NLP hot sellers have not surfaced. Henry Ford's slogan, "You can have any color you want as long as it is black", applies fully for software packages whose utility and cost-effectiveness depends on the mass market. NLP sold as a commodity will be successful only if the setup and the maintenance is in a reasonable proportion to the advantage and productivity gain.

The most effective way to get an NL product out in the market place is to employ what Trout and Ries termed "the bottom-up" marketing strategy, i.e., determining a tactic before developing a fully fledged strategy. Just as pizza empires grew on the premise "delivery in less than 30 minutes", "lean and mean" NLP systems will find easy market niches, however short-term they may be. Eight-megabyte dinosaurs that take weeks to customize are definitely poised to garner the mass market. While NLP technologies on the whole are not only selling new products but are also having to create their markets – the worst possible scenario for success, according to marketing textbooks – short-term gains may be easy for start-ups that quickly respond to small windows of opportunities and are able to move in and out of the market within 2-3 years.

11.2 BUSINESS SECTORS

Apart from NLIs, MT systems and speech systems, NL technology does not have an impact on the high technology market [see Figure 11-1 for the sectors]. Even with the products mentioned, the growth rate is not phenomenal, compared, for instance, to that of DBMSs. Until 1987, for instance, Logos, the largest MT company had sold only 31 systems. Between 1986-1988, Natural Language Incorporated had only 30-40 paying customers. AI Corp's *Intellect* product, however, has sold 550 units between 1981 and 1988. The voice technology market is expected to grow at 20% starting at projected revenues for 1989 at $800 million, according to market analyst Walt Teschner of Tern Systems, a Concord, Massachusetts consulting firm that specializes in voice technologies. The six sectors of the NLP arena are listed with their estimated market proportions in Figure 11-1. The percentages given in Figure 11-1 reflect the research activities based on the number of ongoing NL projects. A large portion of the revenue comes from government contracts. In 1987, the *Commerce Business Daily* and other government related requests for proposals totalled about $12 million in R&D monies for NLP projects.

With the advent of modern day commercial DBMSs the primary concern

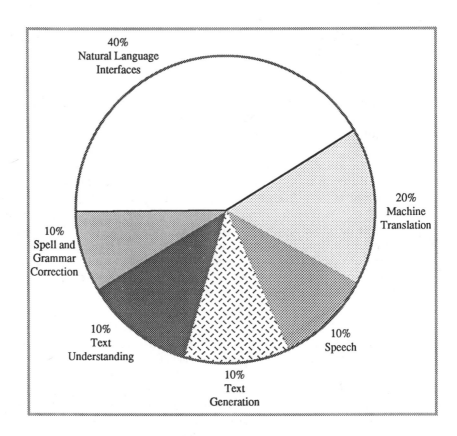

Figure 11-1:   The NLP sectors

has not been the users and their effectiveness but the software and its efficiency. This has created two obstacles that stand in the way of cost effective use of corporate databases: the requirements to (1) learn and (2) frequently use the fourth generation language of your particular DBMS. The presence of these obstacles has created a huge market for easy-to-learn user interfaces.

When people started developing NLIs, the current Macintosh interfaces were not generally available. The training on data base management systems before SQL or any fourth generation language was very hard, and the interface market for even a small amount of NL capability was wide open. Unfortunately, the oversell and the premature introduction of the NLP technology were set backs compounded by the emergence of viable alternatives. The English-like interface that the fourth generation languages promised skewed the expectation somewhat, along with the reluctance of MIS people to introduce a technology that had on its heels the threat of job displacement and an overall demystification of programmers. Internationally, the European market is much more NL oriented, a result of education and the geographical proximity of so many different languages. The first product that can be established will have a major impact on the European market place.

The four strategies for selling NLIs are (1) selling the technology to the upper management of a company and to expert non-technical users, (2) focusing on customization, i.e., consulting contracts while keeping the price of the software to a reasonable amount, (3) targeting large databases whose complexity warrants extensive customization expenditures, and (4) aligning the NL capability with major software vendors by embedding it as an alternative to other available options, into existing products or vertical applications. The common denominators for making NLP hard to sell and for having customers keep coming back are cost and capability. The cost factor arises since companies need to recoup some money fast, while, at the same time, the better part of that money is used for hand-holding the customer through the setup phase and the first trials. The customization effort for even a simple NL application may turn out to be a major undertaking, the support of the installation another step to spending major monies. The capabilities of existing NLP systems have to be balanced against the price that is being charged. Cost and capability concerns on the part of the consumer may become, if properly addressed, major aspects in the marketing and selling results of the technology. A high price tag may be warranted and paid in small niches, while a low price tag along with low capabilities may have a mass appeal. The three niches for NLP technology, especially when it comes to interfaces, are based on the cost/capability interplay.

As regards selling the technology to upper management: executives in need of up-to-date help will embrace NL technology for themselves and their business units. In the past, strong opposition from the MIS departments to unorthodox ways to access data has led to "stonewalling" NL technologies. As the power of the ivory tower individuals in these departments diminishes, a more pluralistic picture emerges. As the functionality of mainframes is now shared by the personal computers and the workstations, the MIS people see a reduction in their clout in decisions about what information processes they will control in the future.

Focusing on customization is a commonly embraced strategy to satisfy customers and at the same time reap handsome profits. NL products do need customization if used as multi-purpose interfaces. In economic terms, the customer wants to be satisficed [sic], i.e., wants his immediate need fulfilled at any cost without going through any agony to achieve it. For the government market, the sheer number of databases, their variety, and the high turnover rate of users make NLIs ideal interface options. The customer accustomed to buying solutions and not tools is often at a loss to know what could or should be done with an NLP system. Even packages like Dbase and R:Base allow consulting companies to reap in hefty fees for customization. The benefit of customizing the software for a particular customer is nevertheless mutual. Spending hidden costs like salaries, etc., on bringing an application up is much less cost-effective than spending upward of $2,000 per day for consulting.

Targeting large databases whose complexity warrants extensive customization was a successful strategy for the IBS system *EASYTALK*. The Hartford's life insurance company felt that their system programmers were spending too much time working as retrieval clerks and not as programmers. After installing an NLI for their corporate databases, the Hartford hopes to increase the productivity of their underwriters and their programmers.

Embedding the NL capability into existing database products that require easy retrieval mechanisms that go beyond, or are being used in addition to, the existing ones is a further marketing strategy. The key for this strategy to work is pricing the NL capability so that it will be viewed as a commodity and a fall-back option. It is a major hindrance to NLP companies becoming successful when they have to market, sell, and support their products independently of the host program. The one-vendor mentality is often perpetuated because of support issues and general service quality.

Another way to market an NLI is to embed its capability into a specific vertical or diagonal application directly. The advantage of having a vertical or diagonal product with NL is that the customization would be taken over to a large part by the company who sells the original package. While the crux of NLP systems consists basically of their setup, modules for vertical and diagonal applications would strengthen the product life cycle in one of two forms: either as optional add-ons, or as part of the customization effort.

A crucial development in the infrastructure of computing, the trend to decentralization and the use of personal computers networked together, opened up a huge market for user-friendly interfaces. While the gods in the MIS departments tried to keep their hegemony, the computerization of the office, coupled with better software and faster hardware, put the computing power in the hands of the end-user. Another good opportunity for the use of NLIs is the recent demand for on-line transaction processing, especially in the areas of banking, travel reservation, and securities. With respect to on-line transaction processing, the desired fast and easy access can be delivered by NLI technology.

11.3 PLAYERS

When General Motors needed an NLI for their internal database, it went out and built Datalog. When A.D. Little needed an unrestricted text parser it built NAS. When the Airline Safety and Reporting System looked at better ways to interface to their vital data repository, it called on Battelle to suggest a solution. In the late 1980s, if you want something special in terms of NLP technology, you better know where to look for it. NLP technology, with the exception of NLIs, is not widely advertised. In fact, there are only a few dozen high technology companies specializing in NLP related technologies, e.g., NLIs, speech technologies, machine translation, grammar and spelling checkers. NLP is part of the R&D market populated by universities, research organizations, and internal R&D departments of all the major computer companies (e.g., IBM, AT&T).

The majority of the R&D contracts, not counting internal R&D, are signed by the US government, in particular, DARPA. The Strategic Computing Program sponsored by DARPA [beginning in 1984] is a multifaceted NLP program including research and development for NLIs and processing of free form text from military messages [see Figure 11-2]. The expected results are two "new generation" systems. Preliminary findings were presented in 1986, at a workshop at USC-ISI, Marina del Rey, California and are detailed in [Sondheimer 86].

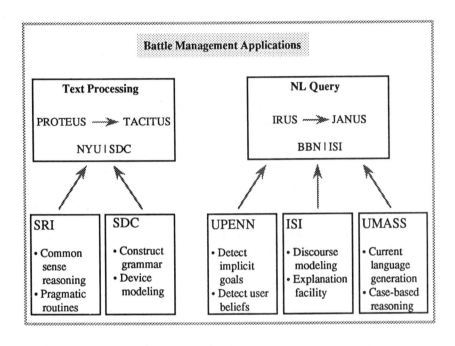

Figure 11-2:   The DARPA NLP programs

11.3.1 NLP Companies

Companies specializing in NLP products often include a wide array of services because many of their customers want something out of the ordinary.

- **Artificial Intelligence Corporation**, Waltham, Massachusetts: Distributor of *Intellect* the first commercially available NLI.

- **Automated Language Processing System, ALPS**, Provo, Utah: Distributor of *Computer Translation System* and multilingual word processors.

- **Battelle/NLQ**, Columbus, Ohio: Distributor of *NLQ*, a natural language query system for personal computer and mainframe based relational databases.

- **Carnegie Group**, Pittsburgh, Pennsylvania: Distributor of *Language Craft* a natural language shell for constructing interfaces.

- **Cognitive Systems**, New Haven, Connecticut: Founded by Roger Schank; products include: *Broker* [access to stock databases], *EXPLORER* [NLI for oil exploration devices], *Le Courtier* [NLI for investments], *ATRANS* [text understanding program that translates and formats bank telexes].

- **Dynamics Research Corporation**, Andover, Massachusetts: Distributor of *Spock*, an NLI [originated at Frey Associates under the name *Themis* for ORACLE databases].

- **Excalibur Technologies Corporation**, Albuquerque, New Mexico: Specializes in neural network technology; sells *Savvy* an NLI for PC based databases and *Savvy/TRS*, a text recognition and retrieval system.

- **Intelligent Business Systems**, New Haven, Milford, Connecticut: venture start-up backed by Olivetti and NCR; sells *EasyTalk*, an NLI for ORACLE that required over 100 man-years of development.

- **Kurzweil Applied Intelligence, Inc.**, Waltham, Massachusetts: Distributor of the *Talkwriter* and other speech recognition software.

- **Logos Corporation**, Dedham, Massachusetts: Distributor of *LOGOS*, a machine translation system

- **Natural Language, Inc.**, Berkeley, California: Distributor of *Natural Language* [previously *Datatalker*], an NLI for databases.

- **Smart Communications**, New York, New York: Distributor of the *Smart Translator*.

- **Speech Systems**, Tarzana, California: Distributor of *The Phonetic Engine*, a speech recognition product.

- **Symantec**, Cupertino, California: Distributor of the most successful PC-based integrated NLI product *Q&A*.

Besides NLP companies whose business is based on proprietary software, many of the large accounting firms (e.g., **Arthur Anderson**) and small businesses (e.g., **Brodie Associates, Elliott Bay Computing**) specialize in consulting related to NLP.

11.3.2 R&D Organizations

R&D organizations overall have a good reputation for quality research. In contrast to NLP consulting companies their speciality is basic research, i.e., exploring the unknown. Based on their experience they may even outperform consulting companies in development tasks.   Among the larger R&D organization with ongoing research in NLP are: **Battelle, BDM, Bolt Beranek and Newman, MITRE, SRI.**   Many computer and computer related companies maintain their own internal research staff in the areas of NLP.

11.3.3 Universities

Universities ordinarily establish a doctrine of how they do things. Many universities have only one method that is accepted.   The better known universities for NLP research are: Carnegie Mellon, Stanford, MIT, University of California [ISI], and University of Pennsylvania).   A good overview of curricula at various colleges is published in [Cohen 86].

11.4 FORECASTS

Howard Austin in an article on "Market trends in Artificial Intelligence" [Austin 84] introduced the idea of a repetition spectrum to assess new technologies such as AI. He describes a repetition spectrum as follows:

> In any society, all fundamentally new ideas are generated by a handful of creative individuals. These ideas are taken up by those who come in contact with the original sources and are "repeated" by elaboration and incorporation into the agendas of the new "owners". If the idea has sufficient persuasive power, its essential core is preserved and spread, repetition by repetition, in larger and larger circles until it completely saturates the society. Individuals and institutions tend to position themselves in characteristic positions along the resulting spectrum. The essential question to ask then, when assessing new technologies, is: where are we on the repetition spectrum? [Austin 84, page 268]

According to Austin's estimation NL system repetitions like Hearsay, SHRDLU, and Lunar are in the ten's of repetitions, DEC and other High Technology companies in the hundreds, IBM having reached a mid point between origin and saturation. Scientists and businessmen are on opposite ends of the repetition spectrum: scientists want to do many different things once, whereas businessmen want to do one good thing many different times. In an area as academically oriented as NLP, the lesson from previous lackluster product introductions clearly should be to bring entrepreneurs as early as possible into the game to define the product, markets, and distribution channels. The failure to realize this fact has led to the lack of market presence of NLP products.

The current impact of NLP technology in the computer marketplace is felt with NLIs, spell checking programs, and machine translation. In the future, text databases, on-line digesting of information, and a strong role in the new telecommunication infrastructure will take precedence over R&D projects. Given that the PC investments for Fortune 1000 companies include over 3 million personal computers, a total investment of hardware and software for PCs of $15.6 billion, and for mainframes $12.6 billion, NLP as the natural interface technology should be making some money. Out of the combined $28 billion investment in end-user computing, roughly one billion dollars is spent on data access tools in the year 1989. It can also be expected that NLP products will create new markets. For DBMS access, executives may consider using NLIs because they require only minimal training.

Unfortunately, the onslaught of claims relating to English–like interfaces has spoiled the market somewhat, but not terminally.   Fortunately, however, executives are more amenable to using keyboards now than ten years ago when it was not part of the corporate culture to be using keyboards.

The entire natural language processing market, with NLIs claiming the lion's share, was expected to grow from $59 million in 1985 to $650 million by 1990 according to DM Data Inc. [May 1985]; according to Datamation [June, 1984], from $10 million in 1983 to $100 million in 1987. The actual sales figures for NLP systems in 1988 for the US were around $15 millions, according to a *Computerworld* article from March 13, 1989, quoting their figures from a study by Cutter Information Corporation, a publishing firm based in Arlington, Massachusetts. The same study predicts an overall increase of software related to AI by 58%.   More optimistic forecasts have NLIs alone topping the half billion dollar mark by 1991 [Johnson 85].

Numbers are misleading, success stories subjective, claims often too optimistic. A case in point is *AI Market*'s predictions from August 1985 that revenues for NLP software would grow by 200% between 1984 and 1985, whereas 1985 actually showed only a 100% increase over 1984. For 1986, *AI Market* [October 1986] predicted a mere 20% increase in revenues, compared to 1985. *AI Market* also predicted in October 1986 that the lion's share of future revenues will be in the sector of integrated NLP products, and that "450,000 software packages, mostly on PCs, will be shipped with integrated natural language interfaces [by 1990]".   Predictions by Dataquest, Inc. [See Figure 11–3] in 1988 are closer to the average of all the above.

Market predictions are hard to make for an area so R&D–oriented and embryonic as NLP. Many of the scenarios that have been proposed are overly optimistic. The technology is still too young to allow firm long–range predictions. The bottom line of the natural language biz is: there is a lot of money in it – on the customer side in terms of cost savings and increase in productivity, and on the vendor side in terms of a wide open market. The pervasive problem with market prediction for NL is that there is no established market. Every time a new NLP product is introduced, it has to help create its own market, which makes it twice as hard for a product to succeed.

In the 1980s, there has been a modest amount of money in the NLI market. More consolidated money makers are speech technologies, spelling–checkers, and eventually grammar–checkers. The big money in the near future will be text databases, retrieval and update. The real pay–off of all the rigmarole and contortions which NLI aficionados, high tech grammarians, and venture capitalists have had to go through to get an NLI operational

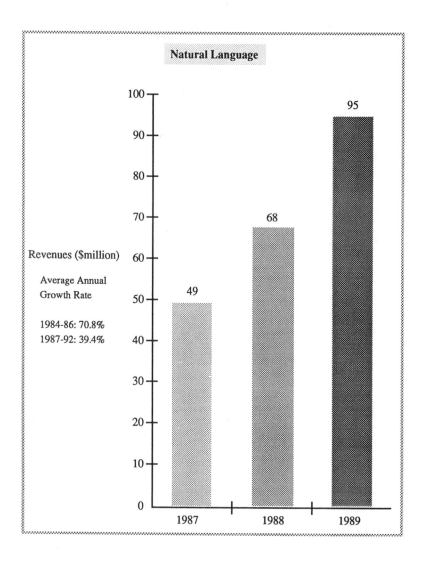

Figure 11-3:   The NLP industry;
Source: Dataquest, Inc., 1988

will come when people will design NL systems that read text, structure it for efficient and effective retrieval, and ultimately become the key to coping successfully with the information explosion. The trend toward the personal computer and the integration into everyday applications software (e.g., Q&A, HAL) will continue. Along with electronic publishing, electronic mail, and more advanced telecommunications, NLP systems will skim, translate, interpret, and help to cut down on time spent sorting information.

11.5 CONCLUSION

NLP is often referred to as a technology in search of an application. While it is true that for the pet applications, like accessing databases via NL, the NLP capabilities may be an overkill, in that other interface modes are simpler and more effective, when it comes to text processing, machine translation, and spell correcting – obvious applications – NLP systems will be commercially viable, if they can be made to work properly and the end-user can be instructed to use optimally the NLP capabilities of the available products.

The current situation is best characterized by the "wait-and-see" attitude of the major US computer companies. The primary reason is definitely that NL products are a high-risk proposition in view of the many potential disasters. The prime reason for taking the risk of selling an NL capability to converse with your programs, thus bypassing fourth generation languages and the command language of the operating system(s), is far too attractive and lucrative a proposition for that market not to be exploited.

Japan and Europe will become the leaders in NLP technology, especially in the area of speech, NLIs, and machine translation. Granted that, at the moment, the technology is not mature enough to make huge profits, but positioning products early, in no matter how limited a way, may prove to guarantee big pay-offs later. It comes as no surprise that the Japanese government will support the ATR telephone dialog translation research project for many years to come without expecting major pay-offs anytime soon. The same is true for Europe's EUROTRA machine translation project that is in its second decade. As the global marketplace becomes multi-lingual as a result of Japanese and growing European economic power, it will become necessary to move from one language to another to realize short-term opportunities. NLP technology is still an expensive endeavor. Pay-offs are not immediate, since basic research is called for to at least assess the limits of the technology for certain applications. Investors generally do not go for low ticket items.

In the short term (1995), the majority of commercial applications will be fourth generation code generators and report writers with a modicum of intelligence.   In the mid term (2000), speech will influence the market to pique investors' interest with all the possibilities of incorporating speech processing into applications ranging from the "Etherphone" to robot control. Text understanding systems will be a mature and prosperous part of the NLP industry.   In the long term (2010), the day-to-day interaction with the computer will be in NL, for a deluge of applications ranging from automated programming to supercomputing. NL will be the computer language of the future. Three major developments will establish NLP products as a new genre of software:

- The emergence of powerful speech technology will obviate the use of the keyboard.

- The world-wide integration of telecommunication and computer technology will make NLP a necessity.

- The change in user attitudes and product quality will increase the demand for NLP products.

The most important lesson that people in the NLP business have learned from the past decades of commercializing software can be summed up in the adage: "When you are working with the cutting edge of technology, the main thing is to stay behind the blade".

11.6 SUGGESTED READING

The most recent book on "Applied Natural language Processing" [Shwartz 87] looks at the possibilities from a Schankian point of view. The book is very good at highlighting the AI approach without discussing the merits of other schools of thought. A somewhat older version of the state of the art books is Tim Johnson's "Natural Language Computing: The Commercial Applications" [Johnson 85].   It contains a wealth of information, unfortunately already slightly dated and at times too anecdotal.   The same holds true for Reitman's "Artificial Intelligence Applications for Business" [Reitman 84] which contains an entire section on "Natural Language Communications".   For up-to-date information, the reader is to consult trade publications (e.g., *Computerworld, Digital News*), newsletters such as *The Spang Robinson Report* that carried valuable data, primarily on NLIs, and *AI Markets*.

CHAPTER 12

NLP - A SCIENCE BY ITSELF.

Personally speaking, I don't really care if we're practicing science as long as we can say we're learning something. [lehn88, page 125]

NLP has been all things to everyone: for the linguist NLP provided a rationale for better grammar formalisms, for the AI researchers NLP meant sexier models, and for the cognitive scientist it became a platform for loftier ideas. Furthermore, for the business world and the government NLP has become the key to having an edge over the competition. This chameleon-like existence promoted fights between the science factions as to the choice of epistemology ("what is the subject of study?") and methodology ("what are the tools for the investigation) [dres76]. The dynamics of the situation did not improve over time, especially when it came to the hefty infusion of monies from industry and government sponsors who were at a loss to know which faction owned the philosopher's stone. Consequently, similar research went on in parallel, often without any real commercial or practical gain. The results in the form of reports or toy systems defied thorough evaluation for lack of sensible gauges. It is for these reasons that NLP must be considered a science by itself. Only then can it promote objective progress without being hindered by ideologies and self-interest.

Before defining what NLP as a science should encompass, let us first ask what linguistics as a science is. Science, by definition shows the order of the subject under study. In linguistics, language is the subject under study. Language lacks, according to Yngve [Yngve 86], a real-world object and therefore cannot be tested against physical reality. Consequently, "language is not something that can be studied scientifically in any strict sense; and it is not an abstraction or model or theory of anything, for there is nothing for it to be an abstraction, model or theory of" [Yngve 86, page 16]. Yngve's contention is that language has to be studied by investigating its functional role in society as a means to communicate knowledge and information [see section 1.3 and Figure 1-5 for a comparison between linguistics and other sciences.]. In my opinion then, it is the functionalism of language that should be at the core of any NLP endeavor. Functionalism in the sense of the information processing tasks that language performs.

NLP in the 1980s shows a bewildering variety of research, ranging from the meticulous analysis of language structure to modeling human everyday language. In general, NLP programs simulate some aspect of how humans use NL or how researchers analyze NL. Various academic disciplines studied NL before the computer age began: linguists looking for universal principles that underlie all languages, philosophers searching for the essence of truth, and psychologists analyzing language as the code to the inner self. The computer as the new metaphor of how the mind works changed the outlook on the study of NL completely: linguists-turned-high-tech grammarians saw the computer as a testing device for their laboriously worked out grammars, while some psychologists and philosophers turned AI gurus saw the computer as part of their theories.

Computer scientists studied formal languages for compilers and started comparing them to natural languages such as English. NLP has always been defined and used to further the specific research interest of various academic disciplines. While researchers are ill-advised to tackle NLP problems using ATNs, NLP is ill-suited for addressing the issue of the psychological realism of the created program, i.e., whether the emulation is a psychological model for how humans perform the NLP tasks. But once NLP is out of the quagmire of self-serving academic politics, what epistemology and methodology is suitable for NLP as a science by itself? What role does the technology play?

12.1 EPISTEMOLOGY

Based on the classic distinction made by McCarthy and Hayes [McCarthy 69] that the AI problem has an epistemological and a heuristic part, AI research has focused on the dichotomy between the representation and the processing of knowledge. NLP systems require large knowledge bases. There have been few attempts at constructing knowledge bases for NLP systems in a principled way: "It is well known that the interpretation of natural language discourse can require arbitrarily detailed world knowledge and that a sophisticated natural language system must have a large knowledge base. But heretofore, the knowledge bases in NLP systems have either encoded only a few kinds of knowledge - e.g., sort hierarchies - or facts in only narrow domains" [Hobbs 84].

AI research brought to the fore what linguists have chosen to overlook: that language is a knowledge based process which requires an account of how the linguistic information processing relates to other cognitive processes as well as to the real world. Just as AI is often defined as the study of what intelligence is and how to put it into a computer, NLP can be defined as the study of what NL is and how to put it into a computer. The analogy ends here, however, for the following reasons: language, and in particular its use, relies in one form or another on intelligence. No, it does not equal intelligence, nor is it a sign of intelligence. Determining what knowledge about information processing one stands to gain from NLP programs should take center stage for establishing a new science in the first place. The real issue for NLP as a science is the role of NLP in information processing including knowledge acquisition, memory organization, and discourse interaction. Without sidetracking on issues such as language universals, computer intentionality or formalism debate, answers to the right questions will no doubt surface. Here are some of the right questions to ask to promote scientific progress:

What is the basic unit of linguistic analysis? - The basic unit of linguistic analysis is the utterance - the string of words governed by syntactic, semantic, and pragmatic principles. It is not the sentence, scripts, or microfeatures. There should be a distinction made between the symbolic level and subsymbolic level of analysis. Speech, for instance, should be analyzed on the subsymbolic level.

What are the specific processes for spoken, written, and typed input? - It is a common misconception that, whatever the basic processing unit is, all aspects involved in understanding NL share the same characteristics. For instance, the argument that it matters little for the overall analysis if an utterance is spoken, typed or written, is misleading since the perceptual processes are different for processing the various modes of input. For speech systems, for instance, there is a lot of uncertainty about the input, whereas with typed input, barring typographical errors, the NLP system can start analyzing at the word level. Moreover, the perceptual cues in the different input modes are different, e.g., intonation, figures of speech, and writing style.

What, if the computer processes NL, does this tell me about human NLP? - The most basic misconception in exploring NLP is starting out with the question, "What can the computer tell us about human cognitive abilities like language?", and then proceeding to model psychologically real processes. The fundamental differences between silicon and carbon based life only allow for a functional comparison and therefore each should be evaluated on its own terms. The issue boils down to setting priorities. For an operational program it matters very little if there are inklings of psychological realism in the way the program processes NL. Even for the theoretical, strictly academic endeavor, it matters little; and yet, many researchers are obsessed with the idea of constructing similes of the human mind, however poorly understood its behavior may be.

12.2 METHODOLOGY

The methodology of NLP is straightforward: develop a theory, program it, and study the behavior of the program to test your theory [Tennant 81, page 3]. Before the computer age, to form a theory and defend it required empirical evidence or stringent logical deduction. With the advent of computer programs, the fact that there was an unbiased device that would repeat the same process multiple times added another method to forming a theory: simulation. Simulation introduced many questions into the process of evaluating a theory, not the least of which was what weight the computer program ultimately carried.

From the academic or scientific perspective the role of the computer program is a controversial issue. "Is the program a theory?", or "Is the theory the program?" are questions leading to fierce disputes among different factions engaged in NLP research. In general, if NLP is viewed as a symbolic process, similar to the processing of formal languages, the computer program assists in testing the power of the formalism ; if NLP is viewed as cognitive process, the behavior of the program may speak to the psychological realism of the theory the program is based on. In the former case, the computer acts as a tool for testing a theory; in the latter, the computer is part of the theory.

In the early 1980s, the AI community adopted the "neat" versus "scruffy" dichotomy to characterize different methodological styles [Abelson 81]. The recent trend in NLP to consider mass processing facilities (e.g., digitized texts and dictionaries) to conduct empirical studies and the immediate adverse reaction of some linguists is reminiscent of this situation. While the "scruffies" have a desire to confront real life problems, the "neats" often feel that such endeavors are futile. To illustrate my point, consider the following tell-tale quotes from *TINLAP 3* in 1987 from two NLP researchers with opposing views who state the problem of NLP as follows:

> For example, why don't a group of us take the best parser, the best semantic interpreter, the best generator, the best inference system, etc., and tie them together? Then let's pick a domain of discourse and make them work for more than a few sentences. Let's beat on them until they work for as much language as they appear capable. [Sondheimer 87, page 119]

> NLP is desperate for good methods whereby contextual constraints can be brought to bear in a timely fashion to help resolve such problems as lexical and structural language analysis. Lexical selection has received far too little attention in generation research. The problem of controlling search remains virtually untouched. [Birnbaum 87, page 122]

Sondheimer in his statement focuses on the quantitative aspect of NLP (e.g., "until they work for as much language as they appear capable"), whereas Birnbaum emphasizes the qualitative aspect of NLP research (e.g., "good methods"). Linguists for the most part strive to tackle the big picture – exploring what makes Language [sic], not language, while AI scientists look at empirically sound models of language research. Linguists brought up in the structural orientation of language investigation are diametrically opposed to the emphasis that AI research has placed on functional aspects of NLP.

From a theoretical perspective the question of what approach to language study the researcher adopts depends on what aspect of language he is interested in. The researchers who are interested in mathematical or statistical aspects of NLP will select theories oriented around one of the many (formal) grammar-oriented models, those who look for psychological or biological based theories will turn to the psychological studies of memory and cognition or neurology research, respectively. The problem with this approach to selecting methodologies is that NLP is bound to become very heterogeneous. If there is no widely accepted and adhered to methodology, how can progress be made and measured?

From a practical perspective, the choice of the programming formalism for NLP is secondary to the question of what approach to choose. Ideally the formalism accommodates the theory. In general, the formalism only supports the computational modeling of a theory. The question of what an NLP formalism contributes to the theory is controversial, often tainted by personal convictions.

One of the reasons for having made so little progress in NLP is the fact that for decades linguists have established the notion of the primacy and autonomy of syntax. Concurrently, they defined the sentence as the significant unit of language investigation, everything else taking a backseat. The skewed picture was only partially attacked when AI researchers, especially Roger Schank [Schank 75], constructed semantic based functioning NLP systems using iconoclastic theories, and when AI engineers revamped linguistic theories (e.g., case grammar) for implementation [Bruce 75]. The latest trend is, however, a regression of sorts, because, as Birnbaum points out, "but now that the linguists (and philosophers) have turned their attention to semantics in a serious way, these *ad hoc* AI theories can and should be replaced by implementations of the far more rigorous products of our brethren science" [Birnbaum 87, page 120].

The AI paradigm provides a good methodology for dealing with the open-ended research issues in NLP. The idea of building programs for problems which are not well understood at the outset is characteristic of NLP. Whereas in the orthodox approach to theory formation, the test/implementation of the theory follows the formulation of the theory itself; for the AI approach, the test/implementation stage is part of the theory formation. The nature of evidence that a functioning program may hold by itself is discussed elsewhere [Obermeier 85b]. Suffice it to say that theories backed by implementations are easily falsifiable. The notion of psychological realism in NLP appears to be the ultimate red herring of the scientific endeavor of finding something truly interesting towards enabling computer programs to use a natural language.

ATNs, for instance, the most unconstrained formalism in NLP as a whole, have been used as tools and abused as similes of the mind. Theoretically, they are much too unconstrained to be used as anything but elaborate, yet elegant flowcharts. Unfortunately, half of the current NLP programs use ATNs as recognizers with backtracking and as generators with unbounded linguistic planning. The argument that if a program shows mistakes or behaviors similar to a native speaker, the theory must be right is fallacious because (1) almost any language anomaly can be illustrated by some deviant idiolect, no matter what; (2) precious little is known about the human mind and its language capability.

Psychological evidence is cited for the Wait-and-See parser that Marcus proposed in PARSIFAL. By the same token, McDonald, in his MUMBLE NL generation program claims that the tactical errors the program makes while putting together a grammatical utterance are evidence for its correctness, proving MIT's new Occam's razor that constrains linguistic theories in Chomsky fashion to syntactic finesse. 20 years ago, in the wake of beginning aphasia studies, it was erroneously held that there are indeed distinct areas of the brain responsible for distinct levels of processing (e.g., syntactic, semantic). An even more fundamental lack of psychological realism for language processing is applicable to laboratory experiments. Ever since Bartlett in his landmark book *Remembering* described how eliciting nonsense syllables and other insane tests must strike anyone, psychiatric patient or not, as bizarre; word recall tests, phoneme monitoring, etc., have been seen as procedures that at least skew the issues of "naturally" occurring language understanding.

The notion of naturally occurring language causes another, more far-reaching fallacy among NL researchers: to equate discourse modeling between humans with that of man-computer interaction. The common wisdom is summarized in a recent article on "Modeling the user in natural language systems" [Kass 88, page 5] as follows: "The use of natural language for communication includes a host of conventions that must be followed in dialog [Grice 75]. A person interacting with a computer via natural language will assume that these conventions are being followed, and will be quite unsatisfied if they are not". This "arm-chair" modeling approach is quite in contrast with empirical investigations described in [Hauptmann 87] that found: "People speaking to a computer are more disciplined than when speaking to each other. There are significant differences in the usage of the spoken language compared to typed language, and several phenomena which are unique to spoken or typed input respectively". Both methods to model linguistic behavior are worthwhile endeavors in academic terms. Their respective pursuit will without a doubt result in different models and theories. The need for an academic discipline called "NLP" is evident to determine what methodology, if any, should be followed, and to prevent that epistemological arguments are fraught by methodological misunderstandings.

12.3 TECHNOLOGY

Technological innovations in hardware and software have created a synergism with the methodology in the form of rapid prototyping. The programming language paradigms are expanding: functional, logical, and now object-oriented systems have been firmly established. While it has always been possible to conceive of different levels of structure and independent knowledge sources, object-oriented programming supports the computer modeling of these ideas. Technology driven innovations, however, are not as significant for advancing the state of the art of NLP as problem driven innovations. The former provide opportunities for the latter. Take object-oriented programming, for instance.

The basic notion of the object–oriented approach to software can best be understood by comparison with the more traditional subroutine approach to programming. The decomposition of a problem in the subroutine approach is in terms of software modules which call on other modules to accomplish specific tasks, while in the object–oriented approach, the decomposition is one of active agents which call other agents to perform behaviors of which they are capable. Even though on first inspection, the approaches seem very similar on the dimension of decomposition, the object–oriented approach is much more amenable to the classic software notion of data abstraction, and in fact, it much more strongly embodies the ability to provide software modularity.

To extend a system written following the subroutine approach, it is often necessary to change a great deal of existing code. However, to the extent the initial problem decomposition was adequate, extending a system written following the object–oriented approach typically will involve creating a few agents in the system or specializing the behaviors of agents already in the system. Not only is this specialization process rather easy to accomplish, but it also offers minimal impact on the remainder of the code, thus demanding far less testing of the modified system (which is the objective of software modularity). This process of specialization provides much of the power of the object–oriented approach.

Because the notion of data abstraction is an integral part of the object-oriented approach, debugging an object–oriented system is typically easier than debugging a conventionally written program. This is because the interaction of behaviors of agents of an object–oriented system is well-defined and standard, thus allowing for testing of agent behavior in isolation to accomplish most of the system testing. Typically, testing the interaction of modules in a conventional system takes most of the time, and occasionally can severely impact the code within modules. In a nutshell: object–oriented programming is powerful because the metaphor of a number of active agents working together to solve a problem is powerful. For NLP, using object oriented programming techniques means having the ability to encode non-linear and multilevel processes without creating new constructs.

By the same token, neural network technology will contribute to NLP by (1) allowing for the processing of large amounts of data, (2) providing techniques to cope with speech, and (3), integrating conventional computing techniques into the connectionist models. Whereas NLP was a symbolic process, after connectionism took the stage, NLP showed a dichotomy between symbolic and subsymbolic processes. From a technological point of view, the future of neural networks apart from theoretical advances, depends on the technologies that support the speed and storage requirements. Currently, a fly has two orders of magnitude faster interconnects per second that the fastest tool available. Improvements in speed will be supported in the short term by the development of digital processing chips, gallium arsenide chips and in the future by optical computing devices.

Because NLP requires large resources to be effective, technological advances are an important aspect of the progress. The change from Assembler language to Lisp, Prolog or C and the improvements in the hardware accelerated NLP research in the past decade.   Clearly, the old algorithms, ATN's, have been shown not to provide the desired results. New ideas and trends do not guarantee immediate solutions to problems.   It is not in the hardware, software or wetware that the solution to NLP lies; it is in the problem driven innovation where scientific progress is made.   Ultimately, it matters little whether the problem is solved in Prolog, Lisp or Smalltalk, or if unification or connectionism is the answer. More often than not, approaches to NLP are selected because they are in vogue in other disciplines. A case in point is the adoption of parallel distributed processing for case grammar analysis introducing a new form (e.g., terminology), but not a new substance. While it is definitely sexier to label semantic primitives microfeatures rather than features, the label will not change their randomness, or, what is even more to the point, show any progress in advancing the state of the art. The very fact that an outdated and controversial theory gets implemented in another paradigm without questioning its validity in the new or in the old paradigm is a sign of how scientists mistake NLP for an add-on to other sciences.   Consequently, NLP has to become a science by itself to make progress possible.

12.4 HISTORY OF NLP

The history of NLP has been controversial with many failures and unrealistic expectations due to the "AI trap" phenomenon. Carver Mead describes the AI trap as:

> You announce that you are going to do a really hard problem. And then you start working on it and you find out that, not only is it a very hard problem, it's ORDERS OF MAGNITUDE harder than you imagined. So then, of course, you do what every good scientist does: you go back to a problem that you can solve. When

I went to school, a professor of mine said, "You keep simplifying a problem until it goes away, and then you go back one." Of course, you can solve that problem by definition, so you solve it. And then you make a little demo of that, which you can make pretty convincing nowadays, thanks to our beautiful digital computers. And then you announced to the press that you've solved the problem [Mead 87].

The "AI trap" might just as well be called the "NLP trap" because similar incidents can be cited, starting with the overblown expectations of early machine translation endeavors that resulted in the ALPAC report, and ending with the many "success" stories of NLIs that are really moderate by commercial standards. If NLP avoids the trap of overstating goals and massaging the data, real progress is possible.

The history of NLP spans four decades [see Figure 12-1]. In 1950, machine translation was the area of interest and funding. The boom ended with the ALPAC report concluding the infeasibility of MT projects. The MT researchers split into two groups: one group continued with computational linguistics and began developing formalisms, the other group focused on the motivating new linguistic theories. Chomsky's mathematical theory of linguistics was introduced. Yngve provided one of the first context-free formalism for implementing grammars.

In the 1960s the new field of AI created hopes for NLP, with the realization that NLP could be the proof for many cognitive issues, not just the Turing test. Weizenbaum and his program ELIZA contributed to a dampening of the enthusiasm. ELIZA [Weizenbaum 66] was based on the idea of modeling the responses of a Rogerian psychologist to his patients. ELIZA created the illusion that it could respond to human input in an "intelligent" manner. In reality, ELIZA could respond only to preprogrammed patterns. Fillmore injected semantic considerations into the study of language. Kay began devising a chart parsing algorithm.

In the 1970s Terry Winograd's SHRDLU program [Winograd 72] showed in a very small application how an NLP program could mediate between a robot and a human. SHRDLU showed the complexity of NLP and its promise. It made use of current technology but did not address problems that were at the core of NLP. The Schankian school of thought dominated the 1970s and later the 1980s. The idea of modeling levels of NLP reaching into memory organization defined a new research program: NLP as knowledge based problem solving. Woods provided an alternative to Schank by using ATNs for NLP. Marcus tested Chomsky's theory of the autonomy of syntax in his deterministic parser Parsifal. The commercial sector showed interest in NLIs.

	NLP Theories and Approaches		Parsing Formalisms		System Applications
1950	'57 Chomsky Syntactic Structures		'58 'Yngve COMIT		**Machine Translation** GAT METAL LOGOS TAUM
1960	'68 Fillmore Case Grammar		'66 Weizenbaum Templates	'67 Kay Chart	**Domain Modeling** ELIZA BASEBALL
1970	'74 Winograd SHRDLU	'75 Schank Conceptual Dependency	'70 Woods ATN Earley	'75 Marcus Determinism	**Natural Language Interfaces**
1980	'80 Gazdar GPSG	'82 Cottrell Connectionism	'84 Shieber Unification PATR-II		RUS INTELLECT MIND EXPLORER PHILQA2 CHAT 80 MARGIE JANUS LADDER IRUS HEARSAY NLQ

Figure 12-1:   Milestones

In the 1980s, the initial success of Intellect, a NLP system for databases seemed to have opened a market for NLP technology. Chomsky's transformational model was challenged. Context-free phrase structure grammars became the new paradigm in linguistics. The unification operation was adopted in formalisms and grammatical theories. AI research was still dominated by Schank. Connectionism introduced the level of subsymbolic processing into NLP.

For the 1990s, the user based modeling of intelligent systems will lay the groundwork for commercially viable knowledge based NLP systems [Kobsa 88]. NL frontends for text databases will act as "filters" for the information seeking public.

12.5 TRENDS

Research in linguistics over the past twenty years has been under the influence of the Chomskyan paradigm of generative grammar which tried to provide a rigorous and concise description of language. The goal of Chomsky and his followers was to decide on formal grounds if a (grammatical) sentence belonged to a language or not. According to Chomsky's theory, the linguistic system can be divided into a native speaker's competence, i.e., the system of linguistic rules of a native speaker, and performance, the applications of linguistic rules. The realm of generative grammar is to study the linguistic competence of an idealized speaker, i.e., the rules which determine the grammaticality of a particular sentence. Linguistic performance, viz., how language is comprehended and produced, belonged in the realm of psycholinguistics.

Research in AI has been based on the assumption that language should be studied by looking at linguistic processes observed in human linguistic behavior. Schank summarized the goal of computational NLP: "Natural language researchers within AI thus had to come to grips with the fact that they would have to build their own theories of the linguistic process" [Schank 81]. Since humans are still the only organisms which understand language with all its complexities, NL research within AI has been dominated by the modelling of linguistic performance.

The gap between AI and linguistics widened when it came to determining what phenomena of language understanding should be investigated and how they could be tested. For the Chomskyan linguist, hypotheses about language were confined to phenomena within single sentences; for the AI researcher, hypotheses about language encompassed all aspects of cognitive processing. Consequently, linguists could establish well-defined formal criteria for testing

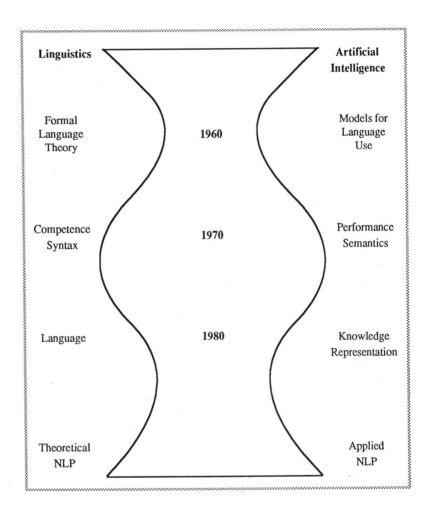

Figure 12-2:   Trends

their hypotheses on carefully selected fragments of English, whereas the AI researchers had to resort to the Turing test or a vague notion of understanding as in the following excerpt:

> A computer understands a subset of English if it accepts input sentences which are members of this subset and answers questions based on information contained in the input [Bobrow 68].

Criticism of Chomsky's syntactically oriented theory arose, however, from within linguistics. After a short and unsuccessful attempt by the generative semanticists to extend Katzian [Katz 64] lexical semantics, Montague [Montague 74] and later Barwise and Perry [Barwise 83] proposed formal semantic accounts for fragments of English. Montague grammar has led to an impasse because his strategy seems to have been "to devise a construct in the formal language for each construct in the natural language" [Brady 83] which thus far has not been applied to a significant fragment of any natural language.

The current state of affairs in NLP is characterized by on-going changes both within linguistics and AI. In linguistics, an increasing number of researchers follow the semantic or pragmatic route while at the same time learning about computers and how they can be applied to NLP. In AI, research is under way to provide criteria of how to evaluate computational theories within cognitive science [Doyle 83, Pylyshyn 84] and the implemented knowledge representation techniques [Touretzky 84]. These endeavors will lead to a better understanding of the programs and their theoretical significance.   AI can draw on results from the current investigation of linguistic methodology, viz., what information processing tasks the various modules of a system perform. AI will also profit from the change in linguistics from transformational grammar to phrase structure grammar which is computationally more tractable.

NLP can also profit from commonly developed tools for different aspects of systems building. The text encoding initiative shows promising beginnings of concerted efforts in the area of encoding and dissemination of machine-readable texts for multidisciplinary research on texts. Research on large bodies of text will bring NLP closer to real life applications and make it more useful than its previous concentration on selected problems.

12.6 CONCLUSION

There ·is not yet a unified field of study called NLP. Rather disparate academic disciplines try to engulf the mainstream NLP thrust. This has lead to serious difficulties in the past and does not bode well for the future. Three major factors have contributed to the disarray of NLP:

- Too much attention was paid to the classic linguistic and computer science disciplines, which used the opportunity to promote their own agendas and grants.

- Commercialization began too early.

- Too many open research problems exist to continue with existing paradigms.

The current state of NLP from a scientific standpoint raises serious questions about its progress. Within each entrenched science dealing with NL (e.g., linguistics, AI, philosophy), NLP has been touted as test case, goal, existence proof, etc. While it is true that more sentence types can be parsed faster than ten years ago, the insights gained from their analysis is qualitatively the same. NLP researchers in general underestimate the problem and overstate the results for two reasons: (1) their primary interest lies in scientifically exciting findings (e.g., quantifier scoping, backward anaphora), and (2) their general habit is to belittle commercial systems. AI researchers, after trying in vain to finesse their semantic theories for implementing their models of NLP are now retreating for lack of success and for want of more manageable problems.

The academic perspective on NLP shows a variety of different views of what language is and how it should be studied. Over the past decades, three NLP research thrusts have formed: linguistics, AI, and neural networks. Cognitive science, the latest hybrid discipline dealing with aspects of language by subsuming all of the above, has done little more than gloss over the fundamental differences in the methodologies of the different disciplines by embracing all of them. Rather than focusing the new field "cognitive science" has diffused the notion of NLP. The study of NLP is neither the search for linguistic universals nor artificial mentalese. It should be the study of how machines recognize/produce natural language. The theories of NLP that can describe most comprehensively the process of language understanding are subsymbolic theories that furthermore embody the idea of neural network modeling of cognition. "Trying to infer the working of the brain from its neuronal structure (whether real or simulated)", according to Gian Carlo Rota from the Mathematics Department at MIT [Rota 89, page 147], "is like trying to infer the working of the Federal Government by examining the structure of buildings in Washington". Using neural network technology is, nevertheless, a way of constructing workable NLP systems, especially with respect to speech recognition.

It is highly unlikely that given the current state of the art an evolutionary solution can be found. As long as people still base their research on ATNs, there is no solution to even the most fundamental problems in sight. If no attention is paid to making the developing technology marketable up front, the field of NLP will remain heterogeneous with academics battling the businessmen. The new science of NLP should have definite elements of both the business world and academia; however, they should together exhibit a synergism that could support new ways of going about the NLP business. One way of looking at NLP would be from an engineering perspective in which the to-be-created artifact could be labeled as an intelligent agent capable of using English without worrying about the psychological realism of the created algorithm.

This chapter suggests a reorganization of NLP as a scientific and commercial endeavor to construct robust NLP systems, and to explore computational modeling of real people on virtual machines.

12.7 SUGGESTED READING

A good overview of computational linguistics, including a description of the genesis of various approaches can be found in the highly readable anthology [Sparck 83]. Deeper issues of the relationship between linguistic and computational aspects in NLP are discussed in [Whitelock 87]. This book contains position papers and transcripts from a workshop on 'Linguistic Theory and Computer Applications' that was held on September 4–6, 1985 at the Centre for Computational Linguistics of the University of Manchester Institute of Science and Technology. The position papers cover topics ranging from the linguistic application of default inheritance mechanisms and computational psycholinguistics to deterministic parsing, and Montague grammar's impact on machine translation. The transcripts from the discussion sessions include lively interchanges on topics such as syntax-semantics interfaces, the lexicon, translation, and speculation of what lies beyond linguistic theory.

EPILOG

This effort shall include the development of a "descriptive terminology" with which software components for processing Natural Language [NL] can be described in a standard way. The Descriptive Terminology shall be a collection of non-subjective terms with associated definitions for describing NL interface components, and procedures for applying the resulting terminology in a consistent manner. [quoted from a request-for-proposal announcement by Rome Air Development Center on November 2, 1988.]

There have been numerous attempts to get a handle on evaluating, if not standardizing NLIs: Harry Tennant [Tennant 79] who introduced the distinction between linguistic and conceptual coverage, IBM by trying to establish a corpus of sentences that would function as a standard set, and other companies have tried in vain to get rid of subjective criteria and to achieve consistency. Benchmarks are in principle double-edged swords: too many variables can skew the outcome. With NLIs in particular and NLP systems in general, the setup may vary considerably, thus leaving it up to anybody's guess how good the algorithm really is. Apart from the lack of standard terminologies and methodologies, the quoted project description points to the underlying cause of the current disarray in NLP: there is no good infrastructure of the NLP technology because it does not constitute a discipline of its own. NLP today has to borrow its descriptive apparatus from many disciplines. What AI people at Carnegie Mellon University and Stanford refer to as "knowledge source", linguists at other institutions refer to as "level of representation". The lack of a common terminology for NLP technology is not the cause but the symptom for the lack of a unified and scientific approach to NLP.

NLP poses hard problems for the scientific and commercial sectors. On the surface, there are problems simply arising out of the sheer tasks of capturing what it takes to process much less to understand language and identifying a lucrative niche in the marketplace. These problems are augmented by the fact that mainstream NLP currently is pursuing the wrong approaches for commercialization of the technology, and the expectation of the computer user is too high for NLP technologies. Moreover, many scientists believe that before commercialization begins, all problems should be solved in a scientifically orderly manner.   In brief, the current state of the art of NLP is determined by people asking the wrong questions for applying NLP technologies. Empirical proof for this statement lies in the little progress that has been made and the touting of ten and twenty-year-old algorithms as the state of the art.

Here are some of the right questions that we raised in the Preface:

Will NLP increase productivity, and if so, how?   All too often a technology is looking for applications. For truly innovative ideas, e.g., spreadsheet, it is a viable way to become successful. For the majority of programs, however, the market orientation should be established before the R&D dollars are spent. Barring breakthroughs of technology, such as the Macintosh-style interfaces and the establishment of standards like SQL, NL interfaces, for instance, would still be second to none as the natural way to access data bases effectively and generically.   The ease-of-use question with NLP products is not a technological problem but a people problem. What the user really needs is a tool that increases his performance without changing his habits too much. By the same token, a structured input screen for updating data bases is easier to use than a NLI because the clerk does not have to think or run the risk of forgetting to input necessary information.

NLIs, for instance will help not only the infrequent end user but also the system programmer. His time is freed from answering user requests.   Even for a "power user" who knows SQL, constructing a query in the proper syntax may take many times longer than typing in the English equivalent. The database as a repository of company information is more effectively used.   The productivity gain is two-fold: the end user access is timely and less costly, and the system programmer can focus on writing application programs. Naisbitt in his book *Megatrends* contends: "The new source of power is not money in the hands of few but information in the hands of many."

What criteria are relevant for evaluating NLP systems?   The idea of economists of satisficing [sic] the customer is based on the all-too-human habit of acquiring necessities without going through the trouble of comparing at great length the benefits of alternatives. Everything else being equal, purchasing behavior is geared towards buying something that at the time fulfills the current need – satisfices – regardless of its becoming obsolete or possibly requiring replacement in the near future. Software manufacturers quickly learned that providing a certain functionality without going overboard on the bells and whistles is the easiest and least painful way of making a profit. The idea that "quality sells" is only of limited validity;

especially with software. The marketplace has established unwritten rules whereby a certain margin of error is acceptable regardless of the question of how little it would have taken to avoid mistakes in the first place.

The only criteria for evaluating NLP systems so far have been extremely subjective: either they work or they do not. Still there is much leeway in determining what it really means that a NLP system works. We have seen that language makes infinite use of finite means. Therefore, many utterances cannot be anticipated by any NLP system unless the processing capability is similar to that of humans including common sense knowledge. Ultimately it will become necessary to require a certain degree of learning from the NLP system. Until then, however, much can be achieved by using the existing systems with the adequate education.

What products are available now and will be in the future? The setup cost of NLP systems is still very high. The identification of vertical and diagonal markets will help to cut down on the initial setup costs because the NLP software has already been customized up to a point. The trade-off occurs where one can provide basic functionality at low cost and high functionality for select applications that have a pay-back commensurate with the customization effort. NLP systems will become successful once they become commodities at a fair price.

Mundane applications, such as spelling and grammar checking are just the beginning for future fully automated document handling. The notion of "shareware" or "groupware", supporting electronic brainstorming over networked computers will increase the productivity of the office of the future. Speech recognition systems will help integrate voice, telecommunication, and computing. Advances in text understanding will allow people to filter information from more resources than ever before. The advent of intelligent manuals and electronic books that "react" to the reader's needs will revolutionize the notion of learning. Many of the innovative applications for computers will be driven by NLP technology.

In the future, NLP technology will become necessary for helping people cope with the information glut and the multitude of interface protocols. The information glut manifests itself on the micro- and macrocosmic levels. With the advances in telecommunications, more people communicate with more people more often. Electronic mail, and voice mail boxes will make it necessary and desirable that low-level decisions - for instance, where to set up a meeting and what the topics will be - are delegated to the smart front-ends to these electronic pools of information. Voice mail boxes eventually extend into intelligent calendars.

The microlevel of communication, personal interactions, will be handled on a low level by NLP systems.   The standards set by the *Integrated Services Digital Network*, or *ISDN* will help integrate voice and data transfer, whereas projects such as the *Etherphone* will help extend the workstation environments to include telephone, recorded voice, and computer data processing. Besides expedience, NLP capabilities satisfy Naisbitt's "high tech, high touch" requirement for integrating technological advances into everyday life without disruption.

On the macrolevel, the sheer number of publications, greatly exacerbated by electronic publishing technology, will make "gisting" and storing of information at one's fingertips a necessity. Hypertext, Judgement or J–space, and cluster analysis will help greatly. The real issue, however, is to integrate these components into a viable NLP system. In the global marketplace, translation capabilities will be required given Japan's growing influence and the cohesion of the European Common Market.

On the fringes of the NLP technology are bionic devices that would aid in cases of impairment or loss of certain language capabilities. Once viable NLP technology is down to the chip level, artifacts supporting aphasics, deaf people etc., will greatly improve the quality of life for the handicapped. NLP systems could become part of computing devices that would serve as companions for the aged. Computer assisted therapy is another way of employing the technology for improving the employees mental health. In some computer assisted programs employees have access to a Therapeutic Learning program that supports their counseling sessions. While this program is a menu–driven expert system that helps people analyze their problems, it shows that people are a lot more open, even trusting, with a computer program. In an interview, an employee using the system pointed out that she felt she had to be totally honest with the program because otherwise it would not work properly. NLP adds an anthropomorphic element to computing that should not be underestimated.

Internationally, the biggest boom in NLP technology can be expected from Europe and Japan, especially in the areas of machine translation and NLIs. Europeans are by and large more language conscious than people living in the U.S. because Europeans have accepted and adapted to the fact that there exists a multitude of languages in a small vicinity. Moreover, the cultural predisposition of computer users (formed by education and habit) for using NLP technology effectively without expecting too much, will help the industry to establish itself. Europeans have thus far been spared the unrealistic hype that undermined the initial ground swell of enthusiasm for the technology in the U.S. Japan experiences a growing demand for machine translation, much more so than for NL interfaces.

In conclusion, NLP technology is here to stay. It will change drastically its own infrastructure as more and more disciplines discover its relevance for their own advancement. NLP technology also will change the infrastructure of everyday computing by providing capabilities for the computer neophyte as well as for the expert on different levels of sophistication. NLP systems, if properly developed, will become the most successful software genre.

REFERENCES

The number of publications on NLP is skyrocketing. A useful bibliography for references including 1986 is in [Gazdar 87]. The best way to keep up to date on the various topics is to consult *Computational Linguistics*, published quarterly by the *Association for Computational Linguistics*, *AI Magazine*, published by the *American Association for Artificial Intelligence*, *Artificial Intelligence*, published by *North Holland*, and *Neural Networks* published by *Pergamon Press* and the *International Neural Network Society*. In addition these three associations sponsor annual conferences whose presentations are published in proceedings that contain recently completed research.

Other sources of timely publications are the large research organizations that publish technical reports on their work, in particular: *Carnegie Mellon University*, Department of Computer Science, Schenley Park, Pittsburgh, Pennsylvania 15213; *Stanford Research Institute*, Menlo Park, California 94025 *Information Science Institute*, 4676 Admiralty Way, Marina del Rey, California 90292; *Bolt, Beranek and Newman*, 10 Moulton Street, Cambridge, Massachusetts 02238.

[Abelson 81]   Abelson.
                Constraint, Construal, and Cognitive Science.
                In *Proceedings of the Third Annual Conference of the
                   Cognitive Science Society*. 1981.

[Allen 87a]   Allen, J.
                Natural Language Understanding.
                Benjamin/Cummings, 1987.

[Allen 87b]   Allen, J., Hunnicutt, M.S., Klatt, D., Armstrong, R.C., Pisoni,
                D.
                From Text to Speech: The MITalk System.
                Cambridge University Press, 1987.

[Appelt 82]   Appelt, D.E.
                *Planning Natural-Language Utterances to Satisfy
                   Multiple Goals. (Technical Note 259)*.
                Technical Report, SRI International, 1982.

[Appelt 87]   Appelt, D.E.
                Bidirectional Grammars and the Design of Natural Language
                   Generation Systems.
                In *Theoretical Issues in Natural Language Processing
                   3. Position Papers*, pages 206-212. 1987.

[Austin 84]   Austin, H.
                Market Trends in Artificial Intelligence.
                *Artificial Intelligence Applications for Business.
                   Proceedings of the NYU Symposium, May, 1983*.
                Ablex Publishing Corporation, 1984.

[Bar-Hillel 60] Bar-Hillel, Y.
                The Present Status of Automatic Translation of Languages.
                Advances in Computers (Volume 1).
                Academic Press, 1960.

[Barrow 79]   Barrow, H.G.
                Artificial Intelligence: State of the Art.
                Technical Report, SRI International, 1979.

[Barwise 83]   Barwise, J. and Perry, J.
                Situations and Attitudes.
                Cambridge University Press, 1983.

[Birnbaum 87]   Birnbaum, L.
                Let's Put the AI Back in NLP.
                In *Theoretical Issues in Natural Language Processing
                   3. Position Papers*, pages 120-123. 1987.

[Bobrow 68]   Bobrow, D.
Natural Language Input for a Computer Problem–solving
   System.
Semantic Information Processing.
MIT Press, 1968.

[Boguraev 82] Boguraev, B.K. and Sparck Jones, J.
How to drive a database front end using general semantic
   information.
1982
University of Cambridge, Computer Laboratory, Technical
   Report No 32.

[Brachman 83] Brachman, R.J. et al.
KRYPTON: A Functional Approach to Knowledge
   Representation.
*IEEE Computer Magazine, Special Issue on
   Knowledge Representation* :67–73, 1983.

[Brachman 85] Brachman, R.J., Levesque, H.J.
Readings in Knowledge Representation.
Morgan Kaufmann, 1985.

[Brady 83]   Brady, M. and Berwick, R.C.
Computational Models of Discourse.
MIT Press, 1983.

[Bresnan 82] Bresnan, J.
The Mental Representation of Grammatical Relations.
MIT Press, 1982.

[Bronnenberg 80]
Bronnenberg, W.J.H.J.
The question answering system PHLIQA 1.
In Bolc, L. (editor), *Natural language question
   answering systems*. Macmillan, 1980.

[Brown 83]   Brown, G., Yule, G.
Discourse Analysis.
Cambridge University Press, 1983.

[Bruce 75]   Bruce, B.
Case Systems for Natural Language.
Artificial Intelligence 6, 1975.

[Carbonell 81] Carbonell, J.G., Cullingford, R.E., Gershman, A.V.
                Steps Toward Knowledge–based Machine Translation.
                *IEEE Transactions on Pattern Analysis and Machine
                    Intelligence PAMI* 3, 1981.

[Carbonell 85] Carbonell, J.G et al.
                The Medsort Project.
                *Final Report on the Automated Classification and
                    Retrieval Project.* , 1985.

[Charniak 72]   Charniak, E.
                Toward a Model of Children's Story Comprehension.
                Technical Report, MIT Artificial Intelligence Laboratory,
                    1972.

[Charniak 75]   Charniak, E.
                Organization and inference in a frame–like system of
                    common–sense knowledge.
                Theoretical Issues in Natural Language Processing.
                BBN, 1975.

[Charniak 81]   Charniak, E.
                Six Topics in Search of a Parser: An Overview of AI
                    Language Research.
                1981
                Proc. of the Seventh IJCAI.

[Chomsky 63]   Chomsky, N.
                Formal properties of grammars.
                Handbook of Mathematical Psychology, Vol. 2.
                Wiley, 1963.

[Chomsky 65]   Chomsky, N.
                Aspects of the Theory of Syntax.
                MIT Press, 1965.

[Chomsky 82]   Chomsky, N.
                Lectures on Government and Binding.
                Foris, 1982.

[Church 87]   Church, K.W.
                Phonological Parsing in Speech Recognition.
                Kluwer Academic Publishers, 1987.

[Clippinger 75]
Clippinger, J.H.
Speaking With Many Tongues: Some Problems in Modeling
Speakers of Actual Discourse.
In *Proceedings of Theoretical Issues in Natural
Language Processing I (TINLAP)*. 1975.

[Clocksin 81]   Clocksin, W.F., Mellish, C.S.,
Programming in Prolog.
Springer-Verlag, 1981.

[Cohen 86]   Cohen, R.
Survey of Computational Linguistics Courses.
Computational Linguistics 12 [Course Survey
Supplement]:1-74, 1986.

[Cullingford 85]
Cullingford, R.
Natural Language Processing.
Rowman and Allanheld, 1985.

[Dahl 81]   Dahl, V.
Translating Spanish into Logic through Logic.
AJCL 7(3):149-164, 1981.

[Damerau 80]   Damerau, F.J.
The transformational question answering (TQA) system:
description,operating experience, and implications.
1980
Report RC8287, IBM.

[Davey 78]   Davey, A.
*Discourse Production: A Computer Model of Some
Aspects of a Speaker.*
Edinburgh University Press, 1978.

[Devitt 87]   Devitt, M., Sterelny, K.
*Language and Reality: An Introduction to the
Philosohpy of Language.*
MIT Press, 1987.

[Dowty 85]   Dowty, D.R., Karttunen, L., Zwicky, A.M.
*Natural Language Parsing. Psychological,
computational, and theoretical perspectives.*
Cambridge University Press, 1985.

[Doyle 83]   Doyle, J.
                *Some Theories of Reasoned Assumptions. An essay in
                rational psychology.*
                Technical Report, Carnegie Mellon University, Dept. of
                Computer Science, 1983.

[Doyle 88]   Doyle, J.
                Implicit Knowledge and Rational Representation.
                Technical Report, Carnegie Mellon University, 1988.

[Dresher 76]   Dresher, B. and Hornstein, N.
                On some supposed contributions of artificial intelligence to
                the scientific study of language.
                Cognition 4, 1976.

[Dyer 83]   Dyer, M.G.
                In-Depth Understanding.
                MIT Press, 1983.

[Earley 70]   Earley, J.
                An efficient context-free parsing algorithm.
                CACM 6:451–455, 1970.

[Fallside 85]   Fallside, F., Woods, W. [editors].
                Computer Speech Processing.
                Prentice-Hall International, 1985.

[Fillmore 68]   Fillmore, C.
                The Case for Case.
                Universals in Linguistic Theory.
                Holt, Rinehart and Winston, 1968.

[Frederking 88]
                Frederking, R.E.
                *Integrated Natural Language Dialogue: A
                Computational Model.*
                Kluwer Academic Publisher, 1988.

[Friedman 71]   Friedman, J.
                A computer model of transformational grammar.
                American Elsevier, 1971.

[Gazdar 81]   Gazdar G.
                Generalized Phrase Structure Grammar.
                The Nature of Syntactic Relations.
                Reidel, 1981.

[Gazdar 87a]   Gazdar, G.
               Linguistic Applications of Default Inheritance Mechanisms.
               Linguistic Theory and Computer Applications.
               Academic Press, 1987.

[Gazdar 87b]   Gazdar, G.
               COMIT ==> PATR II.
               In *Theoretical Issues in Natural Language Processing
               3. Position Papers*, pages 39–44. 1987.

[Gazdar 87c]   Gazdar, G. et al.
               *Natural Language Processing in the 1980s. A
               Bibliography.*
               University of Chicago Press, 1987.

[Gigley 85]   Gigley, H.M.
               Grammar Viewed as a Functioning Part of a Cognitive
               System.
               In *Proceedings of the 23rd Annual Meeting of the
               Association for Computational Linguistics*, pages
               324–332. 1985.

[Grice 75]   Grice, H.P.
               Logic and Conversation.
               Syntax and Semantics 3.
               Academic Press, 1975.

[Grishman 86] Grishman, R.
               Computational Linguistics.
               Cambridge University Press, 1986.

[Grishman 88] Grishman, R., Chitrao, M.
               Evaluation of a Parallel Chart Parser.
               In *Proceedings of the Second Conference on Applied
               Natural Language Processing*, pages 71–76. 1988.

[Grosz 82]   Grosz, B.
               DIALOGIC: a core natural-language processing system.
               *Proc. of the Ninth Intern. Conf. on Comp. Ling.,
               Prague* , 1982.

[Halliday 85] Halliday, M.A.K.
               A Short Introduction to Functional Grammar.
               Edward Arnold, 1985.

[Harris 85]   Harris, M.D.
               Introduction to Natural Language Processing.
               Reston Publishing Company, 1985.

[Hauptmann 87]
          Hauptmann, A.G., Rudnicky, A.I.
          Talking to Computers: An Empirical Investigation.
          Technical Report, Department of Computer Science, Carnegie-
          Mellon University, 1987.

[Haviland 74] Haviland, S., Clark, H.H.
          What's new? Acquiring new information as a process in
          comprehension.
          Journal of Verbal Learning and Verbal Behavior
          13:512–521, 1974.

[Hayes–Roth 79]
          Hayes-Roth, B. and Hayes-Roth, F.
          A cognitive model of planning.
          Cognitive Science 3:275–310, 1979.

[Hendrix 78] Hendrix, D.G et al.
          Developing a natural language interface to complex data.
          ACM Transaction on Database Systems , 1978.

[Hirschman 83]
          Hirschman, L. and Sager, N.
          Automatic Information Formatting of a Medical Sublanguage.
          In Kittredge, R. (editor), *Sublanguage.* deGruyter, 1983.

[Hobbs 84] Hobbs, J.
          Building a large knowledge base for a natural language
          system.
          In *Proc of COLING84.* 1984.

[Hofstadter 79]
          Hofstadter, D.R.
          Goedel, Escher, Bach: An Eternal Braid.
          Basic Books, 1979.

[Hofstadter 85]
          Hofstadter, D.R.
          *Metamagical Themas: Questing for the Essence of
          Mind and Pattern.*
          Basic Books, 1985.

[Hutchins 86] Hutchins, E.L., Hollan, J.D., Norman, D.A.
          Direct Manipulation Interfaces.
          In Norman, D.A. and Draper, S.W. (editors), *User–Centered
          System Design: New Perspectives on Human–
          Computer Interaction.* Lawrence Erlbaum Associates,
          Hillsdale NJ, 1986.

[Israel 83]   Israel, D.
                 Preface.
                 Computational Models of Discourse.
                 MIT Press, 1983.

[Jackendoff 77]
                 Jackendoff, R.
                 X Syntax: A Study of Phrase Structure.
                 MIT-Press, 1977.

[Jacobs 87]   Jacobs, P.
                 Knowledge-intensive Natural Language Generation.
                 Artificial Intelligence 33, 1987.

[Jameson 80]   Jameson, A., Wahlster, W.
                 The Natural Langueg System HAM-RPM as a Hotel Manager.
                 GI - 10. Jahrestagung Saarbruecken.
                 Springer, 1980.

[Johnson 85]   Johnson, T.
                 NL computing: the commercial applications.
                 ovum study , 1985.

[Johnson 87]   Johnson, R.
                 Translation.
                 Linguistic Theory and Computer Applications.
                 Academic Press, 1987.

[Johnson-Laird 81]
                 Johnson-Laird, P.N.
                 Mental Models of Meaning.
                 In Joshi, A. Webber, B. Sag, I (editor), *Elements of
                     Discourse Understanding*. Cambridge University Press,
                     1981.

[Joshi 81]   Joshi, A.K., Webber, B.L., Sag, I.
                 Elements of Discourse Understanding.
                 Cambridge University Press, 1981.

[Kaplan 73]   Kaplan, R.M.
                 A General Syntactic Processor.
                 Natural Language Processing.
                 Algorithmics Press, 1973.

[Kaplan 79]   Kaplan, S.
                 *Cooperative Responses From a Portable Natural
                     Language Data Base Query System.*
                 PhD thesis, University of Pennsylvania, 1979.

[Kass 88]   Kass, R., Finin, T.
             Modeling the User in Natural Language Systems.
             Computational Linguistics 14:5–22, 1988.

[Katz 64]   Katz, J.J., Postal, P.M.
             An Integrated Theory of Linguistic Descriptions.
             MIT Press, 1964.

[Kay 67]   Kay, M.
             Experiments with a powerful parser.
             1967
             Proc. 2nd Int. COLING #10.

[Kay 73]   Kay, M.
             The Mind System.
             Natural Language Processing.
             Algorithmics Press, 1973.

[Kay 82]   Kay, M.
             Machine Translation.
             American Journal of Computational Linguistics 8:74–78,
                 1982.

[Kay 85]   Kay, M.
             Parsing in functional unification grammar.
             *Natural Language Parsing. Psychological,
                 computational, and theoretical perspectives.*
             Cambridge University Press, 1985.

[Kobsa 88]   Kobsa, A., Wahlster, W.
             Special Issue on User Modeling. Guest Editors: Alfred Kobsa
                 and Wolfgang Wahlster.
             Computational Linguistics 14:1–103, 1988.

[Kolodner 84] Kolodner, J.
             *Retrieval and Organizational Strategies in Conceptual
                 Memory: A Computer Model.*
             Lawrence Erlbaum, 1984.

[Kuhns 88]   Kuhns, R.J.
             A News Analysis System.
             In *Proceedings of the 12th International Conference
                 on Computational Linguistics [COLING 88]*. 1988.

[Lehnert 78] Lehnert, W.
             *The Process of Question Answering. A Computer
                 Simulation of Cognition.*
             Lwarence Erlbaum Associates, 1978.

[Lehnert 83]   Lehnert, W., Dyer, M. G., et al.
                BORIS – An Experiment in In–Depth Understanding of
                    Narratives.
                Artifical Intelligence , 1983.

[Lehnert 88]   Lehnert, W.G.
                Knowledge–based Natural Language Understanding.
                *Exploring Artificial Intelligence: Survey Talks from
                    the National Conferences on Artificial Intelligence.*
                Morgan Kaufman Publishers, Inc, 1988.

[Lightfoot 83] Lightfoot, D.
                The Language Lottery: Toward a Biology of Grammars.
                MIT Press, 1983.

[Mann 83]   Mann, W.C.
                An overview of the Nigel text generation grammar.
                In *Proceedings from the 21st Annual Meeting of the
                    ACL.* 1983.

[Marcus 80]   Marcus, M.
                Theory of Syntactic Recognition for Natural Language.
                MIT Press, 1980.

[Marslen–Wilson 78]
                Marslen–Wilson, W. and Welsh, A.
                Processing interactions and lexical access during word
                    recognition in continuous speech.
                Cognitive Psychology 10, 1978.

[McCarthy 69] McCarthy, J. and Hayes, P.J.
                Some philosophical problems from the standpoint of artificial
                    intelligence.
                Machine Intelligence 4.
                Edinburgh University Press, 1969.

[McClelland 86]
                McClelland, J.L., Kawamoto, A.H.
                Mechanisms of Sentence Processing: Assigning Roles to
                    Constituents.
                *Parallel Distributed Processing. Explorations in the
                    Microstructures of Cognition. Volume 2:
                    Psychological and Biological Models.*
                MIT Press, 1986.

[McDonald 81]
              McDonald, D.M.
              MUMBLE, A Flexible System for Language Production.
              *Proceedings of the Seventh International Joint
                 Conference on Artificial Intelligence, August 1981,
                 University of British Columbia* :1062, 1981.

[McKeown 85] McKeown, K.R.
              *Text Generation. Using discourse strategies and focus
                 constraints to generate natural language text.*
              Cambridge University Press, 1985.

[Mead 87]   Mead, C.
              Silicon Models of Neural Computation.
              In *IEEE First International Conference on Neural
                 Networks*, pages I/91–I/106.   1987.

[Mel 88]   Mel, B.W., Omohundro, S.M., Robison, A.D., Skiena, S.S.,
              Thearling, K.H., Young, L.T., Wolfram,S.
              Tablet: Personal Computer in the year 2000.
              Communications of the ACM 30:638–647, 1988.

[Mellish 85] Mellish, C.S.
              *Computer Interpretation of Natural Language
                 Descriptions.*
              Ellis Horwood Limited, 1985.

[Minsky 76]   Minsky, M.
              A framework for Representing Knowledge.
              The Psychology of Computer Vision.
              McGraw Hill, 1976.

[Minsky 85]   Minsky, M.
              The Society of Mind.
              Simon and Schuster, 1985.

[Montague 74] Montague, R.
              *Formal Philosophy: Selected Papers of Richard
                 Montague.*
              Yale University Press, 1974.
              edited with an introduction by R. Thomason.

[Newell 72]   Newell, A. and Simon, H.
              Human Problem Solving.
              Prentice Hall, 1972.

[Nirenburg 87] Nirenburg, S. [editor].
Machine Translation: Theoretical and Methodological Issues.
Cambridge University Press, 1987.

[Obermeier 83]
Obermeier, K.K.
Wittgenstein on Language and Artificial Intelligence. The Chinese Room Thought Experiment Revisisted.
Synthese 63, 1983.

[Obermeier 84]
deHilster, D. and Obermeier, K.
Linguistic Processing for a Cybernetic Model.
In *Proceedings from the Conference on Intelligent Systems and Machines.* 1984.
Rochester, Michigan.

[Obermeier 85a]
Obermeier, K.
Temporal Inferences in Medical Texts.
In *Proceedings of the 23rd Annual Meeting of the Association for Computational Linguistics*, pages 9–17. 1985.

[Obermeier 85b]
Obermeier, K.
Computers and Their Frame of Mind – The Linguistic Component.
Humans and Machines.
Ablex Publishing Company, 1985.

[Obermeier 87]
Obermeier, K.
Natural Language Processing.
BYTE 12, 1987.

[Obermeier 88]
Obermeier, K.
Side by Side – Parallel Processing.
BYTE 13, 1988.

[Oettinger 55] Oettinger, A.G.
The Design of an Automatic Russian–English Technical Dictionary.
Machine Translation of Languages.
Technology Press of MIT and Wiley, 1955.

[Pereira 80]   Pereira, F. and Warren, D.
                  Definite Clause Grammars for Language Analysis – A Survey
                     of the Formalism and a Comparison with Augmented
                     Transition Networks.
                  Artificial Intelligence 13, 1980.

[Pereira 83]   Pereira, F and Warren, D.
                  Parsing as Deduction.
                  1983
                  Proceedings of the 21st Annual Meeting of the ACL.

[Pereira 85]   Pereira, F.C.N.
                  A Structure–sharing Representation for Unification–based
                     Formalisms.
                  In *Proceedings of the 23rd Annual Meeting of the
                     Association for Computational Linguistics*, pages
                     137–144.   1985.

[Perrault 88]   Perrault, C.R., Grosz, B.J.
                  Natural-Language Interfaces.
                  *Exploring Artificial Intelligence: Survey Talks from
                     the National Conferences on Artificial Intelligence.*
                  Morgan Kaufman Publishers, Inc, 1988.

[Peterson 80]   Peterson, J.L.
                  Computer Programs for Detecting and Correcting Spelling
                     Errors.
                  Communications of the ACM 23:356–368, 1980.

[Pollack 86]   Pollack, J., Waltz, D.
                  Interpretation of Natural Language.
                  BYTE 11:189–200, 1986.

[Pylyshyn 84]   Pylyshyn, Z.W.
                  *Computation and Cognition. Toward a Foundation for
                     Cognitive Science.*
                  MIT Press, 1984.

[Raphael 76]   Raphael, B.
                  The Thinking Computer. Mind Inside Matter.
                  W.H. Freeman and Company, 1976.

[Rau 88]   Rau, L.F., Jacobs, P.S.
                  Integrating Top-Down and Bottom-Up Strategies in a Text
                     Processing System.
                  In *Proceedings of the Second Conference on Applied
                     Natural Language Processing*, pages 129–135.   1988.

[Reichman 85] Reichman, R.
Getting Computers to Talk Like You and Me.
Discourse Context, Focus, and Semantics (An ATN
Model).
MIT Press, 1985.

[Reitman 84] Reitman, W.
Artificial Intelligence Applications for Business.
Proceedings of the NYU Symposium, May, 1983.
Ablex Publishing Corporation, 1984.

[Richardson 88]
Richardson, S.D., Braden–Harder, L.C.
The Experience of Developing a Large–Scale Natural Language
Text Processing System: CRITIQUE.
In *Proceedings of the Second Conference on Applied*
Natural Language Processing, pages 195–202. 1988.

[Rieger 79] Rieger, C. and Small, S.
Word Expert Parsing.
6th IJAI , 1979.

[Robinson 80] Robinson, A.E. et al.
Interpreting Natural–Language Utterances in Dialogs about
Tasks.
1980
SRI Technical Note 210.

[Rota 89] Rota, G.C.
Book Reviews.
Advances in Mathematics 73:147, 1989.

[Roussopoulos 79]
Roussopoulos, N.
CSDL: A Conceptual Schema Definition Language for the
Design of Data Base Application.
IEEE Transactions on Software Engineering
SE–5(5):481–496, 1979.

[Rumelhart 86]
Rumelhart, D.E., J.L. McClelland, and the PDP Research
Group.
Parallel Distributed Processing. Explorations in the
Microstructure of Cognition. Volume 1: Foundations.
MIT Press, Cambridge, Massachusetts, 1986.

[Sacerdoti 77] Sacerdoti, E.
                A Structure for Plans and Behavior.
                Elsevier, North-Holland, 1977.

[Sager 81]   Sager, N.
                Natural Language Information Processing.
                Addison-Wesley, Reading MA, 1981.

[Salton 85]   Salton, G.
                On the Representation of Query Term Relations By Soft
                    Boolean Operators.
                In *Proceedings of the Second Conference of the
                European Chapter of the Association for
                Computational Linguistics, March 1985, University
                of Geneva, Switzerland*, pages 116–122. 1985.

[Savitch 87]   Savitch, W.J., Bach, E., Marsh, W., Safran-Naveh, G. [eds.].
                The Formal Complexity of Natural Language.
                D. Reidel, 1987.

[Schank 74]   Schank, R. and Rieger, Ch. III.
                Inference and the Computer Understanding of Natural
                    Language.
                Artificial Intelligence 5:373–412, 1974.

[Schank 75]   Schank, R.
                Conceptual Information Processing.
                North Holland, 1975.

[Schank 77]   Schank, R. and Abelson, R.
                Scripts, Plans, Goals, and Understanding.
                L. Erlbaum Assoc., 1977.

[Schank 81]   Schank, R.C. and Riesbeck, C.K.
                *Inside Computer Understanding. Five Programs Plus
                    Miniatures.*
                Lawrence Erlbaum Associates, 1981.

[Schank 82]   Schank, R.C.
                *Dynamic Memory. A Theory of Reminding and
                    Learning in Computers and People.*
                Cambridge University Press, 1982.

[Sells 86]   Sells, P.
                  *Lecture on Contemporary Syntactic Theories: An
                  Introduction to Government–binding Theory,
                  Generalized Phrase Structure Grammar, and
                  Lexical–functional Grammar.*
                  University of Chicago Press, 1986.

[Shapiro 83]   Shapiro, E.Y.
                  The 5th generation project – a trip report.
                  CACM 9:637–641, 1983.

[Shieber 85]   Shieber, S.
                  *An Introduction to Unification–based Approaches to
                  Grammar.*
                  University of Chicago Press, 1985.

[Shieber 87]   Shieber, S.M.
                  Separating Linguistic Analyses from Linguistic Theories.
                  Linguistic Theory and Computer Applications.
                  Academic Press, 1987.

[Shu 88]   Shu, N.C.
                  Visual Programming.
                  Van Nostrand Reinhold Company, 1988.

[Shwartz 87]   Shwartz, S.C.
                  Applied Natural Language Processing.
                  Petrocelli Books, Princeton, 1987.

[Simmons 72]   Simmons, R., Slocum, J.
                  Generating English Discourse from Semantic Networks.
                  *Proceedings of the Seventh Meeting of the Association
                  for Computational Linguistics* , 1972.

[Slocum 85]   Slocum, J.
                  A Survey of Machine Translation: Its History, Current Status,
                  and Future Prospects.
                  Computational Linguistics 11:1–17, 1985.

[Small 82]   Small, S., Cottrell, Shastri, L.
                  Toward Connectionist Parsing.
                  In *Proceedings from the AAAI–82, Pittsburgh.* 1982.

[Sondheimer 86]
                  Sondheimer, N.K. [ed.].
                  *Proceedings of DARPA's 1986 Strategic Computing
                  Natural Language Processing Workshop.*
                  USC Information Science Institute, 1986.

[Sondheimer 87]
> Sondheimer, N.
> The Rate of Progress in Natural Language Processing.
> In *Theoretical Issues in Natural Language Processing 3. Position Papers*, pages 116–119. 1987.

[Sparck 83]   Sparck Jones, K., Wilks, Y.
> *Automatic Natural Language Parsing.*
> Ellis Horwood, New York, 1983.

[Swartout 83]   Swartout, W.R.
> The GIST Behavior Explainer.
> In *Proceedings of the National Conference on Artificial Intelligence, Washington D.C.*, pages 402–407. 1983.

[Tennant 79]   Tennant, H.R.
> Experience with the Evaluation of Natural Language Question Answerers.
> *Proceedings of the Sixth International Joint Conference on Artificial Intelligence, Tokyo, August 20–23,1979* , 1979.

[Tennant 81]   Tennant, H.
> *Natural Language Processing. An Introduction to an Emerging Technology.*
> Petrocelli, 1981.

[Thompson 69] Thompson, F. et al.
> REL: a rapidly extensible language system.
> 1969
> Proc. of the 24th Nat. Conf. of the ACM.

[Thompson 81] Thompson, H.
> Chart Parsing and rule schemata in PSG.
> 1981
> 19th Ann. ACL.

[Tomita 86]   Tomita, M.
> *Efficient Parsing for Natural Language: A Fast Algorithm for Practical Systems.*
> Kluwer Academic Publishers, 1986.

[Touretzky 84] Touretzky.
> *The Mathematics of Inheritance Systems.*
> Technical Report, Carnegie Mellon University, Dept. of Computer Science, 1984.

[Turkle 84] Turkle, S.
The Second Self. Computers and the Human Spirit.
Simon and Schuster, New York, 1984.

[Unger 87] Unger, J.M.
*The Fifth Generation Fallacy: Why Japan is Betting
   its Future on Artificial Intelligence.*
University of Hawai, 1987.

[Wahlster 86] Wahlster, W., Kobsa, A.
Dialog-based User Models.
Technical Report, University of Saarbruecken, West-Germany,
   1986.

[Waltz 81] Waltz, D.L.
Toward a Detailed Model of Processing for Language
   Describing the Physical World.
In *Proceedings of the Seventh International Joint
   Conference on Artificial Intelligence* , pages 1-6.
   1981.

[Waltz 87] Waltz, D.L.
Applications of the Connection Machine.
Computer :85-97, 1987.

[Waltz 78] Waltz, D.
An English language question-answering system for a large
   relational data base.
CACM 21, 78.

[Waterworth 87]
Waterworth, J.A., Talbot, M.
*Speech and Language-based Interaction with
   Machines: Towards the Conversational Computer.*
Ellis Horwood Limited, 1987.

[Weaver 55] Weaver, W.
Translation.
Machine Translation of Languages.
Technology Press of MIT and Wiley, 1955.

[Weiner 80] Weiner, J.
BLAH, A System Which Explains Its Reasoning.
Artificial Intelligence 15:19-48, 1980.

[Weischedel 83]
Weischedel, R.M., Sondheimer, N.K.
Meta-Rules as a Basis for Processing Ill-Formed Output.
American Journal of Computational Linguistics
9:161–177, 1983.

[Weizenbaum 66]
Weizenbaum, J.
ELIZA-A Computer Program for the study of Natural
Language Communication between man and machines.
CACM 9, 1966.

[Whitelock 87] Whitelock, P., Wood, M.M., Somers, H.L., Johnson, R.,
Bennett, P.
Linguistic Theory and Computer Applications.
Academic Press, 1987.

[Wilensky 88] Wilensky, R., Chin, D.N., Luria, M., Martin, J., Mayfield, J.,
Wu, D.
The Berkeley UMX Consultant Project.
Computational Linguistics 14:35–84, 1988.

[Wilks 87] Wilks, Y.
Machine Translation and Artificial Intelligence.
In *Proceedings of the First Annual Artificial
Intelligence and Advanced Computer Technology
Conference/East, Atlantic City, New Jersey*, pages
14–19. 1987.

[Winograd 72] Winograd, T.
Understanding Natural Language.
Academic Press, 1972.

[Winograd 77] Winograd, T. and Bobrow, S.
An Overview on KRL: a Knowledge Representation Language.
Cognitive Sciences 1(1), 1977.

[Winograd 83] Winograd, T.
Language as a Cognitive Process.
Addison-Wesley, 1983.

[Woods 70] Woods, W.
A Transition Network for natural language analysis.
CACM 13, 1970.

[Woods 72]   Woods, W.
               An experimental parsing system for transition network
                  grammars.
               Natural Language Processing.
               Algorithmics Press, 1972.

[Woods 81]   Woods, W.
               Procedural Semantics as a theory of meaning.
               In Joshi, A., Webber, B., Sag, I. (editors), *Elements of
                  Discourse Understanding.* Cambridge University Press,
                  1981.

[Woods 83]   Woods, W.A.
               What's important about knowledge representation?
               IEEE Computer , 1983.

[Yngve 61]   Yngve, V.
               Random Generation of English sentences.
               In *1961 international conference on machine
                  translation of languages and applied language
                  analysis.* 1961.

[Yngve 86]   Yngve, V.H.
               Linguistics as a Science.
               Indiana University Press, 1986.

[Young 89]   Young, S.R., Hauptmann, A.G., Ward, W.H., Smith, E.T.,
                  Werner, P.
               High Level Knowledge Sources in Usable Speech Recognition
                  Systems.
               Communications of the ACM 32:183–194, 1989.

INDEX